Jim Courtright
of Fort Worth

Timothy Isaiah "Jim" Courtright

Jim Courtright of Fort Worth

His Life and Legend

Robert K. DeArment

TCU PRESS   FORT WORTH

Library of Congress Cataloging-in-Publication Data

DeArment, Robert K., 1925-
   Jim Courtright of Fort Worth : his life and his legend / by Robert K.
   DeArment.
      p. cm.
   Includes bibliographical references and index.
   ISBN 0-87565-292-1 (alk. paper)
   1. Courtright, Jim, 1845-1887. 2. Peace officers--Texas--Fort
Worth--Biography. 3. Frontier and pioneer life--Texas--Fort Worth
Region. 4. Fort Worth (Tex.)--Biography. 5. Outlaws--Texas--Fort
Worth Region--History--19th century. 6. Violence--Texas--Fort Worth
Region--History--19th century. 7. Fort Worth Region (Tex.)--History--
19th century. I. Title.
   F394.F7D43 2004
   363.2'05'092--dc22
   [B97.4/53
                                        2004003697

Cover and text design by Bill Maize; Duo Design Group

Printed in Canada

CONTENTS

Acknowledgments

The following people have been most helpful in my effort to uncover the true story of Jim Courtright:

Jerry Adams, Keller, Texas; Donaly E. Brice, Lockhart, Texas; Harold Edwards, Bakersfield, California; Gary Fitterer, Kirkland, Washington; Linda McDowell, The Butler Center for Arkansas Studies, Little Rock, Arkansas; Kathy Malone, Fort Worth Public Library; Cynthia E. Monroe, Nebraska State Historical Society, Lincoln, Nebraska; Chuck Parsons, Luling, Texas; Charles E. Snyder, Jr., Bowie, Maryland; Shari Stelling, State Historical Society of Iowa, Iowa City, Iowa; and especially,:

Rick Miller, Harker Heights, Texas, who culled countless items pertaining to characters in the Jim Courtright story from contemporary Dallas newspapers and provided me copies;

Victor Westphall, Angel Fire, New Mexico, who generously provided me a copy of his manuscript on the American Valley murders for use in this work;

Fort Worth police officer Kevin Foster, who read the manuscript and made several useful suggestions for improvement;

and Richard F. Selcer of Fort Worth, author of the notable history of that city's early years, *Hell's Half Acre,* who turned over to me all the materials relevant to Courtright's career that he had found in his research, critiqued my manuscript, and wrote the introduction.

Introduction

I was first introduced to "Longhair Jim" Courtright some twenty years ago when I began working on the history of Hell's Half Acre. The "Acre" was Fort Worth's notorious red-light district from its wild and woolly days, and Courtright was one of the most colorful characters from those very colorful days. He is also, I decided, one of the West's *forgotten* legendary gunfighters; that is, his exploits were legendary, but the man himself was largely forgotten. Or perhaps I should say he was unknown. Unfortunately for his place in history, Courtright (his real name) never made it to either Tombstone or Dodge City, the media-created capitals of western gunfighter mythology.

If he is remembered at all today, it is as "Longhair Jim," a colorful sobriquet like "Wild Bill" Hickok, "Bat" Masterson, or "Billy the Kid" that should have helped him attain legendary gunfighter immortality. But he had two strikes against him. First, he practiced his craft in Fort Worth, Texas, which, although one of the wildest towns of the frontier West, never achieved the widespread notoriety of Abilene and Dodge City, Kansas, or Lincoln, New Mexico. Second, his fifteen minutes of fame came from being on the losing end of a gun battle with Luke Short. Popular history likes its legendary gunfighters to be killers, not victims. So Courtright's remarkable story went unappreciated until well into the twentieth century.

In 1929 Eugene Cunningham, a popular western novelist, first brought Courtright to the reading public's attention as the subject of an article in *Frontier Times*.[1] Cunningham wove a fascinating tale out of thin air and fabricated quotes. His "drawling," two-gunned Jim Courtright, who could draw with either hand quick as "a rattler striking," sparked a Luke Short piece in the following month's issue but inspired no biographer to take on either man for many years. Then in 1957 the least likely of western gunfighter biographers, a Catholic Franciscan priest named Father Stanley Crocchiola, tackled Courtright's story.

Father Stanley neatly turned the tables on his subject. Usually, biographers make a name for themselves writing books about western outlaws best known by their aliases (*e.g.*, Butch Cassidy and the Sundance Kid). But Father Stanley in this case was the one with the alias, not his subject, writing under the name "F. Stanley" for reasons that are not entirely clear. His book, *Longhair Jim Courtright: Two-gun Marshal of Fort Worth*, was part hagiography, part romance, and part potboiler.[2] But in terms of a full-length biography, it was all we had until now. And that was the problem.

When we consult bibliographer Ramon F. Adams seminal work *Six-Guns and Saddle Leather*[3] we see only one meager entry for Timothy Isaiah Courtright over the course of nearly eighty years of bounteous western writing, making F. Stanley's 1957 book the source of virtually all information on this obscure gunman until now. F. Stanley turned out to be a moonlighting Catholic friar who simply rehashed family stories. Building a biography around a gunfighter who lost his only face-off is a tall order. In other words, if western historian Thomas Penfield was anywhere close to correct when he estimated that some twenty thousand men were killed in illegal gunfights across the West between 1830 and 1900,[4] Jim Courtright contributed not a single victim to the total. His only known killings were a couple of New Mexico home-steaders. Thus, his qualifications for admission into the "Gunfighters Hall of Shame" are pretty skimpy. But being overrated is not the same thing as being boring or unimportant.

For years, I considered writing a "serious" biography of Fort Worth's hometown gunfighter but was deterred by the apparent dearth of sources. How do you write the life story of a man who scarcely left a paper trail? No one to date has produced a single document over Courtright's signature or even a birth certificate. He is purely a third-person subject for the would-be biographer. Fortunately, Bob DeArment, much like Alex Haley doggedly searching for his family's roots, was not easily intimidated by the paucity of known sources nor by all the nay-sayers (me included) who told him he was on a fool's errand.

The result is a book which puts a long-overdue spotlight on a man who has been forgotten not because he was insignificant but for two very good reasons: 1) Courtright lacked a "Boswell," a clever writer like Walter Noble Burns, Alfred Henry Lewis, or Stuart Lake (chronicler of Wyatt Earp's life) to tell his story; and 2) Courtright, a near illiterate, was unable to write his own legend as did John Wesley Hardin and Tom Horn.

One thing is certain. Timothy Isaiah Courtright's life did not lack for drama. Like many of his brethren in the fraternity of the six-gun, he worked both sides of the law. He was at various times a lowly jailer, city marshal, deputy sheriff, deputy U.S. marshal, "special [police] officer," private detective, hired killer, and racketeer. Contrary to local lore and family history, he was never a U.S. Marshal or a Texas Ranger. He lived out his life on a smaller stage than did men like Wyatt Earp or Bat Masterson. Unlike those two he also lacked a strong circle of men to back him up when trouble came along. He was a lone wolf, apparently rootless until he landed in Fort Worth.

Courtright certainly had a talent for attracting trouble wherever he went. There was the shootout during the railroad strike of 1886, the New Mexico shootings, and the gunfight with Luke Short, just to name the lowlights of his foreshortened lifetime. Depending on your perspective, Courtright was either a "game" man with courage to spare or a vicious bully who preferred to beat up men with his fists rather than shoot them down in cold blood. F. Stanley was obviously an admirer—but his chief source of information was the Courtright family.

Even now T.I. Courtright is still a cipher in many ways. As Bob points out, we still do not know what Courtright did in the Civil War, anything about his family or childhood, or even what provoked the feud with Luke Short that led to his death. (I have my own ideas about that last one.) But those things will probably have to remain ciphers. As Wyatt Earp, Butch Cassidy, and their ilk show us, western gunmen are known by their legends, not their biographical profiles.

Courtright's whole reputation rests on one gunfight, fought out in the shadows on a cold winter night against a man he should have bested. After the former lawman was put in the grave, to great fanfare it must be said, no one even spoke up for him or defended his memory. He left a wife and three children who quickly packed up and left town for good. And the town that had considered him a hometown hero when he patrolled the saloons keeping the cowboys in line soon forgot all about him as it embraced urbanization and civilization.

Then there is the matter of Courtright's character. Truth be told, he was not a nice man. His image would need a major makeover to be Hollywood-ready. He was no mustache-twirling villain, but he was closer to that stereotype than to the steely-eyed, two-gun marshal of Father Stanley's biography. At the end of his life he was running a protection racket, and he probably came calling on Luke Short that night because, as mobsters in the Roaring Twenties knew, if you're going to run a protection racket, you have to rub out a dry cleaner every once in a while. The trouble was, this particular "dry cleaner" shot back.

As I write this, I am listening to the stirring title song from *The Magnificent Seven*. And I am reminded of all the beloved western movies and TV series of my youth, each with is own distinctive theme music, ruggedly handsome hero, and clear moral lessons. The Timothy

Courtright story lacks all of these ingredients for dramatization. "Longhair Jim" has never had his own "biopic," his own theme song, or a group of Hollywood writers to put words in his mouth long after the fact. Probably never will. He will have to be content with a first-rate scholarly biography.

RICHARD F. SELCER
Fort Worth, Texas
November 2002

THE LEGEND
AND THE
LEGEND MAKERS

*"Courtright was a great gunfighter, it is said, and certainly
had a strange and adventurous career."*

William R. Cox,
Luke Short and His Era

In 1975 Harry Sinclair Drago, a prolific author of "factual" Western
books, published a volume entitled *The Legend Makers: Tales of the
Old-Time Peace Officers and Desperadoes of the Frontier*. Wild Bill
Hickok, Bat Masterson, Ben Thompson, Wyatt Earp, Billy the Kid, et
al, the gunfighting frontier figures whose stories he recorded, were to
Drago the "legend makers." But, actually, these men were the legends.
The "legend makers" were men who worked with pen and ink rather
than six-gun and rifle. They were the journalists, newspaper reporters,
novelists, and pulp writers who recounted the exploits of a few frontier
adventurers so skillfully — if not entirely accurately — that they captured the imaginations of millions and made legends of their subjects.

The legend of James Butler "Wild Bill" Hickok began with an
article written by Colonel George Ward Nichols, who met Hickok in
Springfield, Missouri, shortly after the end of the Civil War and
thought an account of the adventures of the handsome Union scout
would make interesting fare for readers of *Harper's New Monthly
Magazine*. Published under the title "Wild Bill," in the February 1867
issue, it immediately made Hickok a national hero. Other writers
dutifully chronicled his later adventures as a scout on the plains and

gunfighting lawman, usually with added embellishment. The legend, spawned by Nichols and nurtured by others, grew and was magnified and unquestionably led to Hickok's assassination nine years later.[1]

The Hickok legend was unusual in that it was spawned at the beginning of its subject's career. Most western legends were not created until after the death of the men they celebrated. William B. "Bat" Masterson was still alive, however, but had deserted the West for a newspaper job in New York City when popular writer and editor Alfred Henry Lewis raised him to legendary status shortly after the turn of the century with a series of magazine articles and a book-length fictionalized account of Masterson's life.[2]

William M. Walton, a Texas attorney, Confederate army officer, and politician, wrote and published a book entitled *Life and Adventures of Ben Thompson, the Famous Texan,* in 1884, the year that Thompson was killed, and the legend of the gunfighting gambler from Austin was ensured.

Newspaperman Walter Noble Burns has the distinction of playing a central role in the creation of two western gunfighting legends. In his book *The Saga of Billy the Kid,* published in 1926, he resurrected an obscure New Mexico outlaw from the dustbin of history and set him on his way to world recognition. His 1927 book, *Tombstone, An Iliad of the Southwest,* first glamorized Wyatt Earp and did much to begin the Earp legend. Another newsman, Stuart N. Lake, finished the job in 1931 with his hugely successful semi-fictional biography, *Wyatt Earp: Frontier Marshal.*

The works of two other writers combined to raise Timothy Isaiah Courtright, an obscure southwestern character of the 1870s and 1880s, to such legendary status that today he is featured in every encyclopedia of western gunfighters.[3]

The first, Eugene Cunningham, attended public schools in Fort Worth, Texas, in the first decade of the twentieth century. There, as a schoolboy, he first heard of a man locals called "Jim" Courtright, who had been city marshal during the early days of the town and had been killed in a famous street gunfight twenty years before. Cunningham began writing western novels in 1924, and by the 1930s his books were among the most successful and popular in the genre.[4] He had not forgotten the stories he heard about the early-day city marshal of Fort Worth and wrote an article about him for a publication of a clothing manufacturer of El Paso, Texas, that was reprinted in a small regional magazine in 1929. Courtright, he said, had been an Indian scout for the

Eugene Cunningham, the western novelist whose most enduring piece of fiction was the creation of the legend of "Long-Haired Jim" Courtright. *Courtesy Robert G. McCubbin Collection.*

army and, in the manner of Wild Bill Hickok, Buffalo Bill Cody, and other notable scouts, wore his hair long and was therefore called "Long-Haired Jim" when he came to Fort Worth to accept appointment as city marshal. Cunningham extolled Courtright's bravery as a peace officer and placed special emphasis on his expertise as a gunfighter. For much of his information he credited Jim Gillett, a well-respected rancher and lawman during Courtright's day. Cunningham quoted Gillett as saying Courtright was "a wizard with the Colts."[5]

The publications in which Cunningham's piece appeared had limited circulation and did little to enhance Courtright's fame as a frontier hero. Where Courtright's name was recognized at all, folks were probably more apt to remember the harsh description Bat Masterson had written for *Human Life*, a slick national magazine of much wider circulation, in 1907. Courtright, Bat said, was "a notorious local character" of Fort Worth, "a sullen, ignorant bully with no sense of right or wrong," who had killed a couple men in that town and a couple more in New Mexico.[6]

But in 1934 Cunningham's most famous book appeared. Entitled *Triggernometry, a Gallery of Gunfighters, With Technical Notes on Leather Slapping as a Fine Art, gathered from many a Loose Holstered Expert over the Years*, it had chapters on a number of western figures, including Courtright. As city marshal at Fort Worth, Courtright "found many opportunities to display both his grim fearlessness and his uncanny speed and accuracy at weapon-play," said Cunningham.

> The old-timers who knew him well used to marvel in my hearing over his skill. They said his hands, snapping to the butts of the .45s in their cut-down holsters, were like racing snakes streaking to their holes. He was a deadly shot with either hand – which was not so usual with gunmen

who "pulled" as flashingly as he. Frequently, the man who was "extra-quick on the draw" figured to make up, by the number of shots he fired, for any lack of accuracy in aim. But not Long-Haired Jim Courtright! And danger, tension, seemed only to increase his coolness, his dexterity.

Quoting Jim Gillett again, Cunningham described Courtright as a man who could not be bluffed, "a gunfighter from the forks of Hard Water Creek." Gillett said he considered Courtright the equal with a six-gun of anyone in the West, including the celebrated pistoleers John Wesley Hardin and Ben Thompson.[7]

Triggernometry became a standard book on the gunfighters of the West and has gone through many editions.[8] The chapter on "Long-Haired Jim" started Courtright on his way to the hierarchy of legendary western gunfighting heroes. But it had not yet had its full impact on perceptions when prolific Texas writer Owen P. White in a 1936 book, expanded on the lead provided by Masterson and described Courtright as a professional assassin whose sales pitch was "I kill 'em for cash." White claimed Courtright "was rated as a cheap murderer [who] had bumped off perhaps a half dozen unarmed claim-jumpers and unoffending nesters."[9]

By the 1940s and 1950s western writers were drawing on the Cunningham portrayal. George D. Hendricks in 1941 wrote: "Everybody knew Jim Courtright was the best pistoleer in Texas.... Courtright was one of the very few who could use two guns with equal speed and accuracy."[10] A Texas Ranger biographer the next year called Courtright "one of the fastest men with his pistols in the entire Southwest."[11] Another chronicler of gunsmoke history assured readers in 1951 that Courtright's gun was for hire and he was "rated one of the world's best professional gunmen."[12]

In a rewrite of his original Courtright article published twenty-eight years earlier, Eugene Cunningham in 1957 told the story again in "Courtright the Longhaired," a piece for *True West* magazine.

But it was Father Stanley Crocchiola, a Roman Catholic priest, who that same year completed the canonization of Courtright as a fearless frontier peace officer and one of the premier gunfighters of the American West. Writing under the pen name "F. Stanley," this unusual cleric for many years had turned out monographs on the early history of southwestern towns and had written several books on the violent men who held sway there. In 1957 he published the first full-length biography of Courtright, calling it *Longhair Jim Courtright: Two Gun Marshal of Fort Worth*. In it he boldly stated that not only was Courtright in the

Father Stanley Crocchiola, who as "F. Stanley" contributed to the Courtright legend. *Courtesy Robert G. McCubbin Collection.*

same league with the storied gunfighters of the West, he surpassed them all with pistol dexterity: "Frontier history has yet to produce a man as fast on the draw as Jim Courtright.... [He] was as fast as the twinkle of an eye when it came to drawing his six-shooters. He wore two guns, butts forward, and drew the gun on the right side with his left hand."[13] The book, written with the aid and encouragement of Courtright's daughter and granddaughter, was an encomium to the man who had been slain on a Fort Worth street seventy years earlier.

Together with Cunningham's *Triggernometry*, Father Stanley's biography firmly established the Courtright legend. Soon western magazines and books were repeating and embellishing the stories of the dangerous gunfighter from Fort Worth called "Long-Haired Jim" and his astonishing ability with pistols. Not everyone accepted Father Stanley's nomination of Courtright to sainthood, however. In an article in 1961 veteran western writer Carl Breihan acknowledged that Courtright was "considered to be the fastest man with a sixgun in Texas" but called him "a hired killer" with a history "of brutal killings which he estimated at forty."[14] And so the legend grew.

Timothy Isaiah Courtright led an action-filled adventurous life in his forty-one years on this earth, but he was neither the saint portrayed by Father Stanley nor the brutal slayer of forty men depicted by Breihan. Like most men of his type, he was neither all white nor all black. Following a noteworthy record as a peace officer in Fort Worth when the town was considered one of the toughest in the West, he became a central figure in the infamous American Valley affair, was charged with murder, made a dramatic escape from the Texas Rangers, and was a fugitive for a year. His later career in Fort Worth as head of a private detective agency, with involvement in the great railroad strike of 1886 and finally death at the hands of a gambler, is less than admirable.

Courtright was a brawler, a drinker, a gambler, and, on one occasion, a cold-blooded murderer. But his wife and children worshiped him, for he was a devoted family man, a loving husband and father who was never known to consort with the women of Hell's Half Acre.

Despite his legendary status created by Cunningham and Father Stanley, the historical record shows that Courtright came out second best in all of the few gunfights in which he participated. From the time he first pinned on a badge and was almost killed by a teenager to his final fatal confrontation with gambler and gunman Luke Short, Courtright never exhibited any real gunfighting ability. He could draw and twirl his weapons with dexterity enough to impress even an experienced Texas Ranger and frontier marshal like Jim Gillett, but Gillett never saw Courtright in action against another armed man, and that is where a real gunfighter proved his worth.

Much of the early history of Timothy Isaiah Courtright as recorded by his legend makers is suspect. Cunningham admitted that little was known except that "he was born in Iowa around 1848, that he served as a trooper under John A. Logan during the Civil War, and through Logan's influence, was later employed as an army scout in Texas, Arizona, and New Mexico.[15]

Stanley expanded greatly on those few details, devoting fully a quarter of his biography to Courtright's life before he came to Fort Worth. Using information provided in 1954 by Courtright's daughter, Lulu May, and granddaughter, Mrs. Henry Meyerhoff, he said that Timothy Isaiah Courtright was born in Sangamon County, Illinois, in the spring of 1845. The son of Daniel Courtright, who had come from Kentucky in 1827, he had several sisters and one brother.[16]

United States census reports for the years 1840 and 1850 confirm none of this, as no Daniel Courtright (or various spellings of that name) family was listed in Sangamon County. In 1850 there was,

Civil War General
John A. Logan, who,
according to legend,
fostered Courtright's
career. *Author's
personal collection.*

however, a three-year-old boy, "Isaiah," living with three older sisters
in the household of Anxil E. Courtright, aged thirty-six, and his wife,
Elen [sic] Courtright, aged twenty-six, in DeKalb County, Illinois.
Perhaps a harried census taker mistakenly wrote Anxil for Daniel, or
perhaps the father's name actually was Anxil. In any event, if this was
Courtright's family, as seems likely, he may have been born two years
later than his descendents believed.

Stanley indicates that at some point prior to the Civil War young
Courtright relocated in Iowa.[17] Here again, the U. S. census reports are
helpful. Isaiah Courtwright [sic], aged fourteen, born in Illinois, was
listed in the 1860 census as living in the Grundy County, Iowa, home
of Chauncey G. Courtwright. This was probably an uncle.

According to Father Stanley's account, when war came in 1861
young Courtright, sixteen years old, joined the Iowa Seventh Infantry
as a drummer boy. Stanley goes on to relate that at the Battle of

The father of T. I. Courtright. His name may have been Daniel or Anxil E. *Author's personal collection.*

Belmont, Missouri, in November 1861, Courtright dropped his drum, picked up the rifle of a fallen soldier, and began shooting the enemy with deadly accuracy, until he fell wounded. His daring and bravery caught the eye of John Alexander Logan, commander of the 31st Illinois, who, after the battle, arranged the transfer of Courtright to his own staff as a scout. At the Battle of Fort Donelson, on the Cumberland River in Tennessee, Courtright was again wounded. He "evidently stopped a bullet intended for Logan, for the latter felt so indebted to him that he continued to regard Courtright as an intimate friend for the remainder of his life."[18] Stanley wrote that Courtright saw action with the 31st Illinois at Port Gibson, Raymond, Jackson,

The mother of T. I. Courtright. Her name may have been Ellen. *Author's personal collection.*

Champion Hill, and the siege of Vicksburg, where he was wounded for the third time.[19]

At the end of the war, in the Stanley recital, Courtright remained in the U. S. Army and for several years served as a scout with Wild Bill Hickok.[20] While stationed in Arkansas, he met fourteen-year-old Sarah Elizabeth "Betty" Weeks and eloped with her to Little Rock. Following his discharge from the army about 1870-1871, Courtright and his wife, a crack shot, joined a Wild West show. When Betty became pregnant, he took her back to Little Rock where her parents cared for her during her period of confinement. A daughter, Mary Ellen, was born there on October 8, 1872. Courtright worked on the farm of his father-in-law for

Sarah Elizabeth
Weeks Courtright,
wife of "Jim." *Author's
personal collection.*

about a year and then moved to his own farm "across the Trinity river about where the Oakwood Cemetery is now located in Fort Worth, Texas."[21] He still wore his hair down to his shoulders in the manner of the Indian scouts of the time. Folks in Fort Worth began calling the man who was to become the town's most famous officer of the law "Longhaired Jim."

The writings of Gene Cunningham formed the basis for this story and Courtright's daughter and granddaughter provided additional details for Father Stanley. Since publication of the works of these original two Courtright legend makers, other writers have accepted and repeated their accounts, some adding further details of their own invention as contributions to the legend.

In his Courtright entry, for instance, one compiler of an Old West encyclopedia writes that after the Civil War Courtright painted G. T. T.

(Gone to Texas) on the door of his Iowa parents' home. "What his ma and pa or both said about his lousing up their front door will never be known."[22]

Although Cunningham and Stanley never mentioned any work with cattle by Courtright, Drago in *The Legend Makers,* said that "Long-Haired Jim" spent a year as a cowboy and went up the trail with a herd to Wichita. At a Red River camp on the way home two of the drovers got into a dispute with Courtright and pulled guns. "With a motion so swift that the eye could not follow it, he slapped leather and his single-action Colt coughed twice. That was all that was required. The suddenly sober crowd gazed at the two men sprawled on the ground and then at Long-haired Jim Courtright. They could appreciate wizardry with a pistol."[23]

No documentation for these tales is offered. Nor can corroboration be found for Courtright's reported adventures during and immediately following the Civil War. It is not certain that he saw service in the Union Army at all. Despite repeated attempts by serious researchers to verify the military service of Courtright (or any variation of the spelling of the name), nothing has been found.[24] *The Roster and Record of Iowa Soldiers in the War of the Rebellion* makes no mention of his membership in any Iowa unit, nor do the recorded recollections of Grand Army of the Republic veterans from Iowa.[25] A search of the Illinois Civil War records disclosed no mention of his name.[26] The National Archives have no record of Courtright's service in either of the Iowa or Illinois military units cited by Father Stanley. The only contemporary evidence of the man's military service is a brief mention in the *Dallas Morning News* of February 12, 1886:

> Jim Courtright, so George Holland says, will go over to Dallas Saturday and go through the necessary formula to entitle him to draw the sum of $3,000, the amount of his

accrued pension as a Union veteran. Courtright was in the federal army during the war and was wounded two or three times.

In his biography Father Stanley quotes this item and remarks: "The fact that his tragic death several months later left his family destitute seems to indicate that Courtright was not successful in obtaining the pension."[27] The fact that no pension file for T. I. Courtright can be found in the National Archives is also significant.

Moreover, Courtright's alleged service as a scout with Hickok cannot be confirmed. After decades of intensive research into the life of Wild Bill, Joseph G. Rosa, the foremost Hickok scholar and biographer, has found no evidence to indicate that Courtright and Hickok were ever associated.[28]

Even Courtright's marriage to Elizabeth Weeks in Little Rock, Pulaski County, Arkansas, in 1866, as reported by Stanley, cannot be verified.[29] The only Weeks family enumerated in Arkansas in the 1870 U. S. Census was that of Ezekial and Malinda Weeks, of Newton County, which is quite some distance from Little Rock. This couple had six children, including daughters Elizabeth J., aged sixteen in 1870, and Sarah A., aged twelve. If either of these two girls later became Mrs. Sarah Elizabeth Courtright, the marriage was obviously several years later than the 1866 date given by Stanley.

At some point early in Courtright's career, his first name "Tim" became corrupted to "Jim," and he was known as Jim, or even James Courtright, throughout his adult life. But no photograph shows him with unusually long hair, and the sobriquet "Long-Haired Jim" is found in no contemporary source.[30] The name seems to have been an invention of Gene Cunningham to provide an eye-catching title for his original 1929 article. Novelists do things like that. Cunningham evidently reasoned that if Courtright scouted on the plains with Wild Bill and Buffalo Bill, both known for their long, flowing locks, then he undoubtedly wore his hair long also. The Indian scouting stories and the association with Hickok and Cody cannot be confirmed, however, nor can the assertion that Courtright ever wore his hair long. The legend begun by Cunningham and Father Stanley is so well rooted, however, that Courtright's impressive tombstone in Oakwood Cemetery, Fort Worth, reads "Jim 'Longhaired' Courtright."

It is suspected that Courtright sowed the seeds of his own legend by spinning fanciful stories of his early adventures to family and friends. These prevarications were accepted as truth and passed on in later years to Cunningham and Stanley. One tall tale that the legend makers missed was Courtright's claim that he had "many years experience as marshal of frontier towns" before coming to Fort Worth, an untruth that was duly reported by a Fort Worth newspaper in 1879. He had, said the paper, "filled the office in Omaha for a number of years to the perfect satisfaction of its citizens."[31] Well preserved records of the Omaha police department, however, contain no mention of T. I. Courtright.[32] A later writer asserted that Courtright was the city marshal at Marshall, Texas, before moving on to Fort Worth, but this report is also groundless.[33]

And so, the history of Courtright before he first pinned on a badge at Fort Worth in December 1875 is sketchy at best. Most of it as reported is likely untrue. But after that date his trail becomes much more defined, and the story of his extraordinary life can be told with much more probity.

MARSHAL OF PANTHER CITY

"He was tall, dark, and forbidding in appearance, and was noted for great courage and equally great cruelty and treachery."

St. Louis Globe-Democrat,
February 14, 1887.

If Timothy Isaiah Courtright in 1873 farmed the land across the Trinity from the frontier town of Fort Worth, as Father Stanley tells us, he tilled the very soil in which he would be buried. And not far from his last resting spot lie the remains of the man destined to kill him. Courtright could not know this, of course, but he did know that he was not cut out to be a farmer. Inevitably he was drawn to the excitement of the boomtown on the other side of the stream.

He soon became a volunteer fireman in the M. T. Johnson Company, an early Fort Worth fire brigade, joined the Odd Fellows lodge, and spent much more time with his cronies in these organizations than he did in the fields. He was a talker, full of tales of derring-do in the war and on the plains. Tall and darkly handsome, he had about him an air of danger that only made him more interesting to other men. When someone suggested he would make a first-class peace officer, he thought that was a splendid idea. On December 14, 1875, he accepted City Marshal Thomas P. Redding's appointment as deputy and jailer.

The legend makers never mentioned the first recorded attempt by Jim Courtright to make an arrest in Fort Worth. It came close to being his last, and the legend would have ended there aborning. Only two days after pinning on his first badge, the man who would be hailed as a premier peace officer of the Old West and pistol wizard without peer came off second best in a shooting incident. He was shot and almost killed by an intoxicated teenager.

Young Richard Alexander "Bingham" Feild was a notorious trouble-maker around Fort Worth, and Courtright should have known he was dangerous. A year earlier Feild had emptied a shotgun load at another lad named John Ogleby. The shooting may have been accidental and the victim recovered, but doctors W. P. Burts and J. T. Feild spent half a day picking shot out of Ogleby's head. Bingham Feild came from a prominent Fort Worth family. His father, Julian Feild, had helped found the city. His brother, Julian Theodore, one of the doctors who minis-tered to Ogleby, was a prominent and respected citizen of the town. Charges were not pressed in the Ogleby shooting.

On the evening of Thursday, December 16, 1875, nineteen-year-old Bingham Feild and a teenage pal, Billy Nance, entered the Club Room Saloon and ordered drinks. The boys were already under the influence of alcohol, "maddened and crazed by liquor," as the *Fort Worth Weekly Democrat* put it,[1] and bartender Lem Grisham refused to serve them. Both pulled pistols, threatened Grisham, and then with-drew into the street and vented their frustration by firing several rounds at the sky.

Jim Courtright was in the vicinity and anxious to prove his mettle as a lawman. He approached the pair in an alleyway off Main Street, announced he was placing them under arrest, and ordered them to put up their weapons. One of the boys — it was unclear which — shouted at the officer to stand back or be shot.

Courtright's judgment in this perilous moment, as in others to come in his career, may be questioned, but it is plain the man never lacked sand. With two revolvers leveled at him, he continued to advance, his own gun in his hand. Nance backed down and meekly handed over his pistol. But as Courtright stepped up to Bingham Feild and reached for his pistol the young man fired from the hip. The bullet struck Courtright near the stomach and ranged upward toward the right shoulder. The pistol fell from his hand and he collapsed on the ground.

Drawn to the scene by the sounds of gunfire, a crowd of men on Main Street swarmed over the two young boys. Some escorted them to the jail, while others carried Courtright to a building where Doctors Burts and Feild, the same physicians who had treated young Feild's last gunshot victim, attended him. Newspapers reporting the shooting held

A map of the country in which Courtright operated. *Author's personal collection.*

out little hope for the officer's recovery. One dispatch from Fort Worth to Texas papers quoted the attending physicians as saying the chances were twenty to one that he would die.[2] But Dr. Feild had a strong personal incentive to save Courtright's life; if his patient died the doctor's young brother might well hang for murdering a lawman. He and Burts worked long and hard to pull Courtright through and in the end were successful.

A justice of the peace named Morris held a hearing into the affair and personally called on the gunshot victim to obtain a "dying state-ment." Courtright laughed at the notion that he was dying and "stated positively that the shooting of himself was entirely accidental to the best of his belief; that it occurred during a struggle for the possession of the pistol, and while he was endeavoring to wrench it from the hands of one of the boys; that neither of the boys had any malice toward him, but on the contrary were his friends." He said that he did not expect to die, but if he should, it was his request that the boys not be prosecuted as he considered the gunshot unintentional.[3]

City Attorney J. C. Scott took note of Courtright's statement and dropped all charges against the boys. The prominence of the Feild and Nance families made the affair something of a cause célèbre in Fort Worth. The editors of two of the city's several newspapers, the *Standard* and the *Mortar*, believed special treatment had been afforded the boys. Both criticized Courtright for not being more aggressive in making his arrests and city officials for not prosecuting the young offenders. There was no public response from Courtright, but Scott defended his deci-sion not to prosecute the case in a letter to Buckley B. Paddock, editor of the *Democrat*, that Paddock published in the December 25, 1875, issue. Another letter from someone identifying himself only as "B" also took the *Standard* and *Mortar* to task and leveled a veiled threat at the editors: "If their sheets are to be used for the purpose of slandering

Buckley B. Paddock, editor of the
*Fort Worth Democrat. Author's personal
collection.*

honest public officials, and prejudging important cases, to the vital injury of innocent boys, and their families and relatives, they will perhaps be held to a stricter accountability than will be pleasant."

The Texas press reported the wounded officer's slow recovery: "Courtright, the Deputy Marshal who was shot a few days ago, is improving, and it is now thought he will recover," said a special dispatch to the *Galveston Daily News* printed in the December 19, 1875, edition. "We understand that Deputy Marshal Courtwright [sic] is recovering from his supposed fatal wound," reported the *Fort Worth Democrat* on January 15, 1876. By February 1, 1876, the *News* of Galveston could report that "Cartwright [sic], the deputy marshal who was shot some time since, is again on the streets." (The press had difficulty with the spelling of Courtright's name throughout his life.)

Courtright was indeed out on the streets and eager for greater things. Like many others, he had been drawn to Fort Worth when it became known that officials of the Texas & Pacific Railroad had chosen the little town the western terminus of its planned line to San Diego, California. The steel rails were originally expected to reach there by January 1, 1874.

Named for a short-lived military outpost established at the site in 1849, Fort Worth had for years been a stop on the route of the Butterfield Overland Mail and the Southern Pacific Stage Line. The turmoil of the Civil War and Reconstruction periods hindered the growth of the town, and the population dwindled to only 175 about 1870. But excitement gripped the area with the announcement of the railroad's coming. People flooded in, merchants and professional men arrived, banks and newspapers opened, land prices skyrocketed, construction flourished, and Fort Worth quickly became the foremost boomtown in Texas. In 1873 it was incorporated with W. P. Burts as the first mayor. Everyone envisioned great prosperity and mushrooming growth, but the Panic of 1873 stopped the railroad's construction and for two years the fulfillment of those dreams was delayed. As an early Fort Worth historian put it, "From the highest point of expectancy, the people descended into the lowest depths of despondency."[4]

During this period Fort Worth acquired the nickname "Panther City." There are several stories of how that came about, but one was the favorite of the residents of the rival town of Dallas, fifty miles to the east. Fort Worth was such a drowsy place, went this tale, that a panther had been found sleeping in the street. Despite the ridicule, folks in Fort Worth took pride in the title. Soon proprietors of stores, meat markets, and saloons were calling their establishments "The Panther."

B. B. Paddock of the *Democrat* added a woodcut of a panther to the front page of his paper. The M. T. Johnson Company, the volunteer fire fighting organization that Courtright joined, gloried in its popular appellation, the Panther City Fire Department.

In early 1876 T&P construction began again with completion of the road to Fort Worth expected by summer. No panthers dozed on the city's streets as the town once again became a hive of activity, and the population swelled to three or four thousand. The regularly scheduled elections of April aroused a great deal of interest in a town again on the move. It was clear to most residents that the elective position of city marshal could no longer be handled by part timers like Edward S. Terrell, T. M. Ewing. H. P. Shiel, and T. P. Redding, the men who had held the office since incorporation.

Before becoming the first city marshal of Fort Worth in April 1873, Terrell had tried his hand, unsuccessfully for the most part, at farming, trapping, horse trading, cattle raising, and shopkeeping. For several years he operated the First and Last Chance Saloon in Fort Worth. Unhappy and equally ineffectual in the marshal's office, he resigned after only six months, and one of his policemen completed his term.

T. M. Ewing was a doctor who, after his election as marshal in April 1874, "split his time between doctoring and arresting criminals."[5] He, too, submitted his resignation after only seven months in office.

His successor, Henry P. Shiel, was a gambler and saloonman whose ties to vice in the city bothered many citizens. Shiel lasted a year but was replaced on October 27, 1875, by T. P. Redding, a barber known to all as "Uncle Tom," and the man who gave Jim Courtright his first law enforcement post in Fort Worth.

Everybody liked "Uncle Tom" Redding, but it soon became evident that he could not control the ever-growing lawless element in town. One early Fort Worth resident summed up Redding's term as marshal

as "more of an appellation than a de facto carrying out of the require-
ments of an executor of the peace" and said, "the boys did rather as
they pleased, regardless of this peace officer."[6] Another old-timer
recalled seeing "cowboys run Tom Redding into a saloon by twirling
their ropes after him or shooting under him."[7]

This was unacceptable behavior for an officer of the law, and by
February 1876 Redding was gone, replaced by John Stoker on a tempo-
rary basis until the April elections. Stoker, with some experience as a
professional lawman, immediately announced his candidacy for election as marshal. Others entering the race for the one-year term of office
were Columbus C. Fitzgerald, J. H. Peters, and D. S. Covert. Also
throwing his hat in the ring was T. I. "Jim" Courtright, who had gained
the sympathy and respect of many with his fight to survive the near-
fatal shooting. His decision not to press charges against the son of the
popular Dr. Feild may also have impressed some voters.

One might wonder why five vigorous and ambitious young men
would vie for a position that on the surface at least did not appear particularly appealing. The salary of the city marshal was meager – only
$25 a month at the time but raised to $50 after the arrival of the railroad that summer. Some of the work was tedious. Bureaucratic paper-
work must have been loathed by a man like Courtright, who was barely literate. Other onerous duties included shooting wild dogs and keeping the streets relatively clear of debris and dead animals. There was
the ever-present element of danger, of course; the list of western boomtown marshals who died with their boots on is long.

But there were benefits. The office carried a certain degree of
prestige. And the skimpy salary could be augmented considerably by a
system of police emolument commonly employed in early western
towns. Arrests of malefactors for minor infractions of the law —
drunkenness, barroom brawling, and the like — were generally

resolved in police court (mayor's court in Fort Worth) by fines of $5 or $10. The proceeds were then divided between the arresting officer, the judge, and the city. Law officers also received a fee for specially assigned duties, such as delivering a prisoner to another legal jurisdiction. Gambling and prostitution, considered social ills but also recognized as necessary to the prosperity of a boomtown, were dealt with by a regular procedure of arrests and fines that amounted to a licensing system. The routine arrest of gamblers, whoremongers, and brothel inmates provided a lucrative source of income for the city marshal and his deputies. Fort Worth, entering its greatest boom period in the spring of 1876, was attracting scores of sporting-world denizens. A large, sprawling district of saloons, dance houses, gambling dens and brothels grew up and became notorious as "Hell's Half Acre." The city marshal particularly profited from the fee system, because a percentage of the fees awarded to his deputies was retained in his account. It is clear that opportunity for substantial economic reward was the major motivator for Courtright and the other contenders for the city marshal's job.

When the polls closed on April 6, 1876, and the votes were counted, Courtright had defeated his closest rival, C. C. Fitzgerald, by the slim margin of three votes.[8] In recognition of his strong showing, the city council promptly appointed Fitzgerald assistant marshal, second in command. William A. "Tip" Clower, who would be involved with Marshal Courtright in an infamous shooting affair later that year, was also given a deputy's appointment.

In this election the voters reelected incumbent Mayor G. H. Day, but J. C. Scott, who had come under criticism for not prosecuting the boys in the Courtright shooting incident, went down to inglorious defeat in the race for city attorney; W. Henry Field received 299 votes to Scott's seventy-two.

When Jim Courtright pinned on the badge of city marshal in the spring of 1876, Fort Worth was ideally located to benefit from two major economic developments in Texas. This was the period when both the longhorn cattle drives to Kansas and the great buffalo slaughter were at their peak. Fort Worth, situated directly on the cattle trail to the Kansas railheads, was the last great provisioning center in the state for the northern-bound cattlemen. It was also the closest mercantile center to the buffalo hunting ranges. Over the next few years the town would become a recreational stomping ground for cowboys, buffalo hunters, railroad workers, soldiers, and the sporting crowd that followed them. Many of these men carried weapons and were quick to use them. Responsibility for maintaining order in a city full of gun-packing hardcases fell primarily on the shoulders of City Marshal Courtright and his policemen, but assistance was provided at times by Tarrant County Sheriff John M. Henderson and his deputies.

In April 1876, a Texas editor bemoaned the frequent use of guns in the state and the strong possibility that the violence, if not curtailed by law enforcement officials, would lead to vigilantism:

> There is always a certain manliness in meeting a foe squarely and striving to the death for the mastery. We do not say that there can be no circumstance where such a thing would not be right and proper, but we do say that the practice upon slight and unimportant [provocation] is murder, and nothing else. . . . The idea of laying [sic] in wait to kill unawares, or seeking to catch your foe at a disadvantage or of "getting the drop," or taking "the go" is base and barbarous beyond conception. Too much, alas! Of this sort of thing has been done in Texas. . . . Good law-abiding people are becoming disgusted and impatient, and if strong

legal steps are not speedily taken to correct it, we fear that the people themselves will resort to extraordinary means, the last resort, vigilance committees, which is only revolution in another form.[9]

The editor of the *Dallas Herald* added his comments in May: "The carrying of pistols is getting to be, here of late, altogether too frequent and demands increased vigilance on the part of the officers of the law.... Men who are in the habit of thus going about armed in a peaceful, law-abiding community are either cowards or bullies, seeking to get up a little cheap reputation by bullying and bluffing quiet people. It is time this nuisance was put down. It's getting to be a bore."

Editor Paddock of the *Democrat* in Fort Worth reprinted the piece and expressed general agreement but did not miss an opportunity to take a swipe at his competitor:

"The *Herald* is right. Pistols are the badge of cowards and bullies, and the only proper and genteel weapon for a gentleman to carry is a pair of brass knuckles such as the editor of the *Herald* carries. Brass knuckles are the thing of course."[10]

In another issue Paddock made his own pithy, sarcastic comment on the use of pistols to resolve disputes. The definition of "a Western settler," he said, was "the contents of a six-shooter."[11]

A few years later in a more serious vein he wrote a lengthy editorial on the subject of guns and their prevalence. If Texas was ever to achieve that reputation for law and order won by other states, he said,

the revolver must go. It gives a false courage – or, rather, it nerves an inherent cowardice. Men carry revolvers, not to fight honorably – at least, fair – duels, where they are used "at the word," but in the hope that the

concealed weapon will confer and advantage in the controversy, which the concealed weapon is so apt to encourage;
that with "the drop" and the pistol, reputation for courage
may be won....Personal satisfaction, personal vengeance,
too often takes the place of an appeal to law. The evil is the
growth of years. It is widespread. It can only be eradicated
by time and hemp, and a liberal use of hemp will greatly
accelerate the work of time.

Let Texas use hemp freely – without regard to fear,
favor or affection. Let it choose men to be judges, sheriffs
and prosecuting attorneys who were not educated in the
revolver school. The people are responsible. If they will not
punish men for taking "the drop," let them instruct their
representatives to repeal all laws against carrying deadly
weapons, and thus place the law abiding citizen on an equal
footing with the coward and the murderer.[12]

In May 1876, a month after the new officers took office, Paddock
lectured Courtright and his deputies on their duties and responsibilities.
Although he was "not disposed to find fault with or censure too severely
our newly elected peace officers who cannot be expected to come from
the private walks of life into a full knowledge of their duties [and] their
powers," a certain instruction was appropriate, he said, "by reason of the
committal of one or two *faux pas* by some of our newly elected officials."
He reminded Marshal Courtright and his deputies that it was not necessary for them to have a warrant in hand or personally witness an offense
to arrest a suspect; the report of an offense by a "creditable person" was
sufficient. If unable to make the arrest without help, officers were
authorized to summon a posse. Although authorized to take suspects into
custody, officers should never "assume judicial powers" but should leave

that responsibility to court officials. "The law protects the officer fully in the discharge of his duty, and will only hold him responsible for a *malicious* infraction of his powers, [but] the law provided for speedy punishment of all peace officers for failing to discharge their duty...."[13]

In that month of May a young horse herder named Charles F. Colcord rode into Fort Worth to "see the elephant" as the expression went. In later years, after a distinguished career as a deputy U. S. marshal, Colcord would make a fortune in the Oklahoma oil boom. But in May 1876 he was a wide-eyed teenager anxious to share in the excitement of Hell's Half Acre. "The railroad men and Irish 'paddies' were there by the hundreds and I think all the cowmen and buffalo hunters from all over western Texas were there," he wrote in his memoirs.

> Lordy, when they came in sight of the town the way those cowboys began to yell and raise the devil! After they arrived in town and had a few drinks some of them got rough and began having some pretty rowdy fun. They would ride at a run up and down the streets shooting their guns and yelling like mad, and sometimes they would ride up the walks and into the buildings.... They gave us all the rein we wanted in Fort Worth and we had a great time. Whatever we did I do not recall anybody ever trying to arrest us – we nearly had the town to ourselves.

Colcord and his friends headed for the dance hall of George and Mag Wood, so recently arrived from Wichita, Kansas, with a bevy of girls that their building was still under construction. "I will never forget Mag Wood's dance hall," said Colcord.

> They were just building this big shack. The floor was completed, the roof and part of the siding was on and

where the siding was lacking the holes were stopped up with wagon sheets and canvas. At one end was a rough bar with five bartenders, all as busy as can be. There was a motley crowd in this dance hall. Mag had about thirty girls that she had brought from Wichita, Kansas. She charged fifty cents a set for dancing and it was a sight to see those old buffalo hunters, cowpunchers and railroad men swing those girls! ...Places like that dance hall took a fellow's money right away from him. At fifty cents a dance and then treating the girl after the set a cowpuncher didn't have much in the way of savings when he left Fort Worth.

Later that night a gunfight erupted. A herder named Adams from the Colcord outfit kicked it off "by jerking out his two six-shooters and firing into the floor and then shooting out the lights." Colcord recalled that "one or two men were killed and several were badly hurt," but his memory seems to have been faulty in this regard.[14] No mention of a deadly shooting in the Woods' dance hall appeared in the local newspaper or the court records in May 1876. Shots may well have been fired that night, but evidently no one was hit.

As W. E. Oglesby, another cowboy veteran of those rough-and-ready days in the cattle town, recalled how Courtright defused a potentially dangerous situation:

Shooting out the lights and using the bar fixtures for a target was a frequent happening in Fort Worth. The cowboys did that to satisfy their devilment emotions and not to be destructive or vindictive. The owner of the place which was shot up could always depend on the boys to settle up the damage. The cowboys were greatly amused by seeing the people duck for cover, as a covey of quail would go, when the shooting started.... Generally no one was hurt during the shooting.

One incident almost turned deadly, however, when a city policeman, whose name Oglesby could not recall, told a group of overly boisterous cowboys to return to camp or he would have to arrest them. They ignored him, and he made a move toward his pistol. A puncher named McClain knocked him cold and took his gun. The cowboys went on with their revelry, shooting at tantalizing targets and riding their horses into the saloons and demanding bar service as they sat in the saddle. When the policeman recovered his senses he left to get assistance under the taunts of the cowboys, who "were riled and wanted a fight."

A large crowd had gathered, expecting to see a gunfight. Soon an officer who Oglesby remembered as "Sheriff Courtwright" arrived on the scene.

> The atmosphere was tense, but not for long. The sheriff walked up to McClain and told him he or his friends need not fear arrest as long as they confined themselves to having fun without hurting anyone, but he would appreciate it if they would cut their play time short under the circumstances. The action of the sheriff saved having trouble and satisfied the cowboys. The boys headed out of town and showed their appreciation for the sheriff's good sense by shooting out the lights in only one block as they rode away. But they were back the next day and settled for the lights.[15]

The arrival of the long-awaited railroad in Fort Worth on July 19, 1876, triggered a new round of drinking and riotous celebration. A drunken cowboy named Fudge became obstreperous in the bar room of the Battle House, and the proprietor tossed him out in the street. Loudly voicing threats, Fudge armed himself with a Winchester rifle and returned. Too inebriated to see straight, he mistook an innocent bystander named E. K. Rea for the saloonkeeper and attempted to shoot him. But Rea managed to grab the rifle barrel and push it aside. Marshal Courtright appeared on the scene, arrested the cowboy, and took him before a justice of the peace who held him under $1,000 bail on a charge of assault with intent to murder.

A man named Sullivan, who claimed some railroad construction importance with five of his own teams working on the road, "considered himself privileged to cut up any amount of disturbance and swore he wouldn't go to the calaboose." But, said the *Democrat*. "Marshals Courtright and Fitzgerald thought differently, and after trying to take him there peaceably, were forced to drag him there. We commend the patience and firmness exercised by the officers in this case, and cannot condemn in too severe terms the action of some of our citizens, who impeded them in the discharge of a sworn duty.... The law must be executed rigidly and inexorably."[16]

C. C. Fitzgerald did not last long as assistant marshal. In September he got into serious trouble and was arrested by his boss. A man named D. C. Brown filed a complaint, charging Fitzgerald with operating a keno game in a saloon in partnership with a man called "Keno George." When they heard about it, Fitzgerald and Keno George went looking for Brown. Fitzgerald found him first and knocked him down several times before George showed up, "sent in a dozen or two more 'daisies,' kicked him in the head severely and bruised him in the face badly." Marshal Courtright and Sheriff Henderson appeared, put an end to the beating "with considerable difficulty," and arrested all the parties.[17]

Fitzgerald lost his job over the affair. He challenged Courtright for the marshal's position at the next election, but finished a poor fifth in a crowded slate of eleven candidates. Fitzgerald was a violent man who had not long to live. In August 1877 he got into a dispute with a black man named Washington Davis. Several blows were struck before guns were pulled, shots fired, and Fitzgerald received a mortal wound.

Shootings were common occurrences in Hell's Half Acre. Often, if no one was killed or seriously injured, they were not even reported in the local press. Overindulgence in alcohol was the primary contributing factor to the high incidence of gunplay and also the deplorable marksmanship that often resulted. An example was a sordid affair in October 1876 when "a party of soldiers in an intoxicated condition" began fighting each other in the saloon and bawdyhouse of Charles and Minnie Kraedler. "Pistols were drawn and two shots fired, both of which took effect, but not upon the persons for whom they were meant." Two of the female inmates were hit, Lizzie Hammer in the abdomen and Lou Stevens in the hand and side. When officers arrived, the soldiers had disappeared. A Doctor Fitzporter was summoned but the Stevens girl refused to let him dress her wounds "and continued her carousal." The doctor, in consideration of "the drunken and nervous condition" of Lizzie Hammer, did not want to risk probing her wounds and sent her to bed to sober up. "It is quite probable that she will die," remarked the *Democrat*.[18]

In December two peace officers visiting the city engaged in a pair of shooting matches that did little to enhance the legend of the deadly accurate gunfighting frontier lawman. A feud had developed between Deputy U. S. Marshal Henry Ware and Sheriff F. E. Wilson of Comanche County, and when the two found themselves in Fort Worth at the same time, violence erupted. On the evening of December 6 they exchanged ineffectual shots in the Trans-Continental Hotel, perforating only the walls, partitions, and bed clothing.

The next morning the two clashed again, this time in a scene beloved by western novelists and movie and television scriptwriters but seldom seen in the historic West: the stand-up, face-to-face shootout on the street. The marksmanship displayed by these frontier lawmen, however, was hardly up to fictional standards. Sheriff Wilson was about to leave on the Comanche stage when he saw Marshal Ware approaching, pistol in hand. Grabbing a double-barreled shotgun, Wilson swung it toward his adversary and pulled both triggers. One shell failed to fire, the other struck "Ware's clothing about the shoulder without doing any injury." The sheriff dropped the shotgun, pulled a pistol, and moved to meet his still advancing enemy. The marshal raised his revolver and fired one shot. The bullet hit Wilson in the wrist of his gun hand and he dropped his weapon. Officers rushed forward before any more damage was done and arrested Deputy Marshal Ware. They lodged him in the jail where he faced a charge of assault with intent to murder.[19]

The Fort Worth jail at the corner of Rusk and Second streets, where Marshal Courtright and his deputies deposited malefactors at this time, had been erected in 1873 when the city was incorporated. Costing less than $500, it was a crude log structure with no running water or toilet facilities. One small, barred window provided the only light and ventilation. Into this reeking, filthy hellhole officers threw those they arrested to remain until fines were paid or sentences completed. There was an often repeated joke in town: Question: "What's the difference between the moon and the Fort Worth jail?" Answer: "The moon is only full once a month. The Fort Worth jail is full every night."[20] When Editor Paddock heard one day in the summer of 1876 that the place had no occupants, he found that newsworthy. "The cal-aboose was without a tenant yesterday," he noted. "Not from the want of any attention, negligence or exertion on the part of our city police, but because the 'vags' have been forced to seek more salubrious climes, and peace and good order reigns in the city."[21]

The city marshal used prisoners to clean up the city streets but not always to the satisfaction of the editor of the *Democrat*, who regularly admonished him for neglecting this major responsibility:

"The city marshal would confer a favor on the entire community if he would have all the loose rocks removed from the streets. It would save animals and vehicles from injury and the multitude, including the tax-payers, would rise up and call him blessed."[22]

"Houston street should be cleaned up. Mr. City Marshal, there is a good deal of rubbish unnecessarily occupying room on that street.... See to it that it is removed."[23]

In an editorial published in early 1877 Paddock was particularly harsh in his criticism, charging that "pools of stagnant water, filth and decaying garbage" in the city streets, and "rocks, wood piles, empty boxes and barrels that obstruct the sidewalks" bore mute testimony that the municipal police force was not doing its job.[24] This appeared shortly before Courtright was to stand for reelection, and he moved quickly to repair any damage to his chances. Only two days later the *Democrat* admitted that "Marshal Courtright has taken steps to have the city cleansed of some of the filth which encumbers it at this writing."[25]

Another form of "filth" concerning Paddock was the licentious and riotous behavior of the dance hall and brothel denizens of Hell's Half Acre. He was well aware, of course, that a great deal of the city's funding derived from fines levied on these vice merchants and the inmates of their establishments, and sometimes commented rather smugly on the practice: "Saturday was an unusual day in the Mayor's office. Quite a

number of females were gently persuaded to pay their periodical trib-
utes to the city treasury. After pleading guilty to the charges made, they
gallantly shelled out their 'rag babies' to the tune of $9.30 apiece, 'rahed
for Fort Worth, and retired with their usual dignity."[26]

Its prosperity and reputation as a town where "anything went"
attracted a number of veteran sporting house proprietors to Fort
Worth. George and Mag Wood were there, as were another couple
infamous in the frontier towns, "Rowdy Joe" and "Rowdy Kate" Lowe,
whose nicknames give a strong hint as to their propensity for disorderly
conduct. Others on hand that first year of Courtright's tenure as
marshal included John Leer, N. H. Wilson, John Stewart, and Jennie
Thompson.

Frontier ruffian Rowdy Joe
Lowe was a prominent
citizen of Fort Worth's
Hell's Half Acre during
Courtright's tenure as city
marshal. *Courtesy Kansas
State Historical Society,
Topeka, Kansas.*

Before coming to Fort Worth the rowdy Lowes managed notorious dives in Newton and Delano, the vice suburb of Wichita, Kansas. In Delano Joe killed E. T. "Red" Beard, another of his type, in a celebrated gunbattle. Wanted for murder in Kansas, Joe moved to Texas, where Kate rejoined him. The couple ran similar places at Denison and Luling before joining the rush to Fort Worth in 1876. Although Kate shared Joe's surname and nickname, she never was legally married to the man, and shortly after their arrival in the Panther City, Joe deserted her for another woman. At Fort Worth on August 2, 1876, he joined with Mollie Field in holy matrimony.[27]

After breaking up with Joe, Rowdy Kate continued to manage a dancehall in Hell's Half Acre before moving on to Weatherford, Texas. The *Democrat* reported in September that "an infernal 'cuss' who does not deserve the name of man, but who, we hear, bears the human form, cut up a nymph du pave at Rowdy Kate's dancehouse night before last. He was pursued by the officers of the law, but his legs which proved longer than the sidetrack of the Texas and Pacific landed him in Dallas at one P.M. He's home now."[28]

Joe, meanwhile, had several business interests. In October he took over management of the Centennial Hotel on Main Street between Second and Third and converted it into a theater. Shortly thereafter he acquired the Red Light Saloon on Rusk Street from John Leer. As Richard Selcer, the foremost historian of Hell's Half Acre, has pointed out, Rowdy Joe Lowe

became the Acre's first vice king and one of Fort Worth's most colorful figures.... His experience and reputation in the Kansas cow towns could be put to good use in Fort Worth. Many of the cowboys who passed through the doors of the Red Light had been regular customers in his establishments on the other end of the Chisholm Trail. He could call them by name and probably even knew what kind of whiskey many of them drank.[29]

Joe Lowe remained friendly with Jim Courtright during these years and never gave him any trouble. The same could not be said of N. H. Wilson, another prominent citizen of the vice district.

On December 20, 1876, Editor Paddock received a missive from Wilson attacking Mayor Day and Marshal Courtright, with a request that it be published in his pages. Paddock complied but, knowing that the "card" was bound to ruffle official feathers, appended a disclaimer intended to distance himself and his paper from any repercussions that might follow. "We give space to a personal advertisement," he said, "for which we disclaim any responsibility, and greatly deprecate any and all matters of this kind. But when a person places his signature to an article of this kind, and thereby assumes all responsibility, there is no course left us but to give them the space desired, at our usual advertising rates."

Wilson's piece, complete with poor grammar, was headed: "A Card: The Way Mayor Day and Marshal Courtright Runs Fort Worth." Wilson accused the mayor of maintaining a financial interest in a keno game in the district and the marshal of directing where and how "legitimate" businesses could be run. The aldermen, he said, were fully aware of these activities and refused to take action against either man. "Yet everybody is screaming morality. I throw up my hands in holy horror," expostulated the saloon and dancehall operator in mock dismay.

The paper no sooner appeared than Courtright, accompanied by a deputy, William A. "Tip" Clower, braced Wilson on Main Street. Wilson's version of what then transpired was given in an interview with a *Democrat* reporter later that day. The saloon man said

Courtright approached and announced he wanted to search him for concealed weapons.

> I objected when he attempted to lay hands on me, and I backed off the sidewalk into the street. Courtright then drew his sixshooter and followed me up. When [he came] near enough, I quickly grabbed hold of his pistol with one hand and drawing mine with the other, struck him a blow on the forehead. "Tip" by this time had hold of me and prevented me from wrenching the pistol from Courtright's hand. At this time, while I had hold of the weapon, he fired, shooting me in the leg.

Wilson said that William Phares, a Dallas policeman who happened to be present, interfered at this point and prevented Courtright from shooting him again while Clower held him. "Courtright and 'Tip' were both under the influence of liquor. In my opinion, Courtright took this way of picking a fuss with me on account of the card I had published in the *Democrat* concerning Mayor Day and himself."[30]

Courtright, interviewed the following day, told it a little differently, of course. After being informed by several persons that Wilson was carrying a pistol, he looked up the man and said he wanted to search him. Wilson declared he had no weapon and stepped back. Saying that "he would discharge his duty," the marshal pressed on.

> Mr. Courtright says that Wilson stood with his right hand in his coat pocket, and as he advanced a second time, Wilson started to draw his pistol, that it caught in the pocket, and Courtright started to draw his pistol. Before he could do so, Wilson had his pistol out and struck him on

the head. The first blow staggered him a little, and as he was rising he shot at Wilson. That at no time did Wilson have hold of his weapon, and that policeman "Tip" caught hold of Wilson only after Courtright had shot.[31]

Whichever version one believes, the Wilson shooting incident adds no luster to the legend of Jim Courtright.

The marshal's bullet had torn through Wilson's thigh, about four inches above the knee, inflicting a painful flesh wound. Courtright also suffered from the blow to the head Wilson had delivered. Neither injury was considered serious.

County warrants were issued for the arrest of the marshal and his deputy on a charge of assault with attempt to murder, but, strangely, Wilson was not charged. Sheriff Henderson served the papers and Courtright and Clower were released on bail pending a grand jury hearing, scheduled for March 1877. Wilson also filed a city complaint against the officers, but when he failed to appear and sign the affidavits the city council dismissed the case.[32]

The grand jury on March 20, 1877, brought indictments against Courtright and Clower, charging, with the usual legal jargon, that "with force [they] did unlawfully, violently and feloniously make an assault upon the person of one N. H. Wilson with the felonious intent... of their express malice aforethought to kill and murder." Trial was set for April 3, 1877. Four prominent Fort Worth attorneys — Junius W. Smith, J. J. Jarvis, C. M. Templeton, and J. C. Scott — represented the defendants. Any violence directed at Wilson, they said, was "in self-defense and to prevent said Wilson, who then had a pistol in his hand and attempting to assault the defendants with same... from committing a violent assault upon [them] and from taking their own lives when they were acting as marshal and policeman. . . in the discharge of their duties." The defense requested a continuance, which was granted until August 21, 1877. At that time William Phares, the Dallas policeman whose testimony was vital to the state's case, did not appear, and attorneys for the state requested another continuance. Another year passed before the trial was finally held.

When the case was called on August 19, 1878, Courtright's lawyers moved to separate his trial from that of Clower. When the court denied the request, they immediately asked that the charges against their client be dismissed. This was also denied, and the trial of both defendants went forward. After hearing the testimony of a number of witnesses, the jury quickly brought in an acquittal.[33]

The Courtright-Wilson dustup in December 1876 seemed to set off a round of violence in Fort Worth that winter. Three weeks later a strong-arm robbery, said to be the first crime of its kind in the city's history, was committed. A man named J. C Lamphier was knocked down and robbed on Third Street. Courtright quickly arrested a suspect, one Charles Allen, lodged him in the city jail, and received the congratulations of the *Democrat*.[34]

Then, three nights later, another dance-hall operator went on a rampage. At about nine o'clock on the evening of January 14, 1877, John Leer, drunk and on the prod, rode his horse through the doors and up to the bar of a competitive dance hall on Houston Street, cocked a pistol, and demanded a drink. Before the proprietors, John Stewart and Henry McCristle, could respond to this intrusion, Leer's horse panicked and backed out of the doorway, throwing its rider. Bystanders took the drunken Leer into the nearby Comique Theatre, where city officers placed him under arrest and escorted him to jail.

After giving $100 bail to assure his appearance at a hearing the next morning, Leer returned to the Stewart and McCristle dance hall. The owners denied him admittance and locked the doors. Leer again unlimbered his six-shooter, broke out several panes of glass, and fired five shots into the building. One ball, after passing through a stove, struck McCristle in the back, but most its force was spent and the wound was not serious. Another bullet hit Stewart in the leg.

Again Courtright's police took Leer into custody and lodged him in jail, where he spent the night. He paid a fine for his spree, but no further criminal action was taken against him, and he returned to Hell's Half Acre and his business interests.[35]

Two weeks after the Leer disturbance an unidentified cattleman delivered a "severe chastisement" in the form of the "bones of the right hand" to the jaw of a troublemaker called "California Bill" and threw him out of the Cattle Exchange Saloon. The city marshal took California Bill in hand and "gave him quarters in the calaboose"[36]

On February 15, 1877, the *Democrat* reported that Deputy Marshals "Tip" Clower and J. H. Peters had "severely beaten" a man named Redmond "for committing an act of indiscretion that would justify the imprisonment of an angel." The nature of Redmond's "act of indiscretion" was left to the imagination of the reader.

In March the nightly revelry in the Acre with its attendant violence continued and was duly reported in the local press: A "war of fists" broke out on Main Street and "resulted in a knock down of one of the parties. The man who maintained his pegs mounted the fellow who was down and flopped his 'wings' and crowed. The Marshal at this time put in an appearance and arrested both offenders."[37]

"Courtright 'snaked in' the rowdy who was shooting in the streets last night."[38]

"More shooting at the usual places in the eastern portion of the city last night…. Wake up early in the morning, hear the gun shots, smell the powder, hear a few stray shots pass your ear, and… imagine you are out on the plains hunting wild game, and not in a city [like] the

Fort, and then [consider] whose duty it is to have such regular and dangerous practice stopped."[39]

The most serious outbreak of violence occurred that month in the early hours of March 6, 1877, at the doorway of Arch Johnson's saloon on Main Street. It involved L. O. Fonvielle, a visitor in town, and Pat Hunter, a "sport" of the district. The two had gambled in the place and when a dispute arose, "abusive language passed between them," and Fonvielle tried to leave. Hunter followed him to the door and "flourished a pistol," a six-shooter. Fonvielle pulled his own weapon, a Smith and Wesson single-shot derringer, and fired. The bullet struck Hunter in the groin, inflicting a dangerous wound. Fonvielle then jerked Hunter's pistol from his hand and fired four more shots, one of which took effect, wounding the gambler in the thigh. Immediately after the shooting Fonvielle left the city. But Courtright, learning that he had holed up at a house four miles from town, went after him and brought him back as dawn was breaking in Fort Worth.[40]

In an interview a few years later W. P. Thomas, one of Courtright's deputies, spoke candidly of those rough days and the problems faced by the Fort Worth police:

> Yes, gentlemen, it is a hard life. You can't expect to please everybody, even by the kindest and most unfaltering adherence to the strict letter of duty. You might detect a man in the very act of committing a violation of the ordinances and perform the duty of arresting and making complaint against him with as much delicacy as you would escort a lady through the streets to her home, and yet, if he had money or friends, there would be some one to find fault with the officer. We do not have as much trouble of this character now as formerly. From the time the railroad

reached Fort Worth [July 19, 1876] up to say one year ago
[1879], the police force passed through many trying
ordeals.... Weapons were plentiful. Every man had them
and almost every man was ready to shoot and cut on the
slightest provocation. We generally managed to land the
disturber in the calaboose, however, and seldom used even
the "billy." Many a man can thank his stars that the law
makes it an officer's duty to turn a deaf ear to his insults....
The wild and wooly ranger of the prairies has been taught
by bitter experience that the city is different from his accus-
tomed haunts – that there are men here who will "take him
in" or take his life.... The dark deeds of reckless desperadoes, confidence men, "thugs," and manipulators of
drugged drinks have gone into the past, never to be revived
in Fort Worth.... The Fort has settled down to a degree of
order and quietness which is hard to realize, and no one
rejoiced over this changed state of affairs more heartily
than we policemen.[41]

Thomas did not exaggerate the trials and tribulations of a cowtown
lawman, but T. I. "Jim" Courtright seemed to thrive on the difficult job.
In the spring of 1877 he stood for re-election to a second term as city
marshal at Fort Worth.

POLICING THE
BLOODY THIRD

"Courtright is reputed to be a man of fearless character, and of a friendly, free-and-easy style among his associates, and in his intercourse with quiet, ordinary people, he was said to be unassuming and pleasant, and the union of these qualities gave him active friends among all classes, and strong sympathizers among some of the better."

W. H. King, Adjutant-General of Texas

In the early months of 1877 as another round of city elections approached, Editor Paddock became increasingly critical of the administration of Mayor Day and particularly of City Marshal Courtright. In his issue of February 9 he inveighed against the city officers:

> Laws, plain and unmistakable, have been violated... ordinances have not been enforced; crime has not been punished; offenders against the law have gone unwhipt of justice; decency has been outraged; good morals and public policy defiled; and a general disregard of the rights and privileges of the tax payer exercised.

In his attack on the officers Paddock avoided mention, however, of the serious charge of assault to murder hanging over Courtright's head. Only two weeks before election day the grand jury handed down the indictment against Courtright and Clower, but the newspaperman did

not report this in his columns, choosing instead to belabor the city marshal for what he considered dereliction of duty in dealing with
Paddock's major concerns — the condition of the streets and the public disporting of dance-hall prostitutes. In an editorial on March 21, the
day following the indictment, he inveighed against Courtright for not
cleaning up the streets and doing nothing about "the daily appearance
of lewd women and their 'friends' in public conveyances [and] the dens
of infamy that are nightly opened on our principal thoroughfare, an
insult to every respectable man, woman and child in the city."

And again on April 3, election day and the day scheduled for the
trial of Courtright and Clower, Paddock continued to berate Mayor Day
and his officers for the deplorable condition of the streets and the ongoing operation of the dance halls. "The city is filled with filth, cesspools
and decaying garbage," he wrote. "Loose rocks of sufficient dimensions
to do serious injury to both animals and vehicles encumber every street
in the city. Several streets have become so obstructed that they cannot
be used." Although the city council had passed an ordinance against the
dance halls, they remained open to "ply their vocations nightly on the
principal streets of the city without molestation or hindrance." While
the mayor, "sworn to see that all ordinances are executed and that the
subordinate officers do their duty ...looks on, with indifference if not
approval... the subordinate officers neglect their duty."

Courtright had announced his candidacy for re-election to the
office of city marshal earlier that month. He was challenged for the job
by no fewer than ten other candidates, including former officers C. C.
Fitzgerald, John Stoker, and Tom Redding.[1]

Mayor Day and City Attorney Henry Field were opposed by two
candidates each.

The Fort Worth electorate seemed little concerned by Paddock's
criticism of the administration or Courtright's legal difficulty. When the

votes were counted, all three incumbents won re-election by a wide margin. Day defeated his nearest competitor by more than two hundred votes; Field overwhelmed his challengers, receiving more than two-thirds of the total ballots cast; and Courtright handily defeated O. C. Cheney, the second place finisher in the city marshal race, 337 to 169.

The town continued to grow, and the size of its police force grew with it. The number of policemen reporting to Courtright varied with the seasonal ebb and flow of transients, but even in the winter when trail herds were not passing through, he had six under his command. All were paid $50 a month, the same salary he received, and all shared also in the distribution of revenue from fines paid. Abram N. Woody, J. H. McConnell, Frank Taylor, J. H. Peters, S. M. Farmer, J. T. Bryant, and E. W. Baker were among those on the force during Courtright's second term in office. Abe Woody became an especially close friend and supporter and figured prominently in Courtright's later Fort Worth adventures.

Until early 1877 the policemen of Fort Worth attended to their duties in regular street clothes, as no provision for uniforms had been made. In January of that year the city council appointed Courtright and Mayor Day as a committee to recommend suitable uniforms for the force. Their recommendation, approved by council, was a gray coat and a hat or cap of the individual officer's choosing. Most selected a black slouch hat. Marshal Courtright created something of a furor in the ranks later in the year, however, when he had the color of the uniform coat changed to blue. This did not sit well with some of his die-hard Confederate deputies who associated the color with the detested Yankee "bluebellies" of the late war and difficult Reconstruction period. But Courtright was adamant, and the blue uniform remained until he left office. Then, at the insistence of the officers, the coat color once again became gray.

Courtright's second term was much like his first, with the continual problem of controlling vice and violence in Hell's Half Acre. For political purposes in February 1877 the city was divided into three political districts with two aldermen to be elected from each ward. The Third Ward, where most of the saloons, dance halls, gambling dens, and low theaters were located, soon became known as the "Bloody Third."

An ongoing source of trouble for Courtright's police during the spring and summer were the cattle drovers flocking into town for a night of carousal before continuing on their arduous journey north to Kansas. Most rode into town wearing weapons and, when they got drunk and belligerent, posed a real threat to order and a serious problem for law enforcement.

In April 1877 a cowboy named Wilson, "while under the influence of liquor" in the Cattle Exchange Saloon, "drew his six-shooter, threatening to shoot Mr. Joe Lowe.... and might have succeeded if policeman Taylor had not put in an appearance and, divesting Wilson of his weapons, took him under the guidance of his protective wing."

While Deputy Frank Taylor was collaring the obstreperous cowboy in the Cattle Exchange, Marshal Courtright was dealing with another on Main Street. The drover, Martin Flannigan by name, having "imbibed an undue quantity of spirituous liquor," was staggering down Main Street when he was spotted by Courtright, who told him to mount up and ride out of town before he got into trouble. Flannigan climbed aboard his horse but, once in the saddle, raced up and down the city streets, voicing loud rebel yells and shooting his pistol. Courtright borrowed a horse, ran Flannigan down, and dragged him off to jail.[2]

In June the *Democrat* reported that "The Marshal, in company with almost his entire police force, was busy all Saturday night last with the troublesome cow boys, who congregated in almost countless numbers at the different dance houses and other places of vile resort. A number of difficulties occurred during the night and most of the offenders were tenderly cared for by the officers in spite of the numerous threats which were made against them."[3]

Courtright was generally quite tolerant of the antics of the visiting cowboys, taking his cue from the establishment, the politicians and merchants who were well aware that the cattlemen's trade was important to the city's business interests. Even that staunch promoter of law, order, and morality, B. B. Paddock, made allowances for the drovers. "The festive cowboy disports himself on the streets now and then," he wrote in the *Democrat* of April 25, 1877. "They are a light-hearted, devil-may-care class of men, and should be allowed as much latitude as is consistent with the good order of the city."

Of greater concern to Paddock, the town fathers, and consequently Courtright, were the increasingly frequent outbreaks of violence in the Bloody Third, the fistfights, shootings, and stabbings. Tin-horn gamblers who had invaded the city with the boom were often a source of trouble.

Ben Tutt, one of that class, entered the Blue Light Saloon and Dance House on Rusk Street on the evening of April 9, 1877, and demanded a free drink from the bartender, D. S. Randall. Seeing that Tutt was drunk and in a dangerous mood, Randall complied. Tutt downed the booze and expressed his gratitude by pulling out a pistol and firing three shots at the bartender. Randall ducked quickly behind the bar to avoid being killed and received only a grazing shoulder wound. Infuriated now, the bartender arose and began hurling bottles at his attacker. Tutt retreated out the door, turned, and emptied his revolver into the saloon in an ineffectual barrage. By this time Randall had found better armament than bottles and opened up with his own sixshooter. He fired three shots at the retreating gambler without effect. Officers later arrested Tutt, but, when Randall refused to press charges, released him with only a warning to behave himself. Tutt was not the behaving kind, however. Again in a state of drunkenness a few days later, he brandished his gun in the Theater Comique and succeeded only in shooting himself in the hand.

Tutt, Randall, and many other Fort Worth shootists seem to have been remarkably poor shots. Under the headline, "A Little Shooting But Nobody Hurt," the *Democrat* a month later reported another altercation in which shots were fired without effect. Courtright quickly arrested the shooter and received Editor Paddock's grudging congratulation: "We concede Mr. Courtright credit for his promptness in the matter."[4]

When Frank Foster and Charlie Smith pulled guns and exchanged shots in the Acre's notorious Waco Tap on January 18, 1878, each managed to hit his adversary, but both survived.

Even an attempt at assassination failed because of poor shooting. The intended victim was John Leer, the saloon and dance-hall man, who in January 1878 expanded his business interests by taking over full ownership of a livery stable on Houston Street that he had formerly operated with one Louis Heller. The terms of the ownership change were evidently not entirely satisfactory to Leer's former partner. As Leer sat at his desk in the office of the livery on the morning of January 9, 1878, Heller came up behind him and "at a distance of not more than ten feet" fired a round from "a Colt's improved pistol at the unsuspecting victim." The bullet tore through Leer's right shoulder and the desk and lodged in a one-inch pine partition. Heller fled but was quickly caught and disarmed by stable employees. Turned over to the officers, he readily admitted his intention was to kill Leer, but "his aim was rendered untrue by nervousness." Leer fully recovered and surprised everyone by refusing to press charges against Heller. However, when he was on his feet and attending to his business again in February he was quoted as saying that no partners were wanted. "He don't like their style," said the *Democrat*.[5]

Weapons other than six-shooters were sometimes employed in the vice district disputes that erupted into violence. When Frank Devere and one "Irish Billy" tangled over the affections of a whore named Willie Reed, "Billy made a suspicious move with his hand as though to draw a pistol, when, quicker than a flash, Frank whipped out his bar-low knife and planted the blade deep into Billy's side…. The wound, though an ugly one, is not expected to prove fatal."[6]

A week or so later two gamblers "came together rather violently" on Main Street. "One of them had three broken knuckles and barely escaped being carved up by a dangerous hatchet in the hands of his bloodthirsty opponent." Both were arrested and gave bond for appearance in the mayor's court.[7]

At three o'clock on the morning of February 13, 1878, a melee broke out in the Mobile Restaurant. Night watchman John Witt was stabbed with a butcher knife and "otherwise bruised by cooks in the establishment." Officers arrested a man named William Hines and charged him with the stabbing.[8]

All this violence resulted in surprisingly few fatalities. An exception was a deadly brawl in the Red Light Saloon in the early hours of Sunday, December 23, 1877, when William Fields got into a dispute with "Indian Dave" Andre and pulled "an ugly looking cotton knife [and] commenced brandishing it recklessly." Fields advanced toward Andre, who drew his pistol. Several bystanders, including John Leer and Palmer Branch, attempted to separate the two fighters. As Branch grasped Andre's revolver, it went off, sending a bullet through the peacemaker's right hand. Andre ran out of the building, but Fields followed, still waving his cotton knife. Indian Dave turned and fired.

Fields went down with three bullets in his body and died that evening.[9]

Deputy Marshal J. T. Bryant later arrested Andre in the Waco Tap but somehow allowed him to escape on the way to jail. The blunder brought forth a letter to the *Democrat* editor that was highly critical of Courtright's police force. The writer, signing himself "Observer," deplored the escape of Andre and pointed out other recent incidents in which he said the officers were negligent: "Christmas night some cowardly ruffians fired their pistols into a house on Houston street [and] no one was arrested for it. The night before last, the same thing happened, by the same parties.... Still no arrests."[10]

Observer's letter was published in the newspaper without comment from the editor. Courtright had risen in Paddock's estimation during the preceding months. Editorial harangues in the *Democrat* about the deplorable condition of the streets and dance-hall depravity had led to noticeable improvement in these areas. Three issues of the paper during one week in May commended the police for their work with the street problem.[11]

The city council had passed several ordinances designed to control prostitution and the marshal and his force of police had enforced the measures. In April two strumpets appeared at a baseball game wearing their professional attire, "which exhibited a little more of their pedal extremities" than was proper at a gathering that included decent women and children. They were promptly arrested and fined $5 each in police court for "indecently exhibiting their persons in public." The *Democrat* lauded the police "for preventing this insult to the ladies and gentlemen on the grounds."[12]

Under the headline, "Closed at Last. The Defunct Dance Houses," the *Democrat* reported in June that Marshal Courtright had shut down all the dance-halls and arrested the owners. Said Paddock:

We heard during the day that the proprietor of one of the houses had said that no police officer in Fort Worth was man enough to arrest him. Expecting some trouble to arise in the efforts of the officers to carry out the functions of the law, we repaired to the scene of the expected trouble, and instead of the usual commotion and noise, so common to the eastern portion of the city, all was tranquil and still and quiet reigned supreme. The dance houses were all closed, the music men have all been discharged and the employees turned off. The Democrat has worked faithfully in the accomplishment of this end, and heartily congratulates the citizens on the final result.[13]

The dance halls did not stay closed, of course. After payment of a $10 fine the owners were released to return to their establishments and open up again. It was a routine that would continue throughout Fort Worth's boom years.

Paddock seemed satisfied with this travesty of justice and heaped plaudits on the city marshal. Courtright, said the editor, "has been vigilant in the discharge of his duty, fearless and brave in meeting danger, has nearly lost his life in effecting arrest, and has been a vigilant, brave and efficient officer."[14] Under fire from the *Democrat* in the past for dereliction in the matter of the dance houses, he had now "come square to the front" on that issue. The paper, said Paddock,

gladly applauds him for having dared to do his duty in the face of the many [intimidations] with which he has had to contend. He has made more warm friends by this act than all others…. He has an efficient corps of policemen under his command, and we look for peace and good order within our limits. All honor to our Marshal Courtright and his assistants. [15]

The prevalence in Hell's Half Acre of gambling, considered by many to be as iniquitous as prostitution, was largely ignored by the *Democrat*, whose editor may have enjoyed engaging in a game of chance himself. (In a history of Fort Worth's early days published many years later, Paddock ridiculed attempts at gambling reform: "The reformer was here then as now and tried to reform every one else but himself, just as they do now with about the same success. The town was 'wide open' to the horror of some and an effort was made at intervals to put a stop to the open gambling house.")[16]

But Courtright's campaign against the vice joints in the summer of 1877 did include gambling dens. "Marshal Courtright was on a rampage last night and before he got through all the gambling resorts in the city closed," reported the *Democrat* of June 28.. Like the dance-hall men, the gambling house operators paid their fines and only three nights later a reporter for the paper toured the district and found the places back in operation.

In an editorial later in the year Paddock explained the paper's position with regard to gaming, professional members of the gambling fraternity, and those who patronized them. As in all professions, he said, there were legitimate and illegitimate practitioners. Professional gamblers, those considered honest and even those "who deal from the bottom, stack the cards, play cold decks, and resort to other tricks [to fleece] their unsophisticated opponent," he did not consider a problem. "If a man chooses to risk his money against that of a gambler's upon the turn of a card, it is no concern of ours. If he is fool enough to engage in a game with a blackleg who is a stranger to him and loses his money by 'ways that are dark and tricks that are vain,' he deserves no sympathy." But criminals posing as gamblers who enticed victims into their dens with larcenous and murderous intent were to be condemned. "We know of no language too severe, no epithet too damning to apply to them."[17]

In a letter signed simply "The Gamblers," members of the fraternity responded to Paddock's remarks. The paper was praised for "its kindly and honorable" position in drawing "a line of distinction" between the sporting fraternity and the criminals element:

> Gambling, though illegal, is a profession followed by many and is tolerated the world over. We know [a law prohibits] gambling, but... we think it to be a bad law, and does not mean what it says. It was not the intention of the givers of that law that gambling should be suppressed in toto, for this is unprecedented and we think impossible [of enforcement]. But they intended to restrict and restrain it to a certain extent [and] it should be restrained.... Gambling is as much or not more restricted in Fort Worth than any other town in the State. We pay hundreds of dollars every month into the city and county treasuries as fines for violating the law.... We simply wish the public to understand that the sporting fraternity of Fort Worth [is] not composed of thieves and robbers, and [does] not like to be classed with such persons.[18]

Among the gamblers in Fort Worth at the time were some of the top professionals in the West. All presumably endorsed the views expressed in this letter. Ben Thompson, the most celebrated gambler-gunman in Texas history, was there, as was his younger brother, William, who also lived by the cards and the gun but always remained in the shadow of his more famous sibling. For more than three years Billy Thompson had been a fugitive from justice. In 1873 he had killed Sheriff Chauncey B. Whitney in the cow town of Ellsworth, Kansas, and fled the state. Rewards were offered for his capture, and in late 1876 he was finally arrested by Texas Rangers and returned to Kansas for trial on a charge of first-degree murder. After his acquittal in September 1877, he joined Ben at the gambling tables of Fort Worth. Interviewed by a reporter for the *Democrat*, Billy was described as having a "pleasant countenance, a sparkling and brilliant eye, an intelligent looking face," and an impressive *"tout ensemble."*[19] A few months later Billy went up to Fort Griffin, Texas, to work the tables. When a report

Ben Thompson, gambler and gunman of wide notoriety, frequented the saloons and dives of the Fort Worth vice district but gave Jim Courtright no trouble. *Courtesy Robert G. McCubbin Collection.*

circulated that he had been killed there, Ben wired friends in the town for verification and was assured there was no truth to the story. Shortly afterward Ben wrapped up his affairs in Fort Worth, put his fine span of black horses stabled at John Leer's Livery up for sale, and, accompanied by "John Chinaman," his servant, left for New Orleans and the Mardi Gras.[20]

Ben Thompson was a true western gunfighter, perhaps the very best. Bat Masterson, who knew Thompson and most of the celebrated frontier gunmen personally, thought so. "It is very doubtful if in his time there was another man living who equalled him with a pistol in a life or death struggle," he wrote.

Billy Thompson, younger brother of Ben, had a reputation as a troublemaker but also behaved himself in Fort Worth during Courtright's time. *Courtesy Western History Collections, University of Oklahoma Library, Norman, Oklahoma.*

Such men as "Wild Bill" Hickok, Wyatt Earp, Billy
Tilghman, Charley Bassett, Luke Short, Clay Allison, Joe
Lowe and Jim Curry were all men with nerves of steel who
had often been put to the test.... These men, all of them,
lived and played their part on the lurid edge of our Western
frontier at the time Ben Thompson was playing his, and it is
safe to assume that not one of them would have declined the
gage of battle with him had he flung it down to any of their
number.... [However] little doubt exists in my mind that
Thompson would have returned the winner in the contest.[21]

The name of Jim Courtright, it should be noted, was not included
in Masterson's list of Ben Thompson's peers.

Although both Ben and Billy Thompson earned their livelihood
by operating games of chance and were notorious gunmen who always
went armed, Marshal Jim Courtright apparently never arrested either
on a gambling or weapons charge while they were in Fort Worth. With
men like the Thompsons, his policy was "live and let live."

Visiting Fort Worth at this time were two other gambler-gunmen
who later were to achieve national celebrity. John H. "Doc" Holliday
was there in July 1877, staying at the Trans-Continental Hotel under
his alias, J. H. McKey. He was recovering from a gunshot wound
received in an Independence Day altercation with another gambler at
Breckenridge, Texas. A cousin, George Henry Holliday, came from
Georgia and checked into the Trans-Continental to help Doc in his
recuperation.[22] The gunfighting dentist probably plied his gambling
trade at Fort Worth, but there is no record that he ever got into trouble
there or was bothered by Courtright or his policemen.

Several months later another gambler and gunfighter, destined for
fame even greater than Holliday's, was in Fort Worth. Wyatt Earp came

to town to see the sights, try his luck at the tables, and visit his elder brother Jim, a dealer and bartender at the Cattle Exchange Saloon on Houston Street. Wyatt never unlimbered his guns in Fort Worth, but on the night of January 25, 1878, in the Cattle Exchange he did display the fistic ability for which he was also renowned. A cowboy named Russell provoked him for some reason, and Wyatt administered what the *Democrat* called "a first class pounding." Officers called to the disturbance arrested Earp, and he gave bond for appearance in the mayor's court. Russell left town hurriedly, and when he failed to appear, charges against Earp were dropped.[23]

Courtright's police were on a campaign at this time to clamp down on weapons toters. In mayor's court a few days earlier four men had been fined $10 and costs for carrying pistols. Another received the same fine for carrying a sword cane.[24]

One of those fined was William H. "Billy" Simms, a well-known Austin gambler who was a good friend and pupil of Ben Thompson. Simms evidently objected to the harassment in Fort Worth and moved on to Denison, Texas, where, within a month he unlimbered his pistol and shot and killed one J. V. George in a fight over a soiled dove named Annie Woods. Simms was quickly cleared on a plea of self-defense, but Paddock, in an editorial entitled "Crime – Society's Wolf," used the incident to rail against the depravity and violence then rampant in Texas:

> We envy not the gambler, rough or libertine who boasts over the success attending the killing of his first man – for of such are the devil's cohorts, and for a certainty will they receive punishment adequate to the enormity of their crimes.Bill Simms [the latest] murderer in Texas... has ever been a gambler, a quarrelsome, troublesome young man, ambitious to 'shoot somebody' – and his selection of a friend

for a victim is only in keeping with his character....
No friendly hand was thrust from under that bed of prosti-
tution to stay the committal of a crime that consigned
George to an unsanctified grave. Texas has already suffered

Billy Simms was another
well-known sport of
Hell's Half Acre.
*Courtesy Robert G.
McCubbin Collection.*

greatly by acts of vandalism and deeds of barbarity. Judge Lynch is a commendable character as compared to the gambler who, with revolver in hand, deals out death according to his individual fancy or compliance with his harlot's decree.[25]

Like the dance-hall men, the gambling house operators of Fort Worth were regularly arrested and fined during this period. The same names kept appearing in police court: Robert J. "Bob" Winders,[26] John Dixon, Charles Hadley, J. A. and A. H. Knight, Charles Cage, J. W. Brown, T. J. Prindle, Charles Lignowski, Dick Townsend, T. J. Randall, Jake Stoker, J. W. Brown and John C. Morris. In 1877 the fine levied for "gaming" was $10 and costs; by the next year it had risen to $25.

Rowdy Joe Lowe, who ran the Centennial Theater in Fort Worth, was both a gambler and a keeper of bawds. He was also a dangerous gunman. Bat Masterson, as noted, considered him the equal of Hickok, Earp, and other celebrated gunfighters of the era. In Fort Worth Lowe was often arrested and fined for running a disorderly house, a euphemism for whoremongering, and for carrying a pistol. In a letter to the *Democrat* in June 1877 he complained that the local press had attacked him unfairly and his theater had been inaccurately described as a den of iniquity; he threatened to leave. "I keep good order in my house," he said, "and if any man becomes disorderly, and there is no officer of the law present, I am very apt to take the law into my own hands. If I am to be subject to newspaper attack for doing this, I want to go to some more law-abiding place of about 40,000 inhabitants, where I can run the same legitimate business and receive the protection of the law, and where a clique will not think it injurious to their town."[27]

During the campaign against the dancehalls that summer, Paddock had an unlikely ally in Joe Lowe, who saw an opportunity to strike a blow at those he considered competitors. In an editorial headed "Good for Joseph," Paddock opined:

> There may be much in Mr. Lowe's moral character to admire, and less to imitate, but we are taught in all things to approve that which is good, and far be it from the Democrat to withhold... praise for good deeds. [Joe Lowe] has been aiding the Democrat in the laudable effort of ridding the city of the dance houses that infest this place. We learn that he has made complaints against some of them, and assisted in the prosecution. The Democrat approves and commends the act, if not the motive. As statesmen sometimes do, it accepts the treason if not the traitor, and wishes Mr. Lowe success in his undertaking. When he shall have succeeded in this, we hope he may himself have become accustomed to the commission of moral deeds, and have absorbed enough of moral elements, so that the Democrat, with what outside assistance we may receive, may be able to reform the reformer.[28]

Paddock may have welcomed Lowe's assistance in the reform campaign, but that did not prevent him from attacking him. "Close the Centennial; close the dance houses, close the gambling houses. Nothing looks worse in public matters than partiality," he wrote only two days after the above editorial appeared. Lowe was indeed having plenty of legal trouble at the time. On July 9 he was in mayor's court, charged with keeping a disorderly house but gained an acquittal. "Joe's always lucky," said the *Democrat*. The following day he was found guilty of running a dancehall in violation of the ordinance then in effect and fined $10. "Let no guilty man escape," remarked the paper. That very day the city council adopted an ordinance prohibiting sale of intoxicating beverages within any show or theater, a measure directly aimed at Lowe and the Centennial.[29]

Jim Courtright always remained close to the saloon scene in Fort Worth. A drinker and gambler himself, he was friendly with most of the sporting men who headquartered in the Bloody Third. While he was marshal he kept his drinking and gambling discreet and never came under attack for these vices. In May 1877 he did submit to arrest for "violation of the gaming laws by playing pool," but this seems to have been a test case to see whether the anti-gambling ordinance applied to billiards or pool. A jury heard the case, decided it did not, and acquitted him.[30]

Courtright certainly was well acquainted also with many of the madams and trollops who plied their trade in the district, but lechery was not one of his vices. He went home every night to his wife and children in their house at the corner of Second and Calhoun streets, on the edge of the Acre. Throughout Courtright's checkered career there was never a hint that he was unfaithful to Betty or anything but completely devoted to his children.

A couple of stories indicate, however, that a pronounced mischievous streak in his nature emerged in his dealings with his wife. While pistol practicing in the yard of their home, Courtright, according to one tale passed down in the family, called to his wife, and when she turned, shot an earring from her ear.[31] This story is undoubtedly apocryphal.

As reported in the press, another prank he tried on Betty backfired. Arriving home late one steamy August night in 1877, he entered his yard and, seeing his wife asleep by an open window with her hand extended on the sill, decided to play a little practical joke. It was an idea, as the Democrat reported, that "came within an ace of ridding our city of the commander-in-chief of the police battalion." Courtright slipped quietly up to the window and began removing two gold rings from Betty's fingers. He had one off and was working on the other when Betty awoke, pulled

> a convenient six-shooter [from] under her pillow [and] brought it to bear on her husband. But for his presence of mind in quickly calling her, she would have shot him dead. Mrs. Courtright displayed great presence of mind, fortitude and courage, and the Marshal should be proud of possessing a wife so fearless and brave. His narrow escape has completely cured him of any further desire to play the role of a midnight robber.[32]

This same window figured in another Courtright story published in the *Democrat* the following March. Weary from his duties, Courtright went to bed early one night and soon "slumbered with much greatness, his enchanting musical sonorous snore filling the air, vibrating from one corner of the house to the other." A neighbor lady, stopping by to visit with Betty, heard the strange sounds. Afraid that her friend might be in some sort of distress, she rapped sharply on the bedroom window. Courtright awoke with a start and, dressed in nothing but a sheet, leaped out of the window. Confronted by this great "white specter," the woman fled with the apparition in hot pursuit. She reached her home, "perfectly exhausted and trembling with fright, while the 'conundrum' wrapped his martial sheet about him, turned about face, and strode toward home with an air that would have put Napoleon to shame, only Napoleon wore pants; this article didn't."[33]

Courtright managed to get through his second term in the marshal's office without resort to his pistol, but he did engage in several brawls. "There was a little pugilistic exercise at the southwest corner of the square yesterday evening," reported the *Democrat* of May 23, 1877. "One of the combatants took a crack at the City Marshal, but he reckoned without his host, and went to the heater to spend the night."

A few months later Courtright's sporting proclivities got him into a fistic battle that did little to enhance his contemporary reputation as a champion of law and order or his later fabricated one as deadly gunfighter. About five o'clock on the evening of August 11, 1877, outside the Cattle Exchange Saloon he tangled with O. C. Cheney, a resident of Hell's Half Acre and one of Courtright's challengers for the marshal's job in the election earlier in the year. Ill feelings over that campaign probably still rankled, but the immediate cause of the fight was an argument over a wager on a horse race. By the time a reporter for the *Democrat* arrived, drawn to the scene by a great hue and cry from the saloon, a large crowd had gathered.

"The first sight that met our gaze," said the reporter, "was the exhausted forms of Mr. O. C. Cheney and Marshal Courtright, covered with blood and fighting for dear life." When a few peacemakers tried to step in and separate the combatants,

six or seven six-shooters flashed in the sun's rays and threats were made that the first man who interfered would bite the dust. Officers McConnell and Woody, with drawn pistols, succeeded in breaking through the dense crowd and made a fruitless effort to separate the two men, but the odds were against them and all their threats and commands availed nothing until Sheriff Henderson, hearing of the mob, rushed to the scene and commanded the crowd in the name of the State to disperse, and at the same time laid hands on the two pugilists and proceeded to separate them, when he was struck in the face with a six-shooter in the hands of Jim Reid [sic], the cattle man. The blow was a severe one, but did not knock him down. Fixed in his determination to put an end to the fight, he paid no attention to the blow and finally, with the assistance rendered by the officers present, succeeded in tearing the two men apart. The fight had lasted fully ten minutes and both men were absolutely used up. Courtright had to be conveyed to his home in a hack. Cheney was equally exhausted and used up, his face and clothes covered with blood. During the struggle Courtright bit the end of his thumb off. No weapons were used by either, but the faces of each presented a sad spectacle to the beholder.[34]

The crowd was in such a state of excitement that, even after Courtright and Cheney were gone, Sheriff Henderson had difficulty restoring order and getting the men to disperse. He appointed deputies, one of whom was ex-alderman P. J. Bowdry, who, "in an effort to quiet the rabble, got his head punched at the hands of Joe Lowe [and] was very fortunate in getting off with only a bruised face. Everybody seemed to be blood-thirsty and were red hot for a fight." It was fully an hour before the officers managed to disperse the crowd, which was estimated at more than three hundred. The reporter thought that most of those who had drawn pistols were friends of Courtright. "It was strange that no shots were fired, and most fortunate, too, for there surely would have been a sad destruction of life."

When Sheriff Henderson accused Jim Reed of hitting him with a six-shooter, the cattleman suggested they fight it out right there. Henderson ignored the proposal, and placed Reed, Joe Lowe, and a number of others under arrest for carrying pistols and disturbing the peace. Most effective in aiding the sheriff, according to the reporter, was Deputy Marshal J. H. McConnell, who displayed a great deal of courage during the melee and deserved much credit for his efficient work. "The whole affair is a disgrace to our city," concluded the newsman, "and those who were prominent deserve the extreme punishment of the law."[35]

The most prominent participant was, of course, City Marshal T. I. Courtright. After regaining his sobriety and patching up his cuts and bruises, he tried to pretend the sordid affair never happened and refused to press charges against Cheney. But a charge of public fighting had been lodged against him, and the case came up for a hearing in the mayor's court on August 14. Knowing he was out of favor with Mayor Day, Courtright demanded a jury. The six men chosen, after hearing the evidence, failed to agree; five stood for acquittal and one for conviction. At a second trial three days later another jury brought in a verdict of acquittal.[36]

But Courtright's legal troubles were not over. County Attorney Sam Furman brought charges of malfeasance in office against him and succeeded in getting a true bill from the grand jury. Sheriff Henderson arrested him on August 25. The charge read that he did "unlawfully and willfully neglect and refuse to arrest and prosecute one [O. C.] Cheney [who had] made an assault upon [T. I. Courtright], marshal of the city [and] a peace officer." A series of postponements delayed a final resolution of the case until August 21, 1878, when it was finally dismissed, one year to the day after it's original filing.[37]

The brawl with Cheney seems not to have tarnished Courtright's popularity with many in Fort Worth. Only two months later, on October 13, a number of prominent businessmen of the city "as a token of appreciation and worth" presented him with "a pair of expensive silver-mounted sixshooters with carved ivory handles and [all the] modern improvements."[38] In the next few months he added two more badges

to his city marshal star. In November Sheriff Henderson appointed him
a deputy sheriff of Tarrant County, and a month later U. S. Marshal
Thomas F. Purnell issued him a commission as deputy U. S. marshal
for the northern district of Texas.[39] These additional law enforcement
responsibilities would lead him farther afield in the months to come.

Chapter Four

THE TEXAS DETECTIVE BUREAU AND THE HUNT FOR SAM BASS

"No braver man than Jim Courtright exists.
He would arrest a circular saw if necessary."

Fort Worth Daily Democrat,
March 30, 1879.

As the city elections of 1878 approached, R. E. Beckham, an up-and-coming young attorney and vocal critic of incumbent Mayor G. H. Day, made a determined bid for the mayor's job. On March 21 at a political debate held in a new county courthouse then nearing completion, Beckham attacked Day in a twenty-minute speech. City scrip, which a year earlier had been equal to U. S. currency, had been devalued to twenty-five or thirty cents on the dollar, he charged. The streets were a disgrace. The city was on the verge of bankruptcy and was without credit. Day, he said, had neglected his other civic duties to concentrate all his attention on the mayor's court, where the fines and inevitable $9.85 costs were divided up by Day and the police. "Why," he demanded, "are not all city officials paid in greenbacks as are the officers? The city administration is just one little police court."

When his turn came to speak, Mayor Day's response to these accusations was feeble. "I come here filled with the milk of human kindness," he said smilingly. "I love everybody here. I offer myself as a sacrifice to the dear people for the good of the country."[1]

The "good people" took Day at his word and sacrificed him. He was soundly defeated in the election and Beckham became the new mayor.

The Fort Worth electorate was clearly in a reformist mood. But, remarkably, incumbent City Marshal Jim Courtright, with two criminal indictments still open against him—the assault to murder charge in the Wilson shooting case and the malfeasance in office charge in the Cheney affair—was not even challenged. He went on to a third term in office without bothering to put his name on the ballot.

B. B. Paddock of the *Democrat* was largely responsible for Courtright's escape from the reformist broom. In the weeks prior to the voting he had directed his customary attacks on Mayor Day and his administration, but there was a marked change in the tone of his remarks about City Marshal Courtright. In February, when residents in the vicinity of the city jail complained about the yelling and profanities emanating from that building, he defended the officer:

> Marshal Courtright was compelled to incarcerate a poor woman, who seemed to be deranged, in the calaboose night before last. Her cries annoyed some of our people, but Marshal Courtright was compelled to provide protection for the unfortunate woman, for the sake of humanity, if for no other reason, and the calaboose was his only resort....
>
> Marshal Courtright is laying himself liable to indictment every time he places a prisoner within the walls of the calaboose. If complaint is made by the citizens residing in the neighborhood of being disturbed or annoyed by hallowing, etc., Jim will be held accountable by the Judge of the District court. It is not right for the city to subject the marshal to this risk. They should take such steps as would definitely settle the calaboose "diffigally" and not longer subject its marshal to the possibility of an unjust punishment at the hands of the law.[2]

The next day Paddock commended Courtright and his officers for having arrested nearly half of the prisoners being held for trial in the county jail. "This fact speaks well of their efficiency as capable officers."[3]

Later in the month Paddock went into his usual harangue about the deplorable condition of the city streets, but made excuses for Courtright:

> It is a frequent complaint that the city marshal does not put the calaboose prisoners to work on the street, and in this way make them pay for a portion of the food which is bought and paid for by the city and consumed by them at their leisure. The marshal, upon several occasions, has expressed a wish to the council to utilize these city paupers, and urged upon them to allow him a guard, but at no time have they lent an ear to his petition, and at nearly every meeting of the council an account is presented and allowed for the feeding of the prisoners, averaging about $100 or $200 a month.... There is no reason why the council should continue to ignore the request of the marshal. One man can guard the street gang, who can be hired at the rate of $1.50 per day. Let this matter receive the attention at the hands of the council that its importance demands.[4]

An amusing bit of doggerel appearing in the pages of the paper a few days earlier indicated that at least some jailed prisoners had been utilized on street work gangs, and one of them had escaped, evidently hitching a ride on a wagon loaded with cotton bales bound for Weatherford. A resident of that town picked up a scrap of paper containing the verse and sent it to Paddock with the note: "As the officer to whom it seems to be addressed resides in your city, I thought the most certain way of reaching him would be by sending it to the *Democrat*." The poem read:

I am going, Courtwright, going,
Yes, my form's receding fast,
Taking the advice of Greeley
Even in spite of this cold blast.
Marshal! Thou shalt not enfold me,
But, one moment bend thine ear,
Listen to a tramp's opinion,
Then let the city hear.

With Fort Worth I am quite disgusted.
Living there is all played out.
Hope your merchants will get "busted"
And your town go up the spout.
Though your people will not help me,
Will no more my stomach fill.
I won't work your streets. But leave you
Proud and independent still.

Let no other city minion
Point their finger as I go.
'Tis not fear of you impels me,
I for freedom strike the blow,
I, who on a bale of cotton
Basking in the sun's bright ray,
Lay contented, I am going
Off to exile in this way.

Marshal! Should you hear the rabble
Dare assail my honest name,
Seek them; say they are mistaken,
I have not impaired their fame.
Tell the, e'en the Gods bear witness
That I'm not inclined to work.
Naught but force will ere compel me.
When I can, I'm bound to shirk.

And for thee, efficient marshal,
Guardian of the city's peace,
Say one kind word ere I leave thee,
Let all harsh ill feeling cease.
Give ignoble, working creatures
All the favors thou canst give.
I can scorn a fate so humble,
I am going West to live.

I am going, Courtwright, going.
Hark! The insulting canine cry.
I must hasten on my journey
Ere the cursed brute draws nigh.
Ah! No more within the city
Shall my heart exulting swell.
So, as I must work or leave thee,
Courtwright and Fort Worth, farewell.[5]

The third term of Courtright's tenure as city marshal at Fort Worth was marked by a distinct change in focus. Increasingly, he left the policing of Fort Worth to his deputies and, wearing his two new badges,

Tarrant County deputy sheriff and deputy United States marshal, became more involved in the apprehension of wide-ranging criminal suspects.

One of the first was Lee Witt, a dangerous character who had triggered statewide attention when he fled Corsicana after the murder of the railroad station agent there. In May 1878 someone recognized Witt in Hell's Half Acre and notified Courtright, who immediately rounded up several of his deputies and went after the fugitive. Tipped off to their approach, Witt mounted his horse and galloped out of town. Courtright and his men rode in pursuit, and a running gun battle ensued. Witt reached the Trinity River, but, before he could cross, the officers closed in and he surrendered. After jailing Witt to await transfer to Corsicana, Courtright determined that two horses in the man's possession at the time of his arrest had been stolen in Dallas County and notified the owners. He received wide acclaim for his prompt action in capturing the fugitive.[6]

Reward notices for wanted criminals particularly caught Courtright's attention. As early as September 1877 he was sending out inquiries about possible rewards being offered for men he had in his sights.[7] A few months before, when two Fort Worth store owners offered a $500 reward for the apprehension of a man named Joe Leonard, whom they accused of robbing them, Courtright and his most trusted lieutenant, Deputy Ab Woody, rode seventeen miles to the home of a Leonard relative in hopes of catching the suspect but missed their quarry by a day.[8]

All of Texas in the summer of 1878 was riveted on the hunt for the notorious Sam Bass and his gang. Bass, a minor Texas gambler and ne'er-do-well, had grabbed national attention in September of the previous year with the hold-up of a Union Pacific train at Big Springs, Nebraska, in which he and his gang got away with $60,000 in gold dollars. Within weeks pursuing lawmen shot and killed two gang members in Kansas and another in Missouri. With a price on his head, Bass returned to Texas, gathered another band, and began a series of daring stagecoach and train holdups in the Dallas area. Soon officers throughout north-central Texas were on the trail of the outlaws.

The only documented photograph of Sam Bass, outlaw and gang leader, who led Jim Courtright and other Texas lawmen on a merry chase in 1878. Bass is standing on the left beside John E. Gardner. The Collins brothers Joe (left) and Joel (right, with pistol) are seated. The photo was taken when the four men were working as cowboys. *Courtesy Robert G. McCubbin Collection.*

In March 1878 Jim Courtright obtained information through an informant that he thought could lead to the gang's apprehension. On his letterhead, "Office of T. I. Courtright, City Marshal, Fort Worth" he wrote to the Texas governor at Austin:

> March 12, 1878
> Hon. R. B. Hubbard:
> Dear Sir:
> Please send Requisition for Sam. Bass Jack Davis and Thom. Nixon the parties who robbed the express car at Big Spring Station on or about the 18th of Sept. 1877 in Nebraska as have recently learned their whereabouts
> Yours truly T. I. Courtright

John Swindells, acting private secretary to the governor, responded the next day: "In reply to your letter of yesterday, his Excellency the Governor instructs me to say that you will have to get the Governor of Nebraska (or of the state where the robbery was committed) to send Requisition on the Governor of Texas, and to appoint you agent. The Governor required this in all cases."[9]

Courtright's supposed line on the Sam Bass gang may have prompted this terse note in the *Democrat* of March 22: "Marshal Courtright left for Dallas yesterday. Business of great importance." Whatever that business, nothing further was reported and Courtright's tip led nowhere.

In June, as the hunt for the Bass gang heated up, Courtright and his friend and deputy Ab Woody obtained ten-day leaves of absence from the Fort Worth city council and joined a posse led by Sheriff John Henderson to aid other officers who had located the gang in Denton County. They left on Friday, June 7 and rode so hard that Woody killed a horse on the journey, but did not catch up with a force led by Denton County Sheriff W. F. Egan until Sunday.

On the evening of June 9 four possemen—Courtright, Woody, and Denton County lawmen John Carroll and Jack Yates—were patrolling the road near the farmhouse of Charles Gray when they spotted a party of horsemen approaching. As the riders, unaware of the lawmen's presence, drew near in the gathering darkness, Courtright thought he recognized the leader as Richard B. Coleman, a Denton carpenter, and called out to him. This was a bad mistake, for the leader was in fact Frank Jackson, a Bass lieutenant, who, alerted by Courtright's call, immediately whirled his horse and disappeared into the underbrush of the Elm Fork bottoms with his cohorts right behind.

Although Courtright remained with the manhunters in Denton County for some time, this was as close as he ever got to killing or capturing any members of the Sam Bass gang. When he returned to Fort Worth he claimed to have thwarted a plan by the gang to rob a Fort Worth bank, but he had blown his chance at lasting fame. His participation in the hunt for the Sam Bass gang became only a footnote in the history of that famous episode. By the time the gang was broken up and Bass killed by Texas Rangers at Round Rock, Williamson County, in July, Courtright's part in the chase was already forgotten.[10]

But the excitement of manhunting and the allure of possible monetary reward now absorbed Courtright, and in the fall of 1878 he made his first effort to enter the detective business. On October 6 an organization called the Texas Detective Bureau announced in the pages of the Democrat that it was open for business in Fort Worth. Its mission was "to discover swindlers and criminals and bring them to justice, wherever they may be concealed." Highly secret in nature, the bureau's "vigilant officers are unknown and indistinguishable, and it is only when their work is proclaimed that the public is aware of their existence." The "honestly disposed" had nothing to fear from the organization, but "a howl [would be] raised against it by those whose evil propensities will not bear the light of day." The bureau's "chief corresponding office" was in the city but no address was given. Parties interested in utilizing the bureau's services were referred to a lock box and assured that they would "receive ample and straightforward information from the efficient officers in charge." Business was solicited from "railroad, express, insurance, banking, steamboat and other corporations, the legal profession, merchants, business houses and individuals."[11]

Since the Texas Detective Bureau was so secretive, its owners and managers were never disclosed, but the major figure in the venture was undoubtedly Jim Courtright, with the financial backing of some of the more prosperous businessmen of the community. Courtright had to keep his identity secret, because he could not openly run a business of this sort while at the same time holding the position of city marshal. Perhaps for that very reason, this first attempt at detective agency operation by Courtright did not last long. After that initial announcement, the Texas Detective Bureau was heard of no more.

Perhaps not coincidentally, that same month the Texas press took note of Courtright's work as a wide-ranging manhunter. On October 17 the *Galveston Daily News* reported that he had nabbed a suspected horse thief, an Arkansas preacher no less, and on the 29th the same paper said Courtright had passed through Dallas with John Mitchell, an escapee from the Texas penitentiary, whom he had captured in Johnson County. "For the benefit of escaping criminals, let it be known that Fort Worth is a dangerous place in which to loiter," said the *Democrat* a few weeks later. "A number of arrests by our officers, which should have been made elsewhere, attest their efficiency in this respect."[12] In November Courtright made an important arrest, collaring a man named Tom Love Culbreth, wanted for murder in Milam County, and claiming the $200 reward offered for the fugitive.[13]

Election time was approaching again and Courtright, who intended to stand for a fourth term as city marshal, recognized that some voters might think he was neglecting his civic responsibilities to pursue these extracurricular activities. To regain the support of Paddock of the *Democrat*, the long-time agitator against the city's notorious dance halls, he mounted raids in late November on the Waco Tap and the Red Light, two of the worst establishments. Paddock's paper told the story in rather jocular fashion. Deputy Marshal W. P. Thomas and A. N. Woody, "in obedience to direct instructions" raided the two "merry resorts." Arrested at the Waco Tap were the proprietor, Lou Bennett, the bartender, D. M. Brown, and Bob Brown, the "rustler," W. T. Andrews, the "cat-gut manipulator," and E. D. Winslow, the "ivory key puncher." At the Red Light the officers nabbed proprietor John Leer and Al Neely, the floor manager, as well as Charles Smith, "cut glass artist," Professor Marcross, "piano beater," and Arthur Hanley, the "fiddling foochoo."[14]

Despite this late attempt to gain support. Courtright's job was in jeopardy and others recognized his vulnerability. In contrast to the previous year when he had been returned to office unopposed, a number of challengers now announced their candidacy. Two of the men who had served as his deputies, Sam Farmer and W. P. Thomas, threw their hats in the ring. Said the *Democrat* in March: "Thomas, Farmer and Courtright are pulling every available cord to insure success at the coming election. Farmer smokes, Courtright takes beer straight, and Thomas drinks lemonade."[15] One-time marshal Henry P. Shiel, J. W. Williams, a former candidate, and a man named G. E. Wheeler also ran. An early entrant in the race, B. M. Melton, later dropped out.

"Who Shall be Marshal?" asked Paddock in a piece emphasizing the importance and uniqueness of the position in a frontier town like Fort Worth:

The welfare of the city is in great measure in the hands of the marshal, who, in looking after its interests, usually acts upon general principles, if he understands his duties, and attends to them, seldom under instructions. The elements of character and qualifications in many respects for fulfilling the duties of the marshalship require a higher endowment than is essential for any other municipal officer, the mayor of the city not excepted.[16]

Courtright's belated crackdown on the dance houses Paddock so detested had the desired effect of gaining the editor's approbation and reelection support. "It is generally acknowledged that T. I. Courtright has performed the duties of his office fearlessly, efficiently, and devotedly," Paddock wrote.

He has used discretion in making arrests, not annoying persons for frivolous misdeeds for the sake of making a fee. That he has done his whole duty may be known from the fact that our city, with its cosmopolitan population, is more orderly than any other its size in the Union. . . . No braver man than Jim Courtright exists. He would arrest a circular saw if necessary. We know of his having arrested five cowboys all armed with their six shooters drawn, but six shooters or shot guns have [no] terrors for Jim. We all know him to be a good man in a good place, and let the people decide whether they will continue to retain him in the position he now holds.[17]

At a public meeting held in Joe Lowe's Centennial Theater shortly before the election, candidates took turns addressing the large crowd in attendance. Courtright, who, in the opinion of a reporter covering the event, "was no speech maker," kept his remarks brief. He chose to use the occasion to attack candidate Shiel, the former marshal, for spending his time gambling when he should have been on duty, "something they can't say of we." He sat down "amidst tremendous applause."[18]

In the weeks leading up to the election it became evident that both Shiel and Courtright were out of the running in this contest, and that the only viable candidates for the marshal's job were S. M. Farmer and W. P. Thomas. The two erstwhile Courtright deputies became involved in a campaign battle, and it was a bitter fight indeed.

Supporters of Farmer filed a complaint alleging that Deputy Marshal Thomas had arrested a man and collected a fine from him without benefit of a hearing or trial. Thomas claimed in his defense that he had acted on orders of Courtright and this was a common practice among the marshal's deputies. An investigating board charged Thomas with corruption and malfeasance in office and turned the matter over to the city council. After heated debate, that body exonerated both Thomas and Courtright of any wrongdoing in a very close vote, with Mayor Beckham casting the deciding ballot.[19]

Backers of Thomas, supported by friends of Courtright, counterattacked by spreading rumors throughout the city that during the Civil War Sam Farmer had been a Union scout and spy, had served in the militia under the detested "chintz bug"[20] administration in Missouri, and had been a policeman in Governor Edmund J. Davis's hated State Police during Reconstruction. The rumors led to a public denial by Farmer of all the allegations in the form of a series of "cards" published in the *Democrat*. His political opponents, led by Courtright's close buddy, Ab Woody, kept up the attacks. Woody went before a justice of the peace and swore to the truth of the charges in an affidavit later published in the *Democrat*. Farmer retaliated by going all the way to Missouri to secure sworn affidavits from men who knew him there that the allegations were false.

The controversy almost came to violence when a man named R. F. Walton made it known around town that he objected to the attack on Farmer and employed some strong language of his own about Woody. Friends of Walton and Woody feared "serious results should a meeting occur between them." Woody was seen carrying a rifle, but when he denied it was intended for use against Walton, tensions relaxed and the "war cloud" blew over.[21]

(It is strange that Sam Farmer's political enemies, in an effort to besmirch his character, would allege that he had served with the Union Army during the War Between the States, when Courtright's claim to the same service never raised an eyebrow in Fort Worth. The only answer to this seeming contradiction is that Courtright made no mention of service with the Union until much later, after bitter passions about the war and later Reconstruction period had cooled in Texas.)

In the election held on April 1 "the contest for city marshal engrossed the largest share of the people's attention." In the morning a rumor going the rounds that Courtright had withdrawn from the race was quickly recognized as false, circulated by Farmer adherents to hurt Thomas's chances. (One wonders if anyone noted that it was April Fool's Day.) There was a big turnout at the polls with voters casting over fifteen hundred votes for city marshal, three hundred more than expected. When the ballots were tabulated, Sam Farmer had won a decisive victory, beating Thomas by 368 votes, and all the other candidates combined by forty-nine. Courtright, with only ninety-two votes, garnered only six percent of the total cast. He finished a dismal fifth, limping in after Farmer, Thomas, Williams and Shiel, and only ahead of Wheeler, who received one vote, presumably his own.[22]

"A CLASH
OF GIANTS"

"Courtright . . . a man of unflinching courage... cool,
calculating and indomitable... an undeveloped lead mine
[with] several ounces of leaden bullets under his hide."

Fort Worth Daily Democrat,
October 27, 1880

Oddly, Courtright's legend makers gave short shrift to the three terms
he served as city marshal at Fort Worth. Eugene Cunningham devoted
only a few lines to the eventful three years, saying merely that during
that time "Jim Courtright found many opportunities to display both his
grim fearlessness and his uncanny speed and accuracy at weapon-
play."[1] Although Father Stanley sub-titled his biography "Two Gun
Marshal of Fort Worth," he told his readers little of Courtright's experiences in the office, filling out the chapter of the same name with extra-
neous information on Wild Bill Hickok, Ben Thompson and Sam Bass.
Neither writer made the slightest mention of Courtright's battles with
Bingham Feild, N. H. Wilson and O. C. Cheney.

This is strange, for Courtright's record as city marshal was actually
quite remarkable. The 1870s were exceptionally violent years in the
cattle towns and mining camps of the West. During the three years of
Courtright's tenure in Fort Worth some of the most famous shootings
involving lawmen of these towns occurred. In 1876 Wild Bill Hickok
was assassinated in Deadwood, Dakota Territory, and gunfighter Clay
Allison shot and killed Deputy Sheriff Charles Faber in Las Animas,
Colorado. The next year Mike Meagher, long-time city marshal of

Wichita, Kansas, killed his only man in a gun battle, and in a Fort
Griffin, Texas, saloon gun battle involving Deputy Sheriff Bill Cruger
five men were shot, three fatally. In 1878 Billy the Kid and cohorts shot
Sheriff William Brady to death in Lincoln, New Mexico, and in Dodge
City, Kansas, cattle herders gunned down City Marshal Ed Masterson,
and police officers Wyatt Earp and Jim Masterson killed another cowboy named George Hoyt. And during this very violent period, the very
peak of Fort Worth's years as a cattle town, Courtright and his deputies
maintained a semblance of order within the town without one of them
ever being involved in a fatal shooting.

Courtright's overwhelming rejection at the polls in the 1879 election did not fit well into the legend Cunningham and Stanley later
tried to create. Cunningham never mentioned elections, stating incor-
rectly that Courtright was originally appointed city marshal and lost
the position because he chose the wrong side in a Fort Worth political
battle, leaving the implication that his political foes simply did not
re-appoint him. Stanley said that his hero had a "disagreement with
political figures in Fort Worth [and] refused to run for another term
of office."[2]

The accounts of the legend makers regarding Courtright's activities in the years immediately following his loss of the city marshal's job
are also confused and wholly inaccurate. According to Cunningham, it
was at this time that Courtright was called to New Mexico and
entered on his adventures there, but actually, this move was four years
in the future.[3]

Stanley attempted to correct Cunningham. He wrote that
Courtright, after leaving office, "did not immediately run to New
Mexico as some writers seem to think." But then Stanley went on to
spin an entirely undocumented and fanciful story. Having previously
reported that following his discharge from the army "about 1870-71,"

Courtright and his wife, "crack shot" Betty, "seem to have joined" a Wild West show for a brief period, Stanley relates how the couple again returned to the world of show business in 1879, joining Buffalo Bill Cody's Wild West Show as sharpshooters.

The billboards advertised Annie Oakley, Lillian Smith, John C. Morgan, Betty Courtright, Jim Courtright, and others. It was while the show was playing in Virginia City that Courtright was shot and injured by the explosion of a pad in the blank cartridge, causing a wound on the forehead just above the right eye. Jim was taken to the Virginia City

Jim Courtright, sporting his city marshal badge and a jauntily cocked hat. *Courtesy Western History Collections, University of Oklahoma Library, Norman, Oklahoma.*

Hospital, where he remained until well enough to leave for home. The show left Virginia City on the day following the accident, Buffalo Bill forgetting all about Courtright and his obligation to him. The people of Virginia City felt embittered of his heartlessness and took up a collection to pay Courtright's hospital bill.... Before Buffalo Bill left Virginia City he and Lillian got into a hot argument over money matters. Lillian upped and left the show, opening a shooting gallery in Virginia City.[4]

Although this story, rich in detail, has been accepted and reprinted by perpetuators of the Courtright legend, it has no basis in fact. Buffalo Bill Cody did not develop his famous "Wild West" show until 1883, four years *after* the Courtrights are said to have performed in it. Annie Oakley did not join the show until 1885, and Lillian Smith was only fourteen when she joined in 1886. In addition, Courtright's activities over the next four years are well documented in contemporary newspaper and court records and no mention was ever made of participation by Jim or Betty Courtright in a Wild West show.[5]

For four years following his defeat at the polls Courtright remained in Fort Worth. He still held deputy U. S. marshal and Tarrant County deputy sheriff commissions and earned some fees working in these capacities. He augmented this meager income by opening a keno game on the upper floor of the Cattle Exchange Saloon, an endeavor that brought him into conflict with John C. Morris, who had been the keno kingpin in the town for several years and resented Courtright's intrusion into his exclusive operation. Morris was a dangerous man with a violent temper, as he proved on more than one occasion. In February 1880 he got into an argument with T. W. Cotton, bartender of the "My" Theater, drew a pistol and shot the man dead. At his trial for murder the following July the jury was out only five minutes before bringing in a verdict of acquittal.[6]

Three months later Morris tangled with Jim Courtright. What transpired was recounted in the pages of the *Democrat* under the headline:

A CLASH OF GIANTS.
HOSTILITIES BETWEEN TWO MEN WHO ARE NOT AFRAID.

The names of T. I. "Jim" Courtright and John C. Morris were familiar to everyone in town, said the story, as both men had "passed through emergencies in Fort Worth calculated to test the nerve of any man." Courtright was described as "a man of unflinching courage. . . cool, calculating and indomitable…, an undeveloped lead mine [with] several ounces of leaden bullets under his hide."[7] Morris was "also a plucky fellow. . . the best man in many a tough contest. . . regarded with no little respect by timid people."

Although everyone in the sporting district knew there was bad blood between the two "giants" over the keno business, a "clash" was avoided until Monday evening, October 25, 1880 when

Morris followed Courtright from the keno room above the Cattle Exchange bar, called for his pistol and displayed it in a threatening manner, at the same time charging Courtright with having circulated dishonorable reports about him [Morris]. From this the two men got warmer and warmer and came near opening fire several times. Finally a proposition was made by Morris that they go into a private room and "shoot it out." Courtright willingly assented and led the way, but something interfered to stop them. It was then proposed that they fight it out

without weapons. A fistfight then ensued in which Morris
was worsted.

City policemen arrived to put an end to the hostilities
at that point. They arrested the combatants and had them
post bonds to appear the following day in the mayor's court.
But both men were still spoiling for a fight. Morris challenged Courtright to a duel, to be fought with knives in a
closed room at two o'clock the next day. The challenge was
immediately accepted. Morris said he was willing to bet
Courtright would not show at the appointed time and
Courtright accepted that bet also. Since both needed all
their cash to make bond, they wagered their gold watches,
leaving the timepieces in the hands of the bartender as
stakeholder.

On Tuesday morning Courtright appeared for his hearing in Mayor's court, but Morris, apparently feeling rather
unwell after his beating, had to send a proxy. Each was
fined one dollar.

Word of the proposed duel spread throughout Hell's Half Acre and
the sporting crowd waited with growing excitement as the appointed
hour neared. Courtright was on the streets early,

looking perfectly fresh and as cool as a cucumber.
Morris was not seen until about one o'clock when he left
his room. . . . It was plainly to be seen that he was in no
condition to meet his antagonist, in consequence of having
drank too deeply. At half past one o'clock Morris was sitting
on the verandah above the Cattle Exchange when
Courtright [appeared], looked up at Morris, who remained

quietly in his seat, and passed into the saloon. Before the two adversaries met, attorney Robert McCart went before Justice of the Peace A. G. McClung and filed a complaint, or "information" as it was called, to prevent the impending duel. McClung issued a warrant for the arrest of the duelists and sent a force of officers to the scene of war. Courtright saw them coming and attempted to get away, but "the police, by a little quick work, overpowered and disarmed him. [They] subsequently returned his pistol, he having given a pledge to use it only in self-defense, and having the right to bear arms." The officers then escorted Morris and Courtright to Justice McClung's office where they were required to post bonds in the amount of $500 each [to] insure appearance in court the next day.

The *Democrat* story closed with an admonition: "There came very nearly a man killed – if not two – in town yesterday, because both were on time and both determined to fight to the death with knives. It is to be hoped that they will cool down now and bury the hatchet. It will be of no advantage to either to take the life of the other, and they ought to take the sober second thought before doing anything rash."[8]

The two men apparently heeded this advice, for the next day the paper reported that Morris, confined to his room by sickness (or the effects of his beating or overindulgence in drink) sent for Courtright, who responded at once. "The two men talked over their difficulty coolly and considerably and agreed to shake hands and become friends again. They both exhibit good sense and commendable liberality in this conclusion."

The disagreement may have been resolved by the two gamblers entering into some kind of partnership. It is clear Courtright continued to run his keno game in the upper rooms of the Cattle Exchange. Only a few days later he pled guilty to a charge of "exhibiting keno bank" and paid his regular $25 fine.[9]

That the two gamblers settled their differences amicably is evidenced by an incident a month later in which they sided each other in a gunfight. The trouble began on the night of November 30 when two black men, Johnson Mays and William Craft, got into a dispute in the vice district and Craft appealed to the police for protection. Deputy Marshal W. B. Hale approached Mays, who drew a pistol and shot the officer. Before going down with wounds to the chin and chest, Hale returned the fire, inflicting a flesh wound to Mays' thigh. Mays hobbled into the El Paso Hotel and locked himself in a room. Drawn to the scene by the sound of battle, Courtright and Morris, acting together, kicked in a window and exchanged shots with Mays, who managed to escape but was later arrested and jailed by City Marshal Farmer.[10]

Courtright and Morris still faced the very serious charge of accepting a challenge to fight a duel. Only the year before the Texas legislature had incorporated into the penal code a stiff punishment for fighting, accepting a challenge to fight, or acting as a second in a duel. Conviction was punishable by a term of not less than two and not more than five years in the state penitentiary.[11] Both Morris and Courtright were indicted under this law. Morris was charged with issuing a challenge to fight a duel with bowie knives, "bowie knives being deadly weapons," and Courtright was charged with accepting the challenge. The defendants were released on $800 bond pending a hearing the following May. At that time W. S. Pendleton, Courtright's attorney, moved to dismiss the charge against his client and the cases were continued until February 1882 when a jury, on a directed verdict from the judge, found Courtright not guilty.

At the time of Courtright's acquittal, charges against John C. Morris were dropped, for the very good reason that the defendant was dead, shot and killed by one of Courtright's fellow deputy U. S. marshals.

Thomas F. Purnell, United States marshal for the northern district of Texas, had originally issued Courtright's commission as a federal deputy marshal. When A. B. Norton replaced Purnell in April 1879, he was immediately inundated with more than one hundred applications for deputy appointments.[12] Many of the men Norton appointed were current or former peace officers who had demonstrated bravery and determination in handling miscreants and were known as "fighting men," but some also had acquired well-deserved reputations as brawlers and saloon toughs. Courtright was one of this crowd, as were W. P. Rayner, Joe Forsythe and Ab Woody, all of whom were deputized by Marshal Norton to serve in the Fort Worth-Dallas area at this time.

William Polk Rayner was about twenty-six when he came to Fort Worth in September 1881 to assume the position of deputy U. S. revenue collector, an appointment he had received by means of strings pulled by his father, Kenneth Rayner, a prominent North Carolina politician and solicitor of the U. S. Treasury Department. The job was apparently too tame for Bill Rayner and he quickly left it to accept appointment as a deputy U. S. marshal. Tall, with dark hair and eyes, Rayner soon became a familiar figure in the dives of Hell's Half Acre.

On December 21, 1881, he tangled with the always explosive gambler John C. Morris. According to the later testimony of Mattie Johnson, madam of a house of ill repute, the two men quarreled over her affections. Hot words were exchanged that day in the clubrooms of former mayor G. H. Day and again in the Occidental Saloon. Shortly after midnight Morris, gun in hand, kicked in the door of Mattie's room and took a shot at Rayner. He missed, but Rayner did not. His answering shot struck Morris in the forehead, killing him instantly. Rayner surrendered to Jim Courtright, who turned him over to Marshal Sam Farmer. At a preliminary examination held by Justice McClung on December 21 Rayner was held on $2,500 bond.[13] He later came clear on the time-honored plea of self-defense.

The shooting brought a Paddock editorial deploring the common practice of pistol packing in Fort Worth. John Morris, he said, was

> in the habit of carrying a pistol almost continually, and others are addicted to the same bad practice. There is a class of our population who do not consider their toilet fully made up unless they are provided with a pistol – which, unfortunately, is brought into use at the very time they are least capable of using it – when they are under the influence of alcohol.

Paddock pointed out that peace officers were among the worst offenders in this regard and argued that they should be prohibited from carrying arms when not on active duty.[14]

No such change took place, of course, and Rayner and other hotheaded badge-toters continued to get into trouble. On February 20, 1882, only two months after the Morris killing, Bill Rayner bullied a man on the sidewalk in front of "My" Theater. He drew his pistol, threatened to shoot the man, and struck him in the face. City policeman Jake Riggles was called and followed Rayner into the theater. Rayner resisted arrest and in a struggle with Riggles, kicked him in the stomach. Both men drew guns, but quick interference by bystanders and the arrival of policemen Ed Maddox and C. E. Garretson prevented a shooting. The next day in mayor's court Rayner was fined $5 for assault and battery.[15] In March he was charged in county court with carrying a pistol and in April pled guilty to a charge of aggravated assault and was fined $25.[16]

The following year Rayner moved on to Silver City, New Mexico. There, in July 1883, the city marshal, H. M. Horn, in recognition of his reputation as a fighting man, enlisted Rayner's help in defending the town and preserving order. "Doc" Cain, a Silver City gambler and gunman, had killed a popular railroad conductor named "Three-Finger Dick" at Deming, and a trainload of irate citizens from that town arrived in Silver City intent on lynching him. Marshal Horn, with the assistance of Rayner and several other special deputies (including Joe Antrim, brother of the famous New Mexico outlaw, Billy the Kid) managed to hold off the mob.[17]

Rayner next showed up in El Paso, Texas, where he served on the police force and presided over a gambling table in the Gem Saloon. But he continued his heavy drinking and belligerent ways and was arrested at least twice for assault. In the Gem on the night of April14, 1885, he picked a fight with the wrong man. In an exchange of gunfire with Robert Bates "Cowboy Bob" Rennick at a distance of six feet, Rayner's shots went wide while Rennick pumped two bullets into his adversary, inflicting a mortal wound. Rayner survived for a time but died on June 7 after weeks of agony.[18]

Joseph Forsythe was another young man in the Courtright or Rayner mold who held a deputy U. S. marshal's commission during these years. Like Courtright and Woody, he was one of the many officers who joined in the search for the Sam Bass gang in 1878. He had first come to notice as a fighting man in November 1875 when he was city marshal at Ennis, in Ellis County, about sixty miles southeast of Fort Worth. On the 6th of that month he arrested a disorderly fellow named Jack Pipen and when ten or twelve of Pipen's pals tried to free him from custody a gunbattle ensued, in which an estimated two hundred shots were fired. Forsythe and his assistant, J. Lamerson, held off the attack with the aid of some of the town's residents. When it was over, two of the gang lay dead and five were wounded. One citizen combatant was wounded seriously, and Forsythe took a bullet through his thigh.[19]

Forsythe was a belligerent sort who had to fight, even if it was with his fellow officers. After his appointment as deputy under Marshal Norton, he tangled with another deputy at Dallas. "Deputy Marshals Maul Each Other," the *Galveston Daily News* headlined the story. "There was war in the camp of the United States marshal to-day. Deputies Forsythe and Alkine passed rapidly from words to blows, the former was knocked down and badly cut on the head with a beer mallet."[20]

Two years later, in February 1882, Forsythe got into a personal dispute with a man named Charles Moore at Ennis that led to another gunfight. Like many of Courtright's affrays, this affair did nothing to substantiate the legend of the deadly accurate gunfighting frontier lawman. The story was carried in a special telegraphic bulletin from Ennis to Fort Worth, where Forsythe was well known.

A most sensational shooting affair occurred here about nine o'clock tonight in which Joe Forsythe, one of the most widely known detectives and recently a deputy United States marshal, was fatally shot by Charles Moore. Both had been drinking, and an old feud was revived early in the day. Tonight the parties met in a saloon and commenced a violent quarrel. They were ordered out. Forsythe called to Moore to "Come out and fight me like a man on the streets." Moore fired two pistol shots, and Forsythe three, without effect. Moore stepped in the saloon and gave his pistol to his brother Benjamin. The latter fired two shots and received three in exchange, none taking effect. By this time Charles Moore returned with a shotgun and discharged one barrel, the load of buckshot taking effect in the right hip and lower part of Forsythe's body, breaking the hip bone and literally tearing his private parts out. Moore was arrested and taken to the county jail at Waxahachie. Physicians say that Forsythe cannot recover.[21]

But recover he did. With or without his "private parts" he continued to be active as an officer. In New Mexico in early 1883 he would work with Courtright in the pursuit of a criminal gang, and later that year would take the job of city marshal at Hunnewell, Kansas.

At its peak as a cow town at this time, Hunnewell was experiencing the usual problems with uproarious cowboys and the city fathers decided they needed a "fighting man" to control them. They sent for Joe Forsythe, described by a newspaper as "one of the few remaining Texas desperadoes," and offered him a monthly salary of $100 to ride herd on the rampaging drovers. They would also pay $75 a month to an assistant of his choice. On August 16, 1883, Forsythe arrived in Hunnewell, bringing with him Hamilton Rayner, brother of Will and a man who was building his own reputation as a tough and fearless officer. Word of their coming had preceded them and the obstreperous cowboys were waiting. Although three Sumner County sheriff's deputies accompanied the new city officers, they had hardly stepped off the train when shooting commenced. Three men were hit, none seriously. But after this tumultuous greeting by the cowboy welcoming committee, things quieted down considerably in the cowtown. The *Sumner County Press* could soon announce that "Jo. Forsythe, the new marshal of Hunnewell, is reported walking around with nothing to do. The outlaws don't care about tackling a thoroughbred.... Under the new marshal and police force, Hunnewell has been, as a matter of fact, as peaceable and law-abiding as the average western town."[22]

In September Forsythe was back in Dallas, where he got into a fracas with Will Rayner. The two met in the rotunda of the Windsor Hotel

> and a scuffle ensued, in which Rayner threw Forsythe
> and got possession of his pistol. Rayner says that Forsythe
> had abused Jim Courtright of Fort Worth, and a friend of
> his. Forsythe says [the trouble] grew out of Rayner charg-
> ing him with being untrue to his brother, who is Forsythe's
> assistant marshal at Hunnewell, Kansas, of which place he
> is marshal.[23]

Forsythe resigned his marshalship at Hunnewell in December, turning over the office to his deputy, Hamilton Rayner.[24] He returned to
Dallas where, over the next two years, he sank into the depths of alco-
holism and violent behavior and was a constant source of trouble for the
city and county officers. In July 1884 Forsythe ran into his old nemesis
from Ennis, Charley Moore, and "war was renewed, though it was
quieted down without shedding of blood." Only four days after paying
a $10 fine for this affair. A deputy sheriff arrested Forsythe for non-
payment of an old aggravated assault fine.[25] In September a justice
fined him four dollars for "abusive language," and in October fined him
$7.50 for fighting another officer, Limestone County Sheriff T. E.
Jackson, who, according to the news account, was "considerably worsted"
in the encounter.[26] Over the course of the next year Forsythe had to
answer to no less than three aggravated assault charges and was arrested
and fined on at least four other occasions for drunkenness and fighting.
He was also remanded to jail for a time for non-payment of his fines.[27] In
the fall of 1885 he disappeared from the pages of the Dallas press and
court records. His ultimate fate is unknown, but brutal, drink-addicted
men like Joe Forsythe generally ended up dead on a saloon floor.

Abram N. "Ab" Woody, a native of Missouri who was also a Union Army veteran, came to Fort Worth about the same time as Courtright. He served under him on the city police force, with him as a federal officer, and would remain his closest friend and supporter during the tumultuous times ahead. Woody was never a desperado type of officer like Will Rayner and Joe Forsythe, but his service was not without controversy.

A farcical affair over a pig in December 1877 resulted in his being charged with aggravated assault. The accusation was brought by James Ashworth, described by the *Democrat* as "a worthy and respected citizen" of Fort Worth. Pigs running loose in the public streets had long been a problem for city officials – R. E. Beckham would make it a major issue in his campaign for mayor a few months later – but when deputy marshals Woody and W. P. Thomas corralled a loose porker belonging to Ashworth and put it in the pig pokey, the respected citizen howled. He demanded that Woody release the animal, but the officer refused unless a "fine" of fifty cents was paid. An enraged Ashworth went directly to the pound where the pig was kept, broke down the fence, and liberated the animal. When Woody attempted to place him under arrest, Ashworth resisted. In the course of a scuffle, Woody struck him over the head with his pistol, Ashworth later claimed in a complaint charging the officer with aggravated assault. At a hearing a month later Woody was acquitted of the charge.[28]

In a more serious affair in November 1878 Woody again used his pistol as a bludgeon. He had arrested S. F. "Charley" Hearn for riding in a buggy with a known prostitute in violation of a city ordinance and, according to the *Democrat* account, "common decency." Woody seated himself in the buggy between Hearn and the woman and set out to seek someone to go the man's bail. Suddenly Hearn attacked the officer, stabbing him in the back with a pocketknife. He made several thrusts and broke the blade before Woody jumped down from the buggy, jerked and "cocked his six-shooter with the intention of... giving Hearn the benefit of the contents, but changed his mind" and swung the barrel at Hearn's head. Although Woody later claimed he had no intention of shooting, the weapon went off, inflicting a scalp wound. "But for the interference of parties near, Woody would most probably have killed him."[29] Woody's forbearance in this fracas is remarkable; there is little doubt that, given the egregious provocation, no bystanders would have prevented Will Rayner or Joe Forsythe from fatally disposing of Mr. Hearn.

In the spring of 1879 a spate of stagecoach robberies near Fort Worth led to a shootout on a Fort Worth street between Woody and Clifton Scott, a man the officer had publicly accused of complicity in the robberies. After the two exchanged angry words, Scott, infamous in Fort Worth and Dallas as a volatile and dangerous gunman, armed himself with a double-barreled shotgun and went looking for Woody. Spotting his quarry across Houston Street talking with a brother, H. C Woody, he leveled the weapon. Someone yelled, "Woody, look out!" which gave the officer just enough time to jump aside before Scott fired. The charge of buckshot passed between the Woody brothers and ripped into the front of the Randall Store. Woody ran for the cover of iron posts in front of Taylor & Barr's as Scott turned loose the contents of the other barrel, missing again.

Aware that the shotgun was empty, Woody "pulled out his Colt's improved 45-calibre six-shooter, and walking to the edge of the sidewalk, took deliberate aim at Scott" and fired. The bullet passed over Scott's head. He fired again and hit a post in front of his target, throwing splinters into his face. Scott ran into Siemer's jewelry store and began to reload his shotgun as Woody emptied his revolver into the store, barely missing Scott and the jeweler.

> Scott had loaded one barrel and was in the act of 'fixing' the other when Ex-Marshal Courtright, with his six-shooter drawn on him, rushed in, followed by Woody's brother, and succeeded in disarming Scott, and by force of strength, pulled him out. Woody, having emptied his pistol, came across and joined them. Had it not been for Courtright, Scott would have re-loaded and appeared again, when Woody would scarcely have escaped his vengeance.[30]

Maybe not, if Scott's marksmanship showed no improvement. The Scott-Woody gunfight is another example of the ineffective shooting exhibited by both officers and notorious gunmen caught up in the excitement of a life-and-death engagement. Even with the deadly scattergun Scott was unable to score a hit on his adversary and Woody, although taking "deliberate aim," emptied every load in his pistol without as much as nicking the man who had just tried to kill him.

The incident also reveals that Jim Courtright was not the quick-shooting mankiller as portrayed by his legend fabricators. He ran into Siemer's jewelry store, gun in hand, knowing that Scott had just tried to murder his fellow officer and very close friend. He saw the man reloading his shotgun, obviously intent on finishing the work he had started. Courtright might very well have opened fire at once, shooting Scott down in his tracks, but he chose instead to disarm and arrest the would-be assassin "by force of strength." Courtright to this point had never killed a man, as far as is known; he seemed in no hurry to dispatch his first victim.

Woody's accusations against Cliff Scott leading to the bloodless gunfight of May 13, 1879 had been precipitated by a series of stagecoach robberies near Fort Worth. They began in February when the Fort Worth to Fort Yuma stage was held up and the passengers robbed within a mile and a half of the city. Highwaymen struck the same stage line again within a week. Two more robberies followed in quick succession, the Fort Concho stage on March 11 and the Fort Yuma coach again on March 19. The latter holdup was particularly bold, as two masked men pulled it off within the city limits and secured all the registered mail.

The stagecoach robbery epidemic came about during the heated election campaign of 1879, and the seeming ineffectiveness of City Marshal Courtright to collar the felons may well have contributed to his losing his job that April. Most people believed the robbers were locals, working out of Hell's Half Acre, and thought that Courtright, with his knowledge of the district and many contacts there, should have been able to ferret them out. As a federal officer, it was also his duty to go after bandits who robbed the U. S. mails. He did make one arrest after the last holdup, taking into custody Charles Freeman, described as "a horse-head dealer" at the Waco Tap and Red Light saloons, two of the Acre's toughest dives, and charging him with highway robbery. Freeman initially paid a fine for carrying a pistol and later for attempting to release prisoners from the county jail, but gained an acquittal in a trial held by the U. S. commissioner on the more serious offense of robbing the mails.[31]

Newly elected City Marshal Sam Farmer energetically pursued the stagecoach robbers, working closely with a deputy U. S. marshal named Seward and Special Agent Amos P. Foster, both on special assignment in Fort Worth to solve the cases. Only ten days after Farmer's election he assisted in the arrest of four suspects, including the proprietor of the Tarrant House, the hostelry in which the others were staying. Two of those arrested, Jack Starrett and Ben Jones, were former drivers on the stagecoach line.[32]

Farmer was also appointed a deputy U. S. marshal soon after his election and, acting in that capacity, he chased other members of the stagecoach robbing gang all the way to Leadville, Colorado. In May he wired Fort Worth that he had killed one of the outlaws and captured two others, effectively wiping out the gang.[33]

In 1880 a Dallas newspaper reported that, following his reelection defeat in 1879, Jim Courtright had to turn in both his Tarrant County deputy sheriff and U. S. deputy marshal badges.[34] It is clear, however, that he retained his federal commission for several years and occasionally was employed by Sheriff Henderson as a special deputy. It was in the latter capacity that on May 7, 1880, he assisted Henderson in the hanging of Isham Capps, a black man convicted of the rape of a white woman the previous February. Eight thousand people assembled on the river bottom a mile from town where a gallows had been erected and witnessed the execution.[35]

But it was as a deputy U. S. marshal that Courtright remained most active in law enforcement. On May 27, 1879, he returned to town after "a long, tedious and fruitless tramp after Ellis, the shark who swindled the City National Bank out of one thousand dollars." Close friend Al Neely, a former policeman and one-time floor manager of the notorious Red Light Saloon and Dance Hall accompanied him on this search.[36]

Courtright passed through town in July with Deputy U. S. Marshal Walter Johnson and Edward DeNormandie of the Internal Revenue Department. They were headed for Dallas with four prisoners charged with violation of the revenue act.[37] In August Courtright, Johnson, and other federal officers were in Palo Pinto County after another band of moonshiners. According to press reports, they destroyed a sixty-gallon still on Buck Creek and took twelve suspects into custody. While the deputy marshals were there, Sheriff S. R. Edmondson enlisted their aid in running down the Jones gang of horse thieves. Sheriff Edmondson's posse, forty-five men strong after the addition of the federal officers, fought a pitched battle with the thieves near Palo Pinto. Larkin Jones was killed, John Jones wounded, and "Old Man" Jones, Enoch Jones and two others captured.[38]

On September 2 Deputy Marshal Johnson and Agent DeNormandie went before United States Commissioner John W. Schenk in Dallas and obtained warrants for the arrest of parties in remote Wheeler County on charges of theft of government property and violation of the internal revenue laws. To assist them in serving the warrants they enlisted Jim Courtright and two other deputy marshals, Womble and Burns. Thus began a strange chain of events that would involve the highest officials of Wheeler County, the state of Texas, the United States Marshal Service, and the War Department, and would fill the pages of newspapers across Texas and beyond in the fall of 1879.

Wheeler County, newly organized in 1879, was the only county in the panhandle of Texas and its law enforcement officers and court officials were responsible for fourteen unorganized counties stretching from Indian Territory on the east to New Mexico Territory on the west and north to the Unassigned Lands. It was very sparsely populated, with Mobeetie, the county seat, located near the U. S. Army post of Fort Elliott, and Tascosa, a cattle town one hundred miles west on the Canadian River, the only settlements of any consequence.

It was later alleged that the warrants carried by Johnson, the posse leader, on his foray north were blank, issued for "nobody in particular, but everybody in general," and names were not filled in until the officers arrived in Mobeetie and began arresting suspects.[39] The raid was mounted because the deputies "were running low in the way of fees, and their plan was to arrest everyone they could on some trumped-up charge, and take them to Dallas, where they could be fined, and the marshal and his deputies would fatten off the fees."[40]

The federal officers took into custody a number of businessmen of Mobeetie and Tascosa and a few pioneer cattlemen of the region, including legendary rancher Charles Goodnight. There were so many arrested that Johnson called on the military at Fort Elliott for assistance. A detachment of black troopers of the Tenth U. S. Cavalry under Lieutenant Henry O. Flipper, the first black graduate of West Point, joined the roundup. Those arrested were charged with selling ammunition stolen from Fort Elliott to the cowboys, or selling tobacco and liquor to them in violation of the revenue laws. They were held at the fort until County Attorney Moses Wiley insisted on a hearing into the charges before Judge Emanuel Dubbs of the state court. There Wiley argued that the warrants, having been filled out after issuance, were invalid, that the purpose of the expedition was "pure blackmail," and requested release of the prisoners on a *habeas corpus* appeal. Judge Dubbs agreed and ordered the prisoners freed.[41]

Johnson, a stubborn and determined man, promptly re-arrested his suspects. Sheriff Henry Fleming thereupon arrested Johnson and brought him before Judge Dubbs, who found him guilty of contempt of court, fined him one hundred dollars and costs, and placed him under $3000 bond for appearance at the next term of court. Johnson returned to Dallas, where he had warrants issued charging the Wheeler County officials with interfering with United States officers in the discharge of their duties. Back in Mobeetie he and his deputies, backed again by Lt. Flipper's cavalrymen, arrested eighteen Wheeler County citizens, including Judge Dubbs, County Attorney Wiley, Sheriff Fleming, and Constable G. W. Easkin. In the dead of night they loaded their prisoners into wagons and started for Indian Territory, beyond the jurisdiction of county or state courts.

Appearing on the stage at this point was a man who would in future years become a close associate and fast friend of Jim Courtright. But the first meeting of Jim McIntire and Courtright, according to McIntire's account, almost ended in a gun battle with the two on opposite sides.

McIntire, who was a Wheeler County deputy sheriff at the time, wrote that he and another deputy, Tom Riley, were the only county officers not in custody, and it was up to them to prevent the removal of the prisoners from the county. "It was 150 miles to the nearest district judge, where a writ of *habeas corpus* could be secured... so we drew up a bogus writ," he said.

That night about 12 o'clock they got their prisoners out of town and started to steal into the Indian Territory with them. They succeeded in getting out of town without being discovered; but when about three miles out, a druggist by the name of Rhinehart [sic: Ira Rinehart] escaped, and, riding back to town, awakened Tom Riley and me. I saddled my horse, and Riley took the horse Rhinehart was riding, and we started in pursuit. About a mile out of town we met Courtright coming back. . . . We sprung the bogus habeas corpus and demanded his arrest, but, instead of submitting, he wheeled his horse and rode for his party. We were right after him, and as we neared the soldiers, Courtright yelled for them to shoot; but we were all running side by side and the soldiers could not tell which was friend or foe. In another second we were right among them, and they were so confused that they did not know what to do.

Taking advantage of our position, we lighted matches and read the habeas corpus, after which we arrested the whole bunch and took them back to town, where we turned the prisoners loose. The marshal and his deputies were "sore" over being knocked out of some nice prospective fees, and soon left town.[42] The Wheeler County affair was an embarrassment to officials of the county, state and federal governments, and most dodged nimbly to avoid responsibility for the debacle. Brevet Brigadier General Richard I. Eskridge, in command at Fort Sill, Indian Territory, where the officers and prisoners were headed before being intercepted by Deputy Sheriffs McIntire and Riley, sent a telegram to General W. T. Sherman in Washington, giving the facts of the case as he knew them. "I have declined to take any of the prisoners into custody, or take any part in the squabble unless ordered by competent authority," he said.[43] Texas Adjutant General John B. Jones and U. S. Marshal Norton held a damage control conference in Dallas, in which it was decided to drop all charges against the citizens and officials of Wheeler County and to let lesser federal officers take the heat. On November 20 Marshal Norton removed Deputy Johnson from office. Tried in county court on charges of false imprisonment, he was convicted and fined five hundred dollars. Agent DeNormandie was fired. A grand jury indicted Lt. Flipper and his superior, Captain Nicholas Nolan for unlawfully permitting U. S. soldiers to be used in the arrest and prosecution of civilians, a violation of the newly passed Posse Comitatus Act. They were tried, convicted, and fined one dollar each.[44]

From the beginning to the end of the Wheeler County imbroglio, Jim Courtright allowed Walter Johnson to take the lead and consequently escaped any punishment or criticism for his role in the affair. Its importance to his later career was undoubtedly the meeting with Jim McIntire, a man who in the coming years would be his close associate as lawman, murderer, and fugitive.

Chapter
Six

LAKE VALLEY MARSHAL

"Courtright was well known as a detective, State Ranger and city marshal. He was a terrible and quick man on the trigger, and was a terror of the country."

Denver Tribune-Republican,
April 27, 1885.

If Jim Courtright was a close associate of Wild Bill Hickok and scouted with him in earlier days, as the legend makers tell us, he certainly would not have missed the P. T. Barnum spectacular that played Fort Worth in October 1880. The featured performer, a female equestrian billed as "Miss Emma Lake, America's Side-Saddle Queen," was the stepdaughter of the celebrated frontiersman and gunfighter who had been assassinated at Deadwood only four years before. Courtright may well have attended the performance – most everyone in town did – but there is no record that he met with Emma Lake and discussed Hickok, her stepdad and his reputed old friend. It would have made a great story for the *Democrat*.

During his years in Fort Worth Jim Courtright was always active in the local Odd Fellows Lodge and particularly the M. T. Johnson "Panther City" Hook and Ladder Fire Company. Many of the leading men of the town served with Courtright as officers of this company, including businessman R. E. Maddox, city attorney W. H. Field, newspaper editor B. B. Paddock, alderman P. J. Bowdry, and attorney J. W. Swayne.

Courtright was acting foreman of the company when he got into an affray with a fireman named Joe Young. On May 3, 1880, a grand parade kicking off the annual German society Mayfest celebration in Dallas was scheduled, and fire companies from surrounding communities participated. As the Panther City fire company prepared to leave for the neighboring town that morning, Young showed up in an inebriated condition. Exercising his authority as acting foreman, Courtright refused to allow Young to accompany the others and wrested his uniform from him. Furious, the drunken fireman produced a pocketknife and stabbed Courtright in the hand and side, inflicting two painful but superficial wounds. "Courtright drew a pistol and would have killed him but for interference of friends."[1]

The incident was another opportunity for Courtright to demonstrate the lightning reflexes and quick-shooting ability the legend makers claimed he possessed, but again he showed none of those qualities.

It was during these months of 1880 that Courtright had his run-in with John Morris and kept his keno game in the Cattle Exchange Saloon. The gambling operation appears to have been a lucrative enterprise as he paid his monthly $25 fine without complaint. He was flush enough in September of that year to be listed on the roll of honor as a $25 contributor to a fund raised to bring the Gulf, Colorado and Santa Fe Railroad into Fort Worth.[2]

In early 1881 Courtright announced his candidacy for city marshal again. He and two other candidates, Benton R. Elliott and John Burford, challenged the incumbent, Sam Farmer. When the ballots were counted in April, Farmer, who had proved to be a popular officer,[3] easily won, receiving 681 votes to second place finisher Elliott's 367. With 283 votes, Courtright was a distant third, only ahead of Burford and his meager eighty-seven.[4]

Contributing to the former marshal's poor showing in the election was the sudden illness of his wife a few weeks before the voting. On March 14 Betty Courtright was struck down with a severe case of meningitis. A week later Courtright left with his family, bound for Los Angeles, where Betty's parents resided. There were now three children, Mary Ellen, in her ninth year, John, familiarly called "Jack," aged four, and the baby, James, not yet two. The *Democrat and Advance* reported that they would be gone for three months and that Jim was saying goodbye to his friends in the city by means of its pages.[5]

He did not stay three months in California but was back within a week, leaving Betty and their three children in Los Angeles. The Courtrights had apparently disposed of their home, for he checked into the El Paso Hotel on his return.[6] If he hurried back to campaign in the race for marshal, he was to be disappointed; his sudden departure from town and the hint that he would be gone a long time, perhaps forever, destroyed any chances he had with the voters.

In the succeeding months he was in and out of the city, working federal cases with his pal, Ab Woody. A report circulated in April that Woody had been killed. "If Ab is killed, it must have been very early after dinner yesterday," wrote Paddock in his paper, "for in the forenoon he and the jolly Jim Courtright were in the *Democrat* office entertaining a number of the boys with a humorous recital of their late trip to the brush."[7]

Soon after Betty and the children returned and the family settled into a new home, tragedy struck. James, the baby, sickened and suddenly died. A funeral notice was printed on the press of the *Democrat and Advance*:

The friends and acquaintances of T. I. and S. E. Courtright
are respectfully invited to attend the funeral of their son,
James W. Courtright,
From the family residence on Calhoun street,
between First and Weatherford
streets, this evening at 4 p. m.
Fort Worth, Texas, Aug. 10, 1881.

FUNERAL NOTICE

———

The friends and acquaintances of T. I. and S. E. Courtright are respectfully invited to attend the funeral of their son,

JAMES W. COURTRIGHT,

from the family residence on Calhoun street, between First and Weatherford streets, this evening at 4 p. m.

Fort Worth, Texas, Aug. 10, 1881,

Funeral notice for the Courtrights' young son.

Courtright was in Graham attending court and just got back in time for the funeral.[8] Shaken by the death of the boy who had been given the first name his father had adopted, Betty took Mary Ellen and Jack back to her parents' home in Los Angeles and stayed there again for several months. Courtright visited them but did not remain long. "T. I. Courtright is again among us," said the *Democrat*. "Jim has been to Los Angeles, California, where his family is now. He says it is a large, fine country, but it is not large enough to hold him, so he has returned to Fort Worth to stay."[9]

In May 1882 Courtright engaged in another of the brawls that characterized his career. With several friends he rode the new line of the Gulf, Colorado and Santa Fe south into Johnson County to do a little fishing in the Cleburne area. Waiting for the train on their return, the Fort Worth fishermen, perhaps attracted by the appropriate name, stepped into Fisher's Lunch House on the Cleburne square. There Courtright got into an altercation with a man named Bud Davis. In a story headlined "A Cleburne Desperado Tackles The Wrong Man," the *Democrat and Advance* applauded Courtright for his fighting ability. Davis, it said,

> succeeded in insulting Jim pretty thoroughly. Jim warned him that he was mistaken in the kind of man he was talking to, but the man was reckless and brought on a fight in which sauce bottles, plates, coffee cups and finally pistols were made use of. Davis, the man who originated the difficulty, struck Courtright with a pepper sauce bottle, and was in turn struck with a plate. Finally, Jim drew his pistol and, in striking his antagonist with it, the weapon exploded, the ball passing through the top of Davis' shoulder, setting his clothes on fire, tearing the crown out of the hat of Davis' side partner, perforating a waiter [a tray for carrying dishes] in the hands of a negro attendant, and then going in the kitchen, hunting around for somebody. The negro out of whose hands the waiter was shot has never been heard of. After the shot Davis closed in on Jim and received a most unmerciful beating with Courtright's pistol. . . . Most any one could have told that man he would be mistaken if he undertook to impose on T. I. Courtright.[10]

This was the story as the Fort Worth newspapermen got it from Courtright and his friends. Other accounts, based on reports from Cleburne, said that Courtright drew his pistol and "shot Davis, inflicting a slight wound in the head, the ball passing through the hat of Bob Blackwell, who was a looker-on…. [Courtright claimed he struck]

Davis over the head with his pistol [and] the lick... caused the pistol to explode. This is doubted."[11]

In any event, the sound of the shot brought local policemen running to the scene. They disarmed and arrested Courtright and took him before a magistrate, who released him on bond of $100, pending a hearing on May 26. Courtright returned to Cleburne on that date and at a trial pled guilty to an assault charge and paid a fine of $5 and costs. Davis, arraigned on the same charge, entered a plea of not guilty. After hearing testimony in the case, the court exonerated him.[12]

Courtright may have bludgeoned Davis with his six-shooter and in the process fired accidentally, as he claimed, or shot at the man, nicking him and taking the hat off the head of a bystander, as others reported. In either case the Bud Davis affray, like Courtright's previous clashes with Bingham Feild, N. H. Wilson, O. F. Cheney and John C. Morris, did not conform to the myth of his amazing gunfighting ability as promulgated by the legendists, so they simply ignored it.

Courtright had established a reputation throughout the frontier as a tough, fearless fighting man, however, and only a month later city officials of Caldwell, Sumner County, Kansas, offered him the city marshal's job at that cow town. In announcing the offer on June 27, the editors of the *Democrat and Advance* seemed convinced Courtright would take the job. "He is assured a good salary and sure pay. He will accept the position and make a good officer. For his long experience as a peace officer and his cool bravery qualify him for such a position."

As an end-of-the-trail cattle town, Caldwell had a record for violence surpassing Newton, Ellsworth, Wichita, and Dodge City, the other important Kansas cow towns. In the two years preceding the offer to Courtright no less than four current or former city officers had been gunned down within the city limits. The death of the latest, City Marshal George Davis, on June 22, created the vacancy Courtright was asked to fill. A local Kansas paper deplored the violence in an editorial that same week:

> From July 3, 1879 to June 22, 1882, there were just forty murders committed in Sumner county. By this we mean forty murders of which we have a record.... The cause in thirty-four instances is directly traceable to whiskey and lewd women.... In every instance [the killers'] devilish hearts were fired to evil by bad whiskey and prostitute women, both of which were placed within their reach only by means of flagrant violations of the laws of the state. . . . How long is this state of affairs to continue? Is this debauchery, this murdering to go on perpetually? Let an end be put to it at once and effectually.[13]

What was needed to accomplish that job, in the words of a Caldwell resident, was "a man ready to lay down his life at any time, [one] who knew no fear, whose highest ambition was to be dreaded by man, and who rushed to the front of battle [determined] to come out of the conflict victorious."[14] For the first time Caldwell officials looked beyond the bounds of their own town for such a man and of course turned to Texas, a state renowned for its fighting men. They tapped the former city marshal of Fort Worth, but Jim Courtright decided he was not their man – not for $50 a month – and passed on the offer. Within a week B. P. "Bat" Carr, lately of Colorado City, accepted the position at Caldwell.

Courtright turned down that job offer, but it was clear that after twice being soundly defeated for reelection as city marshal at Fort Worth, he was looking for greener fields. During this period he reportedly found a marshal's job at Mesilla, in southern New Mexico. "After he was fired from his job in Fort Worth [sic] he drifted again," Bill Cox tells us. "His next important appearance in Western history was at Mesilla, New Mexico.... Again Courtright did a good job. In fact, he worked himself right out of the position. Their badmen departed, the community no longer needed the services of a gun-totin' marshal."[15] There is no record that Courtright ever served as an officer in Mesilla, but in late 1882 he did pin on a badge in New Mexico, not in an old Mexican town like Mesilla, but in a brand new silver mining camp some fifty miles to the northwest, at a place called Lake Valley.

There had been a small lake there once, hence its name, but in 1882 water at Lake Valley was a scarce commodity. "Water is conspicuous by its absence and the dust is terrible," wrote a visitor in November, two months after the town's founding.[16] The fourteen-mile ride from Nutt Station, the nearest railroad point, to Lake Valley had cost him $2 and he had to spend $1.50 more for a night's lodging.

> The family washstand was a feature of this hostelry. It consisted of a cracker box and a tin basin in the back yard, a chunk of rosin soap, a filthy towel and a barrel of water with a dipper. A cautionary notice tacked on the barrel informed the guest that 'water was very scarce.'. . . At present the people are supplied with water by carts, which bring water about a mile from the well. People are building a reservoir about a mile from the town, and are laying iron pipes through the streets. The town has two marshals...."[17]

Courtright was one of those marshals; the other was Jim McIntire, the man he had first known as a Wheeler County deputy sheriff back in 1879 and the man with whom he would be closely associated the next few years.

Both Courtright and McIntire were called Jim, although neither had been given that name by his parents. As Courtright had discarded the name "Isaiah," so McIntire had dropped the name "Isaac" and both had adopted "James" as a first name. This was one of many characteristics the two men had in common. Both were tall, dark, and considered handsome. The surnames of both were commonly misspelled in press reports. Born and raised in the North, both came to Texas after the Civil War in search of adventure and found it in the saloons and gambling halls of the frontier towns. Establishing reputations for fearlessness and ability with a gun, they both drifted into law enforcement.

Jim McIntire, who hooked up with Courtright in Lake Valley, New Mexico, and then was linked with him in the American Valley murders. *Courtesy Western History Collections, University of Oklahoma Library, Norman, Oklahoma.*

McIntire, born in Ohio in 1854, was some eight years younger than Courtright. At the age of nineteen, having "developed an ambition to be a cowboy and see life on the plains as portrayed in the dime novels" he had been reading, he left home, made his way to Texas, and struck Fort Worth in 1873, the same year Courtright settled there.[18] At Weatherford he was employed by cattleman J. C. Loving as a cowboy to help work stock on his ranch in Jack County, northwest of Fort Worth.[19] Fighting Indians was part of a north Texas cowpuncher's job in the early 1870s, and McIntire did his share. This led him into service with the Texas Rangers and police work. He was a deputy sheriff of Wheeler County when his first meeting with Courtright in 1879 almost resulted in a gun battle between lawmen. Later he was city marshal at East Las Vegas, New Mexico, during some of the most riotous years in that tough town's history. He had also hunted buffalo, raised sheep, kept saloons, and gambled professionally in his nine years in the West, and still found time to marry a girl named Kitty.

A newspaper a few years later described him as "a remarkably fine looking young man about thirty years of age. He is six feet tall, erect, and broad-shouldered, and has a pair of dark, keen, fighting eyes. The expression on his face is anything but forbidding, and his manners are very quiet, his address pleasant, and taken all in all, he doesn't look like a bully or desperado, although he does look as if he would be a bad customer if he were aroused."[20]

McIntire had come to the marshal's job at Lake Valley from Socorro, where he had been operating a gambling saloon. Lawyer and newspaperman Albert J. Fountain, a major investor in the mines at Lake Valley, reportedly hired him on the recommendation of James B. Gillett, city marshal at El Paso, Texas.[21] "Jim McIntire... is marshal here... and holds the reins with a steady hand," wrote a Lake Valley visitor to the *Las Vegas Optic* on November 1, 1882. For holding those reins he was paid a whopping $300 a month.[22] (Unincorporated at the time, Lake Valley had no municipal officers or treasury; the city marshal was evidently compensated from funds contributed by local businessmen and the Sierra Grande Mining Company, the area's largest employer.)

Lake Valley may have been short on water, but it did not lack drinking establishments. One of the few women living there in 1882, Mrs. Ellen Lucy Capp, recalled that eighteen saloons provided libation for the five hundred residents. Miners worked around the clock. "Had to keep them busy, you know, to keep 'em from drinking and fighting and raising Cain. Great old times."[23]

Albert J. Fountain was instrumental in luring Courtright to New Mexico. *Author's personal collection.*

McIntire's "steady hand" was apparently not enough to control the Cain-raising of the miners, for soon he was joined by Courtright, hired by Fountain, according to the legend makers, on the recommendation of Jim Gillett. As Cunningham told the tale, Fountain offered the Lake Valley job to Gillett at double what he was making as marshal at El Paso. Gillett declined the offer, but reportedly told Fountain:

I know just the man for you! Jim Courtright, the old Army scout. He's a man who can't be bluffed. And, when he has to be, he's a gunfighter from the forks of Hard Water Creek. As good as anybody I ever heard of – and I'm not barring John Wesley Hardin or Ben Thompson or anybody else. He's been marshal up at Fort Worth but lost his job through politics. If he'll come to Lake Valley, I guarantee that it won't be long after his arrival that you'll see your hard cases hightailing for a healthier climate.[24]

Stanley repeated the story in his *Longhair Jim Courtright*.[25] In their effort to present the lone hero image of "Longhaired Jim," both writers neglected to mention that Jim McIntire had preceded Courtright as Lake Valley marshal and the two men served together as co-marshals there.[26] Conversely, McIntire, in his autobiography published twenty years later, ignored Courtright's employment. Perhaps he was still irked because he had to share that munificent $300 salary with the man from Fort Worth. McIntire developed a strong dislike for Fountain, as he made clear in his book, and the genesis of this animosity may well have been Fountain's hiring of Courtright.

It is not clear just when Courtright joined McIntire at Lake Valley. He was still in Fort Worth, holding his office of deputy U. S. marshal, in August when he fell and suffered "a severe contusion." By November

Jim Gillett was impressed by Courtright's dexterity with his six-shooters. *Courtesy Western History Collections, University of Oklahoma Library, Norman, Oklahoma.*

he was in Lake Valley, although it was well into December before the *El Paso Lone Star* took note: "T. J. Courtwright [sic], late city marshal at Fort Worth, has accepted the marshalship of Lake Valley."[27]

Ten days later the same paper reported: "William Young, charged with stealing ore from the Sierra Grande Mining Company, Lake Valley, was arrested by Marshal McIntyre [sic]. Threats were made of lynching Young, but he was protected by the militia."[28] In his autobiography McIntire made no mention of this incident. He devoted only a few pages to his Lake Valley experiences, including an account of his pursuit of a pair of Mexican thieves who had stolen two horses and two mules from prospectors. When he shot at them, he said, the thieves deserted the stolen animals and took to the brush. But McIntire's horse fell, pinning him to the ground, and it was only after some effort he freed himself and returned to town with the prospectors' animals. "They bought a few rounds of drinks as a solace for the fall I had received," wrote McIntire, "and we had a good time for the rest of the afternoon."[29]

The legend makers tell us that Courtright, while serving as Lake Valley city marshal, killed two ore-thieves "in a running gun battle" and "it has been said," dispatched three other rustlers and ore thieves to Boot Hill.[30] No substantiation of these claims can be found in contemporary sources. They are likely derived from Courtright's later confused and deliberately distorted accounts of events that took place in the spring of 1883.

Despite the claims of his mythmakers that Courtright "tamed" Lake Valley – "the 'bad men' were smitten with the fear of sudden death. They 'high-tailed' for places where no Jim Courtright was riding herd on civic affairs. Lake Valley became downright peaceful...."[31] – the town and the nearby Cottonwood Ranch were in fact at the time the headquarters of the John Kinney gang, characterized by one eminent historian "as blood-handed an assembly of bandits as ever was found in the American Southwest."[32] The depredations of this cutthroat band, thirty or forty strong, became so blatant that the governor of New Mexico, Lionel Sheldon, directed units of the territorial militia to root them out and kill or capture them all. The Doña Ana County militia, familiarly called the Mesilla Scouts, led by Major Albert J. Fountain, took the lead in this campaign. The Mesilla Scouts were mostly Hispanics and the unit was derisively referred to by many Anglos (including Jim McIntire) as the "Greaser Militia." Governor Sheldon also called on the regular army for support, but the Posse Comitatus Act, the measure that had gotten Lieutenant Flipper in trouble in Texas a few years before, prevented the military from acting. The governor did receive help, however, from Alexander L. Morrison, Sr., recently appointed U. S. marshal for New Mexico and eager to please. Morrison issued deputy marshal commissions to a number of men with gunfighting reputations, including

Courtright, McIntire, and an old Courtright compadre from Texas, Joe Forsythe. The three were also employed by the Sierra Grande Mining Company as guards to protect ore shipments and at least one, McIntire, held appointment as a deputy sheriff.[33]

On March 21, 1883, Fountain led his Mesilla Scouts, out of Las Cruces by special train to Nutt Station, which they reached about three o'clock on the morning of March 22. "The men were furnished with forty rounds of ammunition," Fountain wrote in his report to Governor Sheldon,

> and each carried two days' rations for the entire com-
> mand and a sufficient supply of reserve ammunition was
> carried in pack mules.... I had positive information about
> fifteen notorious rustlers and my detectives informed me
> that they were fully resolved to resist arrest. I had warrants
> for most of these men.... The command arrived at Nutt
> Station (a five-hour ride by rail out of Las Cruces) and
> about an hour was occupied in disembarking men and
> horses. At midnight the command took up its line of march
> for Lake Valley. At Nutt Station I was joined by Courtright
> and Forsythe, employees of the Sierra Mining Company
> sent to meet and guide me.[34]

At Nutt Station Fountain received information from his "detectives," undoubtedly Courtright and Forsythe, that many of the gang were at Kingston but several for whom he had warrants were currently disporting at Lake Valley. Taking a detail of five men, he left immediately with Courtright and Forsythe for the town. The rest of the command followed with orders to encircle the town and prevent the escape of any of the wanted men.

At Lake Valley Courtright, who knew the wanted men by sight, searched the saloons while Fountain and his militiamen waited outside. He found William "Butch" Leland[35] gambling in Bennett's saloon. According to newspaper reports, the outlaw had been having a run of luck at poker and was considerably ahead of the game, but his fortunes changed drastically from the moment Courtright collared him and turned him over to the militia.

John Watts,[36] another for whom Fountain had a warrant, got wind of the militia's arrival and managed to get his horse from a stable before being captured. A third wanted man, one Burke, succeeded in slipping out of town.

Fountain's men bound the hands of Leland and Watts, mounted them on one horse, and rode out to the nearby Daily ranch, where they stopped and prepared coffee. Here the two prisoners died, shot down, it was said, as they attempted to escape. Fountain wired Governor Sheldon:

"Lake Valley, March 22. – Before daylight this morning after the moon had gone down, the two rustlers captured last night, John Watts and William Gilliard [sic], alias Bill Bush, made an attempt to escape, while the men were unsaddling their horses to go into camp. They ran up the road about 200 yards, when the company fired upon them, riddling them with bullets. Fountain, Major.[37]

The militiamen left the bodies lie where they fell and moved on toward Kingston, where the major portion of the Kinney gang was believed to be located. Courtright and Forsythe evidently accompanied Fountain, while McIntire remained in Lake Valley. When news of the killings of Watts and Leland reached town, McIntire, who still was a deputy sheriff, summoned a jury of inquest, headed by Justice of the Peace Jay Barnes, and led a large number of citizens to the scene. The condition of the bodies was not consistent with Fountain's report that the two men were shot at a distance of two hundred yards. Both bodies were "terribly mutilated," according to witnesses.

> **Zillard [sic] had ten bullet holes in his body and head. His face was badly powder burnt. He was shot in the face, the ball entering at the nose, passing downwards, carrying away the lower jaw and into the breast, indicating that he had been shot from above while lying down. There were marks of a boot heel on the nose, and elsewhere on the face and body. John Watts was similarly used up, his face being terribly burned and disfigured. Those who served upon the coroner's jury state that the pockets of the dead men were found turned wrong side out and that the boots of one of the men had been removed.[38]**

In his autobiography Jim McIntire added further gruesome details. "They stripped the bodies of clothing and cut them open, filling the cavities with tobacco spit; then placed quids of tobacco between their teeth. They left them lying in the middle of the road, with a placard on each one stating that any who moved them would be treated likewise."[39]

Lake Valley citizens were outraged. A meeting was called for that night but "was stopped by Deputy Sheriff McEntire [sic], who advised the men to keep quiet and behave themselves, which they did."[40]

A man named John Shannon was particularly vocal in his condemnation of the killings and reportedly stalked the streets, rifle in hand, calling on others to join him in a war on the "Greaser Militia." Major Fountain was making raids in the neighborhood of Hillsboro when he learned of the disturbances at Lake Valley. He dispatched Sergeant Leandro Garcia and a squad of men to return to Lake Valley and arrest any troublemakers. On March 23 Garcia's squad, accompanied by Joe Forsythe, rode into the little community, quickly identified the outspoken Shannon as the main agitator, and took him into custody. He too, according to Fountain, attempted to escape and was shot by his guards at a distance of one hundred yards.[41]

"His remains were found where the guard left him, a short distance above Young's boarding house," reported the *Lake Valley Herald*.

> A wagon was sent for by the citizens and he was brought to the morgue, where a large crowd had assembled. He had several wounds in the body and a shot through the head, the ball entering at the rear, passing directly through and issuing at the forehead. It carried away the frontispiece, and scattered the brains in the road…. Shannon was known to be a harmless man, although one who was given to loud talking…. He was never known to injure anyone and was regarded as weak and childish. His death creates a feeling among his friends which it will be hard to eradicate. The squad which is doing this work is composed of five Mexicans, under the command of J. H. Forsythe, one of the Sierra Grande guards.[42]

Although the "Greaser Militia" went on to round up John Kinney and many members of his outlaw gang in what became known as the "Rustler War," the brutal killings at Lake Valley, particularly that of John Shannon, who was not an outlaw, brought Albert Fountain under severe criticism in the New Mexico press. Typical was this piece in the *Silver City Enterprise* of April 6, 1883:

It is thought by the people [of Lake Valley] that the killing was altogether unnecessary. Even if it were necessary, there is no excuse for the militia to leave the bodies of their victims lying where they fell, without burial. This is barbarous, and it would be better to do away with the militia altogether than to have citizens murdered under the cloak of their authority. [Major Fountain] is responsible for the action of his company, and a great deal of hostile feeling is expressed against him at Lake Valley.

In response to the complaints that the actions of his militia had been cold-blooded and cruel, Fountain demanded a court of inquiry to investigate the allegations. Governor Sheldon directed that a special court be convened at Lake Valley, but before that could be accomplished a Doña Ana County grand jury held hearings in the matter. After examining more than thirty witnesses, the jurors refused to bring indictments. Instead they issued a report praising the governor for calling in the militia and requesting that the units remain in the district longer to weed out more outlaws. Sheldon then cancelled his court of inquiry directive, citing the grand jury report as proof that no crimes had been committed.[43]

Many citizens of Lake Valley were unconvinced, however, and some still muttered about revenge. Courtright, McIntire and Forsythe, who as lawmen had aided and abetted Fountain and his militia, heard the grumblings and thought it prudent to move on. Forsythe left to pursue his raucous career in Kansas and Texas and his eventual slide into oblivion. Courtright and McIntire remained together. Within weeks their names would be inextricably linked as they became involved in one of the most infamous murder cases in the history of the West.

Chapter Seven

THE AMERICAN VALLEY MURDERS

"It is certain that if any attempt is made to arrest Courtright here a bloody tragedy will ensue, Courtright being determined not to be arrested, and in this resolve is backed by a host of friends, who are desperate men."

Dallas Daily Herald,
June 26, 1883.

Legend has it that the involvement of Jim Courtright in the infamous American Valley murders of 1883 came about when he was summoned to the region by John A. Logan, his old Civil War commander, who had maintained contact with his former scout over the years.[1]

Following his distinguished service in the war, Logan went on to a successful career in the United States Senate, and by 1883 his name was being mentioned in Republican Party political circles as a possible candidate for the presidency.[2] Early that year a New Mexico cattleman named John P. Casey made the long trip to Washington for the express purpose of interesting Logan in the purchase of his ranch.

Casey was tall, aggressive, and persuasive. Born in County Cork, Ireland, he had come to Albuquerque in 1880 by way of Canada and Texas. After scouting out the range country, in early 1881 he moved a cowherd he had acquired in Texas to a wild, sparsely settled region some 130 miles west of Socorro and established a ranch headquarters at the forks of Largo Creek. Naming the place American Valley and his new ranch the American Valley Cattle Company, he began filing on all the land adjacent to streams and creeks, for whoever controlled the water in that arid country also controlled the surrounding rangeland for as far as cattle could travel to get to that water. Within a short time Casey could claim a vast cattle empire stretching about sixty-six miles north to south and seventy-two miles east to west. To insure that this great land was speedily surveyed, Casey took on as a partner Henry M. Atkinson, who had been appointed surveyor general for New Mexico by President U. S. Grant in 1876 and reappointed by President R. B. Hayes in 1880. He also needed help in stocking and managing this

Senator John A. Logan became embroiled in the American Valley affair. *Author's personal collection.*

John P. Casey planned
to establish a cattle
empire in American
Valley. *Author's personal
collection.*

huge ranch, so he entered into a "verbal partnership" with a Texas cattleman named William C. Moore, whom he met in July 1881.[3]

An air of mystery always surrounded Moore, a man in his early
thirties, whose pleasant appearance was marred by one distinguishing
feature—a cast in his left eye. He seemed very conscious of the defect
and always wore his hat pulled down over the left side of his face.
Moore had worked cattle in California and Wyoming before becoming
general manager of the big LX spread in the Texas panhandle in 1877.
Although he was reluctant to talk about his past and stories circulated
that a few dead bodies littered his back trail, Moore quickly gained the
respect of veteran Texas cattlemen for his range knowledge, leadership

ability, and ruthlessness in dealing with cattle thieves. But even as he carried on a relentless war against rustlers, Moore was stealing his employer's stock. By the time D. T. Beals and W. H. Bates, the LX owners, discovered his duplicity in the summer of 1881 and fired him, he had built a large herd of his own and panhandle cowboys were calling him "Outlaw Bill." Undaunted, in August 1881 Moore married the daughter of a Dodge City doctor, moved his stolen herd onto new rangelands in Hutchinson County, and began construction of a large stone house for his bride. This became the headquarters of his Adobe Walls Ranch. Convinced by the persuasive John P. Casey that in New Mexico there were opportunities for even greater wealth, in February 1882 Moore sold his ranch for $75,000, a huge amount for this period. In September of that year Moore purchased a third interest in the

W. C. Moore was John P. Casey's partner in the American Valley cattle ranching venture. *Courtesy Western History Collections, University of Oklahoma Library, Norman, Oklahoma.*

American Valley Cattle Company, paying Casey and Atkinson $25,000 in cash, in addition to 850 head of cattle and twenty horses.[4]

The "Rustler War" was raging in New Mexico that year and when the American Valley ranchers complained of cattle losses to Governor Lionel Sheldon, the chief executive responded by issuing commissions to Casey as captain and Moore as first lieutenant of Company C, New Mexico Volunteer Militia, with authority to fill the company's ranks with their own cowboys and arm them with Sharp's rifles provided by the territory.[5]

John P. Casey, Governor Sheldon, Senator Logan, and Surveyor General Atkinson were all Republicans. When President Chester A. Arthur on March 2, 1882, appointed Alexander L. Morrison, Sr., United States marshal for New Mexico, Casey gained another powerful ally.

The commission of W. C. Moore as an officer in the New Mexico militia. *Author's personal collection.*

Not only was Morrison a strong Republican, he was also, like Casey, an immigrant from Ireland. Fifty years old, he had arrived in America in time to see action in the Mexican War and had served in New Mexico. After the war he settled in Chicago. Popular with the Irish bloc of voters, he was elected to the Illinois legislature. Senator Logan of Illinois was his patron, and it was through the auspices of Marshal Morrison that Casey was introduced to Logan.

When Casey conferred with Logan in Washington he told him that a St. Louis firm had offered $800,000 for the American Valley holdings, with $100,000 down. Logan, who was interested in obtaining owner-ship of the ranch, thought his Chicago stockyard friends could come up with a better offer. He agreed to accompany Casey to New Mexico to look over the property.

The two men reached Santa Fe on April 24, 1883. Included in their party were Casey's partners, W. C. Moore and Henry M. Atkinson; U. S. Marshal A. L. Morrison; Henry W. Lawton, acting assistant adju-tant-general of New Mexico; C. C. Campbell, a Chicago politician, Logan cohort, and potential investor; and William H. Patton, who also had a financial interest in the American Valley ranchland.

New Mexico's well-publicized "Rustler War" concerned Logan and his prospective buyers, who understandably wanted assurance that herds they ranged in the American Valley would not be decimated by cattle thieves. To provide that assurance, Casey and Moore asked Morrison to assign deputies, experienced manhunters and seasoned fighting men, to the job of ridding their range of rustlers. So Senator Logan did not send for Courtright to come to American Valley, as legend has it. The call went out from United States Marshal Morrison to his deputies in Lake Valley, Courtright and McIntire. There is no reason to believe John Logan, if he remembered Courtright at all, was aware he was in New Mexico, and he certainly knew nothing of Jim McIntire.

Like Courtright's legend makers, who could not resist the urge to tie their hero's name to the famed Civil War general and nationally known United States Senator, Jim McIntire claimed in his autobiography with typical braggadocio that he was the man Logan selected for the American Valley job and Courtright simply tagged along:

> I went to Albuquerque, where I met General John A. Logan, who had come down to that country to look over the Western Slope of New Mexico, which an Eastern syndicate he was connected with had recently purchased [sic]. Logan offered $10 per day to go with him on a scouting trip over the slope. Jim Courtright... was also hired in a similar capacity."[6]

If McIntire and Courtright were paid $10 per day, the money surely came from the ranch owners and not from Logan or the prospective buyers.

What Logan, his financial backers, and probably Morrison and Atkinson, did not know was that Casey and Moore had larger and darker plans for the imported gunmen than simply putting heat on cattle thieves. Atkinson's surveys, begun earlier in the year, indicated that by adding some 3,400 acres of water-fed land to the vast American Valley ranch holdings, the owners could gain control of over three million acres of fine grazing lands. Already they had forced about ninety settlers of the twelve-year-old community of Rito off the land and made the little town the new headquarters of the company. But two young men, partners in a small ranching operation at Gallo Springs in the American Valley, were proving to be a problem.

In December 1881 Alexis "Aleck" Grossetete and Robert Elsinger, both twenty-four-years-old, had set up residence across Gallo

Mountain from Casey's cattle empire. Grossetete, of French descent, had come to New Mexico with his mother Clotilde from Lawrence, Kansas. In Durango, Colorado, he had met and befriended Elsinger, formerly of Illinois. The two men hit it off, and Elsinger accompanied the Grossetetes on to New Mexico. As partners they moved into the American Valley, built a stone house at Gallo Springs, and felt secure in their claim to the property under provisions of the preemption acts that guaranteed settlers on unsurveyed land the right to file for a patent to that land after it was surveyed. In May 1882 John P. Casey, his brother James, and a party of horsemen stopped at the Grossetete

Alexis Grossetete and Robert Elsinger, the victims in the American Valley murders. *Author's personal collection.*

house and accused the homesteaders of squatting on American Valley Company land. When Grossetete and Elsinger cited their preemption rights and refused to leave, John Casey offered to buy the rights, but they turned this proposal down also. The Casey brothers left, grumbling that the matter would be settled later. The young homesteaders ignored the implied threat and went about their affairs. In October Grossetete sent for his mother, three younger brothers, Fred, Alfred, and Gus, and three younger sisters, Eulalie, Adella, and Josephine. The following April he married Clemence Pourade, daughter of a French Canadian trapper and mountain man, in Socorro.[7] It was plain Aleck Grossetete and his partner were determined to stay right where they were.

A saying going the rounds, "All he wants is what joins him," was a cynical comment on the greed displayed by some big cattlemen of the time. It certainly applied to John P. Casey. The small operation at Gallo Springs adjoined John Casey's huge ranch and, as he negotiated for the sale of his holdings to Logan and the Chicago investors, Casey kept thinking that the addition of the Grossetete and Elsinger land would greatly sweeten the deal. It might even make the difference in getting the deal through at all.

Action was needed immediately to resolve the problem. At Casey's request, Marshal Morrison sent for the noted gunmen, Courtright and McIntire, ostensibly to hunt down rustlers but actually to aid his partner, "Outlaw Bill" Moore, and brother, James Casey, in the elimination of the problem at Gallo Springs.

In the beginning Courtright and McIntire probably believed their mission in the American Valley country was to chase cattle thieves. In an exchange of telegrams with John P. Casey about April 30 McIntire, still at Lake Valley, reported that a band of rustlers led by D. L. Gilmore, a former Casey employee, had just left Nutt Station to raid the cattle country west of Socorro. Casey told McIntire to bring

Courtright and a posse, meet W. C. Moore at Socorro, and search out the trail of Gilmore and the suspected cattle thieves.

On May 2 the "posse" from Lake Valley, consisting of Courtright, McIntire, and another Jim, a man named James Fointaney, met Moore at Socorro. Little is known of Fointaney, but he was reputed to be an experienced gunman.[8] Moore rented fresh horses from a Socorro livery and led the little posse directly to Rito and the American Valley ranch headquarters, more than a hundred miles away. On the way they passed Alexis Grossetete and his new bride in a buggy on the way from Socorro to their new home at Gallo Springs. The parties did not know each other, and the only exchange between them was a polite nod and tip of the hat. All were unaware that within a few days the young bridegroom would lie dead, murdered at the hands of three of the others.

Moore, Courtright, McIntire, and Fointaney arrived at the ranch headquarters at Rito on the morning of May 5. That same day another party passed through Albuquerque on its way to the ranch. Led by John Casey, the group included Logan, Atkinson, Morrison, Campbell, Patton, and a few other dignitaries. They would stay that night at Fort Wingate and go on the next day with an escort of troopers from the fort.

Meanwhile, Bill Moore on the afternoon of the fifth was leading a scouting expedition, ostensibly to look for signs of Gilmore's alleged rustlers. Riding south in the direction of Gallo Mountain with him were Courtright, McIntire, Fointaney, James Casey, Dan McAllister, Mueller Scott, and nine cowboys from the ranch.

James Casey was described as tall, with a sandy complexion, mustache, and goatee. Of "nervous disposition," he was said to have "exerted a malignant influence on the affairs of his brother John."[9]

Twenty-nine-year-old Daniel H. McAllister had come to New Mexico from Salt Lake City, where he was a deacon in the Mormon Church. His wife, Rhoda, described as a beautiful blonde, was the daughter of Brigham Young by his third wife. At American Valley McAllister became a justice of the peace and foreman of the Casey spread. In June 1882 he had been promoted to ranch manager, but on May 1, 1883, only a few days before the gathering at Rito, Mueller W. Scott had replaced him as manager.[10]

The promotion of Scott was the idea of W. C. Moore, who had known Scott in Texas. A veteran buffalo hunter, Scott still was armed with a fifty-caliber Sharp's buffalo rifle.[11]

The Moore party spent that night at a Casey line camp known as Harry's Cabin. To the surprise of many, in the morning Moore ordered only five men—Scott, Casey, McAllister, McIntire and Courtright—to saddle up and follow him. He told the others to remain at the camp and

Daniel H. McAllister turned state's evidence in the American Valley murders. *Author's personal collection.*

instructed Fointaney to see they obeyed orders. "Don't do any shooting while we're gone," he said. "And if you hear any shooting, don't leave. If we need help, we'll send for you."[12]

Harry's Cabin was about eight miles from the home of Aleck Grossetete and his partner, Robert Elsinger. Moore, grim-faced and determined, led the way directly there.

He stopped the party once to announce that their mission was to dispose of two "squatters." Both were to be killed and each of the six men was to fire into their bodies so that all six would be equally guilty.[13]

Moore and his riders were all wearing pistols. Other armament included the heavy Sharp's buffalo guns carried by Scott and Casey, Courtright and McIntire's .44-caliber Winchesters, and shotguns that Moore and McAllister carried. Calling a halt some distance from the Grossetete house, Moore sent Casey and Scott ahead to see if the homesteaders were there. They returned a few minutes later to report that Grossetete and Elsinger had gone to the house of Manuel Romero, a neighbor, to borrow a plow.

Moore led his gunmen down the road to Romero's and soon encountered the partners coming back, driving a wagon drawn by a team of black mares. With weapons drawn, the six gunmen surrounded the wagon. McIntire loudly announced he had a warrant for the arrest of the two men but did not produce it. He took a pistol from Grossetete and a rifle from Elsinger and ordered them to unhitch the mares from the wagon and mount them bareback. The party then rode on toward the house. As they approached a narrow ravine, Moore ordered them to leave the road and follow it. About a half mile from the road he called a halt.

Without another word, Moore rode up behind Grossetete, placed the muzzle of his pistol behind the man's left ear, and fired. The bullet passed through the young man's brain and out his right eye, killing him instantly. His lifeless body slid to the ground. Seeing his friend and partner brutally murdered before his eyes, Elsinger kicked his horse's flanks and made a desperate attempt to escape, but four rifle bullets, fired almost simultaneously by Courtright, McIntire, Scott, and Casey, slammed into his back, and he too fell to the ground, dead.

McAllister had not pulled his trigger. The hard stares of the others reminded him that all were to participate in the killings. He drew his pistol and fired a round into Grossetete's dead body.

The six men left their victims where they lay and headed back to Harry's Cabin. On the way Moore stopped them. "We need to do something to make sure no one squeals," he said. "I want you all to repeat after me: 'If I reveal anything that has transpired today, may you all kill me.'" Each man took the oath and they went on.[14]

On that fatal Sunday, May 6, John P. Casey's party of dignitaries was making its leisurely way from Fort Wingate to the ranch headquarters at Rito, a point they did not reach until May 8. During those crucial days the family of Alexis Grossetete was frantically searching for the missing men. Joining in the search were neighbors Manuel Romero and his father, and, ironically, the alleged rustlers from Lake Valley, D. L. Gilmore, John W. Sullivan and Jerome "The Kid" Brandon. On May 10 they found the bodies of the dead men, brought them back to their ranch, and assisted Grossetete's distraught mother, bride, and three young brothers in the burial.

When word of the murders reached Rito, Moore told the visiting contingent of notables that the Gilmore gang of rustlers must have committed the crime. That morning, while Moore and John P. Casey conducted Logan, Morrison, and Patton on a tour of the ranch land, James Casey went out with a posse in search of the suspected cattle thieves. Riding with him were Courtright, McIntire, Fointaney, McAllister, Scott, and ranch cowhands Jack Haines, Hank Andrews,

Charles F. Jewett, John Blair, and John H. Woods. They found and arrested Gilmore, Sullivan, and Brandon. They also took into custody Manuel Romero and his father on charges of violating revenue laws. In a surprising move later that day Courtright and McIntire also arrested a number of the cowboys from the Casey and Moore ranch, including Andrews, Jewett, Blair, and Woods, who had just served with them as possemen, on charges of complicity in the crimes.[15]

The John P. Casey party and its military escort soon left on the return trip to Albuquerque and Santa Fe. Before leaving, Marshal Morrison put Courtright in charge of the prisoners and instructed him to take them by wagon to San Juan, a point on the railroad some seventy-five miles east of Fort Wingate. There he was to wait until Casey and Morrison reached Albuquerque and made special arrangements for railroad transportation for Courtright and his charges.[16]

Word of the murders had preceded Logan's arrival at Albuquerque and reporters rushed to interview him at the depot. "I enjoyed the trip hugely," he said, "but I'm looking so much like a rustler I'll not stop over to see Albuquerque."[17] He did not stop over to see Santa Fe either, for his sharp political senses told him the affair in American Valley was about to explode into a major scandal, and he wanted no part of it. He hurried back to Washington as fast as railroads could carry him. His senses were right and the scandal did explode, but he managed to stay clear of it.[18]

On May 17 the special train arrived in Albuquerque with a bevy of prisoners brought from Fort Wingate and San Juan by Marshal Morrison and his deputies, Courtright and McIntire. Lt. W. C. Moore and members of the territorial militia assisted in the transport. They turned the prisoners over to Bernalillo County Sheriff Perfecto Armijo for incarceration while the grand jury, then in session, heard the evidence against them.

Within two weeks many of the suspects, including the Casey and Moore cowboys, were released when the grand jury found there was insufficient evidence to warrant indictments.[19] Feelings ran high during this period. About eighteen of the American Valley ranch hands quit in a body to protest the actions of their employers. Frank Hoagland, one of those cowboys, publicly threatened the life of John P. Casey and had to be disarmed by the Albuquerque police. Pistols were taken from several others. When Clemence and Clotilde Grossetete arrived in town and started to check into the Rio Grande Hotel, they found that Casey was staying there and immediately turned around and stormed out. They had no doubt who was responsible for the murder of the young Gallo Springs ranchers. "I can't stay in the same house with that man," Clemence declared.[20]

After hearing the testimony of many of those present in American Valley in early May, the grand jury did bring indictments, however. They indicted John P. Casey on five counts, and his foreman, Dan McAllister, on eight, of cattle stealing and brand altering. Both were arrested and released on bail.

This blew the lid off the case, for McAllister was sure that Casey, with his powerful political connections, would never be convicted or even go to trial, while he would become the scapegoat and get a stiff sentence. He went to Neill B. Field, a prominent attorney from Socorro, and told him the entire story of the double murder. Field sent him to the district attorney, C. C. McComas, who offered McAllister immunity from murder prosecution if he testified against the other five participants. Although he confessed he was in fear of his life because of the blood oath Moore had forced him to take, McAllister agreed to relate his story to the grand jury. Following his testimony, murder indictments were quickly handed down and arrest warrants issued for W. C. Moore, James Casey, Mueller Scott, Jim McIntire, and Jim Courtright.

Scott and Casey were taken into custody that very day. In a bizarre turn of events, John W. Sullivan, recently deputized by Sheriff Armijo, arrested two of the men who had a few days earlier had him incarcerated, charged with cattle theft.

Somehow Moore got wind of the indictment—rumor had it that there had been a grand jury leak—and fled Albuquerque. He avoided the railroad depot that he knew would be watched by Sheriff Armijo's deputies and had Bob Harris, an American Valley cowboy, drive him in a buggy to Santa Fe. There he boarded the train and went to Las Vegas, where the editor of the *Las Vegas Optic* interviewed him before he purchased a saddle horse and continued his flight eastward. Along the way, he left a trail of worthless checks drawn on Socorro and Las Vegas banks. Soon telegraph lines hummed with demands for his apprehension. A renowned manhunter, Tony Neis of the Rocky Mountain Detective Agency, followed his trail for a time but came back empty-handed.[21]

Courtright and McIntire had returned to Lake Valley. On May 26, with warrants in hand for their arrest, Socorro County Sheriff Pete Simpson and Rocky Mountain Detective Agency operative William Abbott went by train to Nutt Station and took the stage for Lake Valley. On the way they met the stagecoach coming the other way. Courtright was aboard. They placed him under arrest and took him back to Lake Valley. Thinking that he might try to escape if he knew he was charged with murder, they told him he was wanted back in Albuquerque as a witness in the grand jury hearings. At Lake Valley the officers learned that McIntire had gone to Kingston. Turning Courtright over to a deputy sheriff, they took the stage for the nearby mining camp.

But a copy of *Albuquerque Daily Democrat* telling of the murder indictments handed down by the grand jury had been on the stage from Nutt Station, and Courtright read it. He got word to McIntire at

Kingston, and when Simpson and Abbott arrived there they found McIntire had already departed. They returned to Lake Valley on the next stage only to learn that Courtright had slipped away from his guard and also disappeared. Chagrined, the sheriff and detective had to go home and report that two more of the accused murderers had gotten away.[22]

Courtright and McIntire, fugitives now, headed for the Mexican border. It was a harrowing journey across the bad lands of southern New Mexico, as described by McIntire in his autobiography.

> We traveled all that night and until 3 o'clock the next afternoon without water for ourselves or horses. The weather was extremely hot and our suffering was intense when we reached a water-tank on the line between El Paso and Deming.... We traveled all day across the "Bad Lands" under the broiling sun. Our horses were again suffering for water, and there was no relief in sight, only a great sandy desert on all sides as far as the eye could see.

They finally came to a railroad section house and obtained some food and water from the Chinese railroad workers there. The food, McIntire remembered, amounted to

> some pickled pork, which seemed to contain more salt than pork, and a pan of bread which was merely flour and water baked as hard as a rock.... We made an attempt to eat the bread, but a file wouldn't touch it. We couldn't break it with our hands, so we laid it on our bootheels, taking our six-shooters and breaking it in pieces. We then took the pieces and soaked them in water until they were soft enough

to eat. The bread and pickled pork did not make a very delicious repast, but we were hungry enough to eat anything.[23]

They crossed into Old Mexico but had not gone far when they encountered a force of Mexican soldiers who chased them back toward the American side. About the first of June they re-entered the States at El Paso. There, according to McIntire's account, they were warmly greeted by "a lot of Texas Rangers, all old friends." Although the story of the escape of Courtright and McIntire, wanted for the murders in American Valley, was reported in the Texas press and a rumor circulated that the governor of New Mexico had offered a $1,000 reward for their capture,[24] the Rangers, McIntire said, "would not think of attempting to arrest us or 'give us away.' While we were with them, we were as safe as we could be anywhere."[25]

Courtright sent for his wife and children, who had remained in Los Angeles while he was in New Mexico, and they joined him at El Paso on June 8.[26] Together with McIntire, who had made arrangements with his wife to meet him at Fort Worth, the Courtrights then proceeded by train to the Panther City. According to the McIntire account, "to keep under cover," they paid $15 for the exclusive use of the smoking room at one end of the coach. They stopped over two days at Colorado City before going on to Fort Worth, where "excitement ran high, but the people were our friends, and we were not molested." Just to be sure, however, McIntire said he and Courtright concealed themselves

in a thicket just back of the graveyard until the excitement died down, as we were liable to be surprised and captured at any time. We remained in the thicket during the day, and slept in the graveyard at night, with a grave for a pillow. Mrs. McIntire, together with my friend's wife, would bring us provisions, and we were completely lost to the people of Fort Worth. Two nights, when we were making a lodging-house out of the cemetery, it rained, and we slept in a vault.[27]

Whether or not the two men hid out for a time as McIntire related, by June 20 Courtright was openly on the streets. A dispatch of that date from Fort Worth said that

An officer from New Mexico passed through the city today on his way to Austin to obtain requisition papers from Governor [John] Ireland for the arrest of J. Courtright and McIntire, who are accused of murdering two rustlers near Albuquerque. The officer says $1,000 reward is offered. It is certain that if any attempt is made to arrest Courtright here a bloody tragedy will ensue, Courtright being determined not to be arrested, and in this resolve is backed by a host of friends, who are desperate men. Courtright says he would be murdered as soon as he crossed the line. Serious trouble is expected daily. Courtright seems to have the sympathy of the community in his trouble, being well known here as city marshal for four years [sic].[28]

The Texas press took up Courtright's refrain. He and McIntire would be murdered before ever standing trial if they were taken back to New Mexico, so they would fight arrest and extradition to the death. "Two officers are in the city tonight with the avowed intention of arresting Courtright and McIntyre [sic]," said a June 25 dispatch from Fort Worth. "But it will be next to impossible, as the men have hundreds of friends who will secrete them and if necessary take the offensive in aiding the men to escape. An arrest means certain death at the hands of a Mexican mob."[29]

An El Paso paper echoed the theme: "Courtright and McIntyre [sic], who were implicated in the murder of Grossette [sic] in the American Valley, N. M., and who escaped from the officers at Lake Valley, passing through this city in their flight, are now at Fort Worth. They have been secreted by their friends, who have intimated that any officer who tries to arrest them will be killed."[30]

Beyond threats, Courtright managed through his friends to mount a serious legal effort to prevent his extradition to New Mexico. At his urging, Tarrant County attorney W. S. Pendleton drafted a petition requesting Texas Governor John Ireland to deny any extradition requests from New Mexico for Courtright. The stated reasons for the requested denial were that at the time of the killing of "two Mexicans," Courtright "was a peace officer, aiding the sheriff in arresting the ruffians"; that a fair trial could not be had, "owing to the disturbed state" in New Mexico, and in recognition of "Courtright's great services to law and order during the 'hurrah' days of Fort Worth."[31] Many of the foremost citizens of Fort Worth signed this petition, including Sheriff W. T. Maddox, city attorney J. W. Swayne, Judge R. E. Beckham. Colonel A. J. Chambers, and Henry M. Furman. The newspaper reporting this added that "three rangers were in the city last night to arrest Courtright, but vigilant friends, who watch all trains, notified him of their arrival, when he was quickly [taken to] a place of safety. The entire community would warmly applaud Governor Ireland should he deny the Mexican judge's request."[32]

It is plain that Courtright was appealing to the longstanding prejudice of many Texans against "Mexicans" that extended back to the Alamo and the Texas War for Independence. The victims in the American Valley affair had become "Mexican rustlers" in his account, a "Mexican judge" was demanding the return of Courtright and McIntire, who, if returned would meet "certain death at the hands of a Mexican mob." He told everyone he was wanted back in the territory because he had killed two Mexican criminals at Lake Valley (a fiction that later became part of his legend). Texas newspaper editors printed this fiction. They should have known better, because the American Valley murders and Courtright's involvement in them had been big news across the country.

Jim McIntire, in his autobiography written two decades later, was still using the same tactic. He would have the reader believe that he had been persecuted and driven out of New Mexico by the villainous members of the "Greaser Militia." Although the murders in American Valley were probably the most important events in McIntire's life, they are not mentioned in his book, and. other than Courtright, the names of the other participants in those murders—Moore, McAllister, Scott, and James Casey—never appear.

On June 29, Texas Attorney General John D. Templeton arrived in Fort Worth from Austin and "was closeted" with Courtright and McIntire, who explained their version of the controversial affair. Templeton, a long-time resident of Fort Worth who knew Courtright well, said on returning to Austin that he would lay the whole matter before the governor and let him decide.[33] His recommendation must have been to deny the New Mexican requisition, for Governor Ireland did not grant it and for a time New Mexico officers did not appear in Fort Worth. When a deputy sheriff from the territory did show up in July he denied that a requisition had ever been issued for Courtright and McIntire and insisted that W. C. Moore was the only one wanted for the American Valley murders.[34]

With the situation cooled, McIntire went on to Wichita Falls, where he bought an interest in a gambling house, while the

Courtrights, who had been living with Jim's old friend, Ab Woody, went out to find a house of their own. It is worth noting that both Courtright and McIntire seemed well supplied with cash at this time. No doubt John P. Casey had taken care of them financially for their services in his behalf.

In July Courtright, having secured new appointments as deputy U. S. marshal and Tarrant County deputy sheriff, was back in the law enforcement business. On July 7 he assisted Deputy Sheriff W. P. Thomas in the arrest of Harrison Weaver, "a desperado who was wanted for the theft of several fine Angora goats," in the southern part of the county. The officers hid in a corncrib until Weaver approached and they "got the drop on him." The goat thief "tried to draw and resisted strenuously, but was compelled to yield [and] is now in the county jail."[35]

Although the records do not show that Courtright held a permanent position as city policeman during this period, the current city marshal, William M Rea, evidently made him a special officer, as he was involved in a number of local police actions, acting well beyond his authority as a county or federal officer.

On the night of July 11 he was in the Horse Head Saloon in Hell's Half Acre when a melee broke out centering around William Randolph, a black man. Bartender Joe Griffin threw an ice pick at him and "Bonny Campbell, a desperado, slipped up and deliberately shot Randolph through the right breast," inflicting a fatal wound. Although this was a municipal and not a federal matter, the papers reported that "Deputy United States Marshal Courtright at once arrested Campbell and lodged him in jail."[36]

In October Courtright unlimbered his pistol and made the only shot in his whole career that might have entitled him to the accolades as a pistol wizard later bestowed upon him. After imbibing freely from his own stock of beverages, saloon owner W. R. Sanner pulled his six-shooter and turned it loose. Two city policemen ran to the scene, closely followed by Courtright. Sanner fired three more shots in the direction of the officers, one of them barely missing Courtright. Jerking his own six-gun, Courtright fired one round, hitting Sanner in the wrist of his pistol hand, sending his gun flying. Said the newspaper account: "The remarkable shot of Courtright is the talk of the city."[37] Whether this was an example of Courtright's marvelous marksmanship or just a lucky shot will never be known. The man's legend makers never mentioned the incident, thereby missing a fine opportunity to prove their hero's pistol prowess.

In another saloon dustup a month later Courtright arrested one of the wealthiest and best known men in Fort Worth. James D. Reed lost his right arm fighting for the Confederacy in the Civil War, but the handicap did not prevent him from leading cattle drives to the Kansas railheads or building successful ranches in Goliad and Stonewall counties. He made his home in Fort Worth in 1877 and was one of the most respected cattlemen in town. Like many of his kind, however, he was prone to fighting and use of a pistol. A case against him for shooting a man in the leg at Little Rock, Arkansas, the previous March was still pending when he tangled with a professional gambler named Jace Wilson over a poker game in Hell's Half Acre. It was a very big game indeed; Reed was said to have dropped $9,000 to Wilson. After losing a large pot, Reed, in a fit of rage, reached over the table with his only hand, grabbed the gambler by the mustache and "pulled it until tears ran from Wilson's eyes."[38] This broke up the game and caused a commotion in the house as players and onlookers sought exits. When the police came running, Reed dropped Wilson's mustache, drew his six-shooter, and pointed it menacingly in their direction.

Out of fear of Reed's pistol or reluctance to place one of the wealthiest and most influential men in the city under arrest, the officers backed off. "Jim Courtright was sent for and arrested [Reed] and took him to the calaboose and disarmed him," said the newspaper account. "Reed threatens to shoot Courtright, and Wilson, who is a game man, threatens Reed. A serious difficulty is apprehended at any moment."[39] The affair blew over, however, with no damage except to Reed's wallet and Wilson's mustache.

An inveterate manhunter, Jim Courtright's ambition had always been to run a detective agency in Fort Worth, and he had not been discouraged by the failure of his short-lived Texas Detective Bureau in 1878. He tried again in 1884, establishing an investigative company he called the T. I. C. Commercial Detective Agency. The letters T. I. C. were his initials, of course, but, to capitalize on the famous all-seeing eye in the Pinkerton National Detective Agency logo, he substituted a human eye for the letter "I" on a sign he had painted on the side of his headquarters office at the corner of Houston and Second streets.

A dispatch from Fort Worth printed in the *San Antonio Daily Express* of July 10, 1884, announced the opening: "The famous Jim Cartwright [sic] has established a detective agency here, and is receiving much encouragement." To assist him in the enterprise, he enrolled his pals Ab Woody, Jim Maddox and John Price.

Business was slow in the first months of the year. In January he worked with Dallas private detective and bounty hunter Jack Duncan, who had achieved some fame a few years earlier when he tracked down and assisted in the capture of the most notorious Texas desperado, John Wesley Hardin. Duncan came to Fort Worth seeking a man named Frank Mooney, who had been peddling bogus goldbricks in Dallas, and Courtright aided him in the capture. An experienced manhunter and detective, Duncan was also clever and loath to share any reward money with others. When he wired Austin to see if Mooney was wanted there, an answer came back that the man should be held for Travis County officers. On the corner of the telegram was written "$500 reward." Before turning the telegram over to Courtright so that he could use it to continue holding Mooney, Duncan tore off the corner with the notation, hoping to that he could collect the money without the other detective's knowledge. It was a trick Courtright himself might have used, had he the opportunity. In the end, however, the Travis County officers denied that any reward money had been offered for Mooney and neither detective benefited financially from the affair.[40]

Dallas was plagued in July by a series of burglaries and attacks on white women by a pair of black felons. The Dallas police were hot on their trail, and at one point city officer Ed Cornwell got close enough to take a shot. He thought he had winged one of the culprits, but they got away and were believed to have fled to Fort Worth. Announcement of a $1,000 reward for their capture got the attention of Courtright. Utilizing the services of a black informant, he focused on two new black arrivals in the city, one of whom had a recent gunshot wound in the leg. Courtright's operatives kept the suspects under surveillance while he notified Dallas. Officer Cornwell and Dallas County Deputy Sheriff B. H. Winston came to Fort Worth and interrogated the suspects in the offices of the Commercial Detective Agency. Convinced they had the right men, they took them with them back to Dallas and locked them up. There the citizenry was in an uproar over the crimes, and there was much talk of lynching on the streets. But, after more questioning, Dallas officials concluded the two men were innocent and released them. Many were disappointed by this turn of events, none more so than Jim Courtright, who once again missed out on a sizeable reward.[41]

But in the following months Courtright would have more to concern him than unfulfilled reward opportunities. The New Mexican

authorities had not forgotten the American Valley murders. The repercussions of that affair would reach a climax in 1884 and rock Fort
Worth to its foundations.

Chapter Eight

THE GREAT ESCAPE

*"Jim Courtwright [sic], the luckiest man in the west,
has again played hazard with fate and won."*

San Antonio Daily Express,
October 21, 1884.

For a year after escaping the law in New Mexico Jim Courtright closely followed newspaper accounts of unfolding events relative to the American Valley affair in the territory and kept a wary eye over his shoulder. On October 8, 1883 James Casey and Mueller Scott went on trial in Albuquerque, charged with the murder of Robert Elsinger. Of the six men involved in the murders of Elsinger and Alexis Grossetete, Casey and Scott were the only ones available for trial. McAllister had been granted immunity for his testimony; W. C. Moore, Jim McIntire and Jim Courtright were still fugitives from justice.

District Judge Joseph Bell heard the case. District Attorney C. C. McComas led the prosecution, assisted by Neill B. Field, and, as an indicator of the importance of the case, New Mexico Attorney General William Breeden. Three able lawyers, S. M. Barnes, John H. Knaebel, and Frank Chavez, made up the defense team.

"Of all the murders that have occurred in the Territory of New Mexico during the last five years," commented the *Albuquerque Morning Journal* of October 9, "it is safe to say that none has attracted the widespread attention, nor filled our home people with a deeper feeling of horror, than the brutal murders of Grossetete and Elsinger."

A parade of witnesses testified for the prosecution, including D. L. Gilmore and the Grossetete neighbors who found the bodies, a number of Moore and Casey cowboys, Clotilde[1] and Clemence Grossetete, and, of course, the star prosecution witness, Dan McAllister. Chief witnesses for the defense were John P. Casey, Henry M. Atkinson, and the defendants, James Casey and Mueller Scott

The case went to the jury on October 13. On the 15th the foreman reported that the jury was hopelessly deadlocked. Judge Bell dismissed the members and sent the defendants back to jail to await a new trial. According to newspaper accounts, the jury vote was eleven to one for conviction.[2]

A second trial, in which the defendants were charged with the murder of Grossetete, began two days later in the same court. Counsel remained the same except that William B. Childers joined the prosecution. Testimony little different from the first trial brought the same result: a deadlocked jury. Casey and Scott were never tried again for the murders.[3]

Unable to convict the two men they had in custody, the New Mexico officials now turned their attention to the three fugitives who, it was believed, were equally guilty of the murders, and had demonstrated that guilt by fleeing the territory. In a bitter editorial published a few days after the Casey and Scott trials an Albuquerque newspaper called on Governor Sheldon to offer rewards for the apprehension of the fugitives:

> Why is it that if a man kills a sheep, or commits some other petty offense, and runs away, a reward is promptly offered by the governor for his apprehension, and yet that man Moore, who is believed to have been the ringleader of the worst gang of land pirates and murderers that ever infested the Territory, was permitted to take himself away at

his leisure, and no effort is made to find him or bring him back? ...Public opinion holds this man as the responsible author of the murders and assassinations which have made the name of the American Valley infamous.[4]

The governor got the message. The very next day he issued a proclamation offering a five hundred-dollar reward for the capture of Moore, Courtright, and McIntire.

Moore simply disappeared after painting his trail across New Mexico and Kansas with bouncing checks. Despite the reward on his head, lawmen and bounty hunters never captured him. In 1890 Socorro County Sheriff C. A. Robinson thought he had Moore located in the state of Washington and wrote the New Mexico governor, requesting expense funds to go after him, but nothing came of it. Five years later famous Pinkerton detective Charles A. Siringo, while working another case, spotted Moore in Juneau, Alaska, but made no effort to arrest him. There were later reports that Moore was killed in Alaska, but these were never confirmed and what happened to "Outlaw Bill" after he fled in the wake of the American Valley murders remains a mystery.[5]

New Mexico authorities may not have known where McIntire was located in the fall of 1883, but they could not have been unaware of Courtright's well-publicized presence in Fort Worth. Two months passed following Governor Sheldon's reward proclamation, however, before lawmen from New Mexico showed up in Fort Worth looking for the fugitive. A telegraphic dispatch going out from Fort Worth to papers around the state on December 22 explains their hesitancy in approaching Courtright's domain:

There is great excitement in the city to-night over the fact that five officers from New Mexico are here with the

avowed purpose of arresting and taking back with them
Deputy United States Marshal Jim Courtright, who is
accused of murdering two Mexican rustlers some months
ago. A number of Courtright's friends are heavily armed and
will back their man to the death before he will be taken.
Courtright's lawyers advise him not to submit to arrest. For
it means murder at the hands of a Mexican mob. The sentiment of this community is entirely with Courtright, and at
least five hundred men would be willing to fight in his
defense. The only fear is that he will be kidnapped, and the
vigilance of his friends is exerted to the fullest extent to prevent this. Courtright has proven himself fearless and useful
to this city, and his friends are therefore of the better class.[6]

Perhaps intimidated by the threat of having to face five hundred
friends of Courtright "willing to fight in his defense," the New Mexico
officers left town without making the arrest.

The next month a Fort Worth reporter interviewed an attorney said
to be interested in the prosecution of the American Valley murder case.
He said that newspaper reports were untrue that Texas Governor
Ireland had refused to honor a requisition for Courtright, or that New
Mexico Governor Sheldon had failed to issue a requisition because he
did not really want the fugitive returned. New Mexico authorities knew
where Courtright was, said the lawyer, and a requisition for him would
be issued at the proper time.[7]

In February 1884 correspondents reported from Fort Worth that
Captain S. A. McMurray and four Texas rangers were in the city to
arrest Courtright, "who is wanted so badly by the authorities of New
Mexico on a charge of killing two Mexican rustlers." McMurray was
said to have a warrant and a requisition for the fugitive, but Courtright's

friends told the rangers he had been notified of their coming and was "now hundreds of miles from this city, where the Texas process can not reach him. ...If he is not gone, serious trouble is feared, as Courtright and his friends consider it certain death for him to be taken to Albuquerque, and Courtright says he had rather die right here."[8]

Two months later the rangers were back again. "It would seem that the pursuit of Jim Courtright by the New Mexico authorities would never cease," said the *Dallas Weekly Herald* in April.

> A day or two ago four rangers met A. W. [sic] Woody and told him they were going to Fort Worth to get a bad man when Woody suggested they go to Courtright to get his assistance. "That's the very man we're after," was the reply. Now, any one who knows Abe Woody and Jim Courtright knows they are firm friends; men who have often faced danger together, and men who will die fighting for each other if necessary; so it will not be surprising to know that Woody informed Courtright of the fact that the rangers were after him.

When Courtright and Al Neely rode out of town on "a fishing picnic" three rangers followed them. Courtright, said the paper, pulled up his horse, "deliberately loaded his Winchester, held it across his knee, faced the horsemen, and waited." The rangers turned around and rode back. "Courtright has always made but one statement in regard to the matter: 'If I go back I will be murdered by the Greasers, and I prefer to die where my friends are. I will not be arrested alive, that's all.' It is said the great inducement for Courtright's arrest is a reward of $2,000...."[9]

There was not that much money on Courtright's head, but the reports were enough to get the attention of publicity seekers and bounty hunters. In September three men showed up in Fort Worth and boasted around the saloons that they had come from New Mexico to kill "Jim Courtright, the famous detective." Word quickly reached Courtright, of course, and he and his detectives went looking for the strangers. They were not to be found, but before leaving town they had been seen in whispered conversation with two black men. A night or two later these two showed up at Courtright's house. When Betty opened the door and saw two men with pistols drawn, she slammed the door shut and bolted it. She sent Willie Carlisle, a neighbor boy who happened to be in the house at the time, out the back door with instructions to run to town and notify her husband. Courtright hurried home to find

Courtright and his young
friend, Willie Carlisle.
Author's personal collection.

the two men still in his front yard. On seeing him approach, one ran. The other was lying down, still holding a pistol. Covering him with his own weapon, Courtright "wrenched the pistol away and beat him over the head with it, inflicting eight or ten wounds."[10]

"It is almost certain that the negroes were hired by the New Mexicans to kill Courtwright [sic]," reported a paper. Andy James, the man Courtright had pistol-whipped, was thought to be "in a dying condition." Officers throughout north Texas were on the lookout for his companion, who had high-tailed it for Indian Territory.[11]

Meanwhile the New Mexico authorities were making another attempt to take the fugitives. On September 27th C. C. McComas, district attorney at Albuquerque, requested Governor Sheldon to issue requisitions for Moore, Courtright and McIntire "at the "earliest possible convenience [as] the thing is now ripe here for execution." City Marshal Harry Richmond of Albuquerque would be sent for the fugitives, and the requisition was to be "so drawn as to enable Richmond to act in person or to designate any party or parties to act for him." Courtright and McIntire were known to be in Texas and Richmond had "reliable information" that Moore was also in that state.[12]

Governor Sheldon issued the requisition and Harry Richmond went to Austin and succeeded in getting Governor Ireland to issue a state warrant for the arrests and authorization to use Texas rangers to assist in those arrests. None of the officials could foresee that their actions would precipitate one of the wildest scenes in Fort Worth history.

On Thursday, October 16, Marshal Richmond arrived at the camp of Company C, Frontier Battalion, Texas Rangers, near Wichita Falls, a hundred miles northwest of Fort Worth, and conferred with Captain George H. Schmitt, commanding. Together they hatched a plan to take the two fugitives into custody and get them out of Texas. To prevent word of the arrest of one suspect alerting the other and permitting his escape, they decided to arrest Courtright in Fort Worth and McIntire, who was in Wichita Falls, in simultaneous raids. Richmond would go to Fort Worth with two rangers and on Saturday, October 18, take Courtright into custody and hold him at the railroad station. As soon as the arrest was made they would wire Schmitt at Wichita Falls. He would then nab McIntire and take him by train to Fort Worth. The two parties would meet at the Fort Worth depot and that evening Richmond, with his prisoners and an escort of ranger guards, would board another train, bound for El Paso. There other New Mexico officers would meet him and help him convey the prisoners on to Albuquerque. It was a fine plan, designed to whisk both fugitives away in a day, but it would go terribly awry.

Lieutenant Grimes and Corporal Hayes of the rangers accompanied Richmond to Fort Worth. Aware that Courtright had often been quoted in the press as vowing he would not be taken back to New Mexico alive, they considered him very dangerous. The arrest itself would have to be done with caution. In order to avoid having to move their handcuffed prisoner through town and alerting his many supporters, they decided to resort to subterfuge. They would lure Courtright to the railroad station, make the arrest, and hold him there until Captain Schmitt arrived with McIntire. Then the two prisoners could be quietly placed on a westbound train.

On Saturday morning the officers arrived in Fort Worth, took a room at the Ginocchio Hotel, adjacent to the Union Depot, and went in search of their quarry. They found him in the offices of his detective agency. His assistance was needed, they said, in identifying a man they were after. They asked him to go with them to the depot where the suspect was expected to make an appearance. Courtright agreed, but insisted that Jim Maddox, a deputy sheriff and one of his detectives, go along. Maddox was not at the offices at the moment and Courtright, accompanied by the officers, set out to find him. This development did not fit well into the plans of the officers, for they wanted to get Courtright alone to make the arrest. The waste of time was also important, as Captain Schmitt had to be notified soon so that he could arrest McIntire and catch the one o'clock train from Wichita Falls and be in Fort Worth that evening. But they reluctantly went with Courtright to find Maddox, whom they finally located in the Occidental Hotel. All went together down to the depot.

The train carrying their suspect was not yet due, said the officers, so they asked Maddox to remain at the depot while they took Courtright to their second-floor room in the hotel to show him some photographs of other wanted men. Maddox said he was leaving anyway, as he was not feeling well.

In the hotel room Courtright studied the photographs. When he looked up, the muzzles of three six-shooters were pointing at him. Announcing that he was under arrest, the officers relieved him of his weapons, slapped manacles on him, and chained him to a chair. Leaving the others to guard their prisoner, Grimes went to the Western Union office to notify Captain Schmitt of the capture, so that the next phase of the plan, the arrest of McIntire, could be put in motion.[13]

McIntire, who was running a gambling operation in the White Elephant Saloon in Wichita Falls, was taken easily. "I was in a little side-room of the saloon carving a turkey for the free lunch," he remembered, when "the Rangers rushed in from three doors and covered me with their guns. They allowed me time to straighten up my business, then took me to their camp just below the town.... The next day they took me to Fort Worth."[14]

Schmitt had to wait until the next day, because the delay in effecting the arrest of Courtright caused him to miss the one o'clock train to

Fort Worth. He wired Grimes that it was necessary to change the plans. The rangers in Fort Worth would have to hold Courtright overnight and await Schmitt's arrival with McIntire on Sunday.[15]

Meanwhile, back in Panther City, Courtright's wife and friends missed him. Learning from Maddox that he had last been seen with the rangers at the depot hotel, they soon discovered that he was being held there under arrest. "The news spread all over town like a flash," recalled an old Fort Worth resident. "In ten minutes you couldn't push a needle between the crowd that gathered about the place. Every kid three feet high had a gun on and said they would like to see them take Jim Courtright away from here."[16]

Newspapers later reported that five or six hundred excited men gathered outside the hotel.[17] Lieutenant Grimes estimated the crowd numbered "at least one thousand or fifteen hundred." They filled the lobby of the hotel and surged forward. Only the rangers on the stairway with drawn guns prevented their advance. One man stood on the depot platform and made a speech, urging the crowd to take Courtright from the officers to prevent his "being taken to New Mexico to be murdered." The mob cheered wildly. The building "fairly shook with their yells." When a ranger stood at the window and tried to calm the crowd, they hooted him down and demanded to see Courtright. Taken to the window, the prisoner waved to the crowd with manacled hands. What one paper called a roar of "exquisite abandonment" went up. A shout of "Let's turn him loose and give him a gun" brought another roar of approval.[18]

In his report of the affair to the Texas governor, Adjutant-General W. H. King would later say that during this critical period "an open, lawless and dangerous attempt at [Courtright's] rescue was made by a large crowd while he was held prisoner at the union depot." He believed only the "coolness" of the rangers, the intervention of a district judge, and the assistance of the local officers prevented the mob from forcibly releasing the prisoner.[19]

The entire police force under City Marshal W. M. Rea and all the deputies of Sheriff Walter T. Maddox had been called out to maintain order. "From 15 to 20 officers came to the room where [Courtright was confined], shook hands with him, and expressed their sympathy for him," the rangers later reported. The sheriff's brother, Jim Maddox, was particularly outraged by the turn of events. He "was the first man in the room. He seemed to be very angry and told Courtright not to think he had anything to do with his arrest and that if he had known the 'racket' that Lt. Grimes was going to arrest him, that he would have prevented it."[20]

At the urgent request of William Capps, Courtright's lawyer and personal friend, Judge Hood issued a writ of habeas corpus. Sheriff Maddox attempted to serve it on Lt. Grimes, who refused to accept it, saying he had no authority in the matter, having turned Courtright over to Richmond, and he and Hayes were only assisting the New Mexico officer in guarding his prisoner. Richmond also rejected Judge Hood's writ with the argument that a state requisition took precedence over the writ of a local court. Stepping to the window, Sheriff Maddox notified the crowd of this response. This further incited the mob. Threats were made that if the officers did not immediately turn Courtright over to the local officers, the hotel would be set afire. Alarmed by this reaction, Richmond and the rangers agreed to hold Courtright over until Monday when a ruling on the habeas corpus writ could be made in Judge Hood's court. Meanwhile they had to get their prisoner out of there. They made arrangements with Sheriff Maddox and Lawyer Capps.[21]

The attorney descended to the railroad depot platform where he addressed the crowd, urging its members to disburse and let the law take its course. While Capps temporarily diverted the mob's attention, the rangers and sheriff's deputies hurried Courtright down a back stairway of the hotel, placed him in a hack, and, with the horses at full gallop, took him to the county jail.

The crowd followed and there were some tense moments at the jail as Sheriff Maddox recalled:

> I was never in so much danger in my life as at the jail. City Marshal Rea... was on the outside of the room door, and I was on the inside, where the Rangers, with loaded revolvers, were standing over their prisoner. They were all determined men. I could feel the swaying of the door as the crowd on the outside pressed against it. A cordon of policemen had been placed around the entrance of the jail, but the people walked right through them and came up to the door. I knew that the moment the door burst open the Rangers would open fire on the attacking party and the crowd would retaliate. I, being between the two, would have been a target for their bullets. I opened the door and succeeded by firmness and sensible talk, in getting the crowd to move back and wait for the development of the remedy of habeas corpus. Marshal Rea was with me and his personal influence had much to do in calming matters.[22]

Courtright was not an ordinary prisoner and he was given special treatment. He was not locked in a cell like a common criminal, but kept in the sheriff's quarters at the jail, where he was permitted to receive visitors. He slept overnight there under the watchful eyes of his guards. On Sunday, at his request, they took him for breakfast and lunch to the Merchant's Restaurant at 41 Main Street, a café that claimed in an advertisement to offer "the world's best chicken sand-wich" for ten cents. Crowds lining the street cheered his passage.

During the day a reporter for the *Fort Worth Daily Gazette* inter-viewed Courtright and his captors. He thought Harry Richmond "nerv-ous," Corporal Hayes unable to take his eyes from the prisoner, and Courtright "the coolest and most collected man in the room." Asked if it was true that the New Mexican authorities wanted to prosecute Courtright for killing "three or four" Mexican ore thieves, Richmond said the report was false, that Courtright was wanted as a material wit-ness in the trial of Casey and Scott, charged with the murder of two Anglo ranchmen. Courtright snorted that Richmond's response was "nonsense," although he was careful not to answer the reporter's ques-tion directly. "Heavy rewards are not offered for witnesses," he said, "and I am wanted on a charge of murder. Knowing the bitter feelings between Americans and Mexicans, I am convinced that I could not have a fair trial. The assertion that I am wanted as a witness is only made to allay the public feeling in this city."[23]

Assisting in the guarding of Courtright were many of his friends, including Jim Maddox and Ab Woody, two of his detectives. They were in and out of the sheriff's office all day. At some point one of them passed the word to Courtright that a bold plan for his escape was underway.

Richmond and the rangers took their prisoner to the Merchant's Restaurant at six o'clock that evening for supper. The place was packed with almost a hundred Courtright friends and supporters, but a hush fell as the officers and their prisoner took seats at a reserved table. Courtright sat at one end, Richmond at the other, and the Rangers on either side.

Lt. Grimes was anxious to get the meal over with, as Captain Schmitt was due in with McIntire at seven and he wanted to meet his superior at the depot and discuss the change in plans. In addition, he was troubled by the size of the crowd in the restaurant and an air of expectancy that seemed to radiate from it. Restlessly, he got up and walked to the front door to see how many others were massed in the street.

As if on a signal, Courtright dropped his napkin to the floor and bent over to pick it up. Hidden under the table, directly in front of his place, were two loaded pistols, hanging from nails. When he straightened up, the pistols were in his hands, pointed at his startled guards. Even with the muzzles of two six-shooters in the hands of a "desperate man" aimed directly at him, Corporal Hayes attempted to draw his own weapon, but someone behind him knocked it from his hand.

At the same moment men grabbed at Grimes, trying to pin his arms to his side. He managed to pull two revolvers, but, finding himself surrounded, with pistols menacing on every side, he dropped his weapons back into their holsters and raised his hands.

Courtright, meanwhile, was backing to the rear doorway through an aisle opened for him by his friends. At the door he whirled, and, mounting a saddled horse left in the alley for him, galloped off. His supporters quickly closed in, blocking any attempt by the guards to follow.

The cry "Courtright has escaped!" arose on all sides. People came running from every direction to join the throng already there. The crowds impeded Courtright's progress, and, yelling for them to get out of his way, he fired several shots into the air. Near the corner of Second and Commerce, his horse stumbled, throwing him, and injuring his leg. Fortunately for Courtright, the tumble took place just across from the Panther City fire station, where he had many friends. The firemen ran out, caught his horse, and helped him remount. He continued on, riding hard.

And that was the last Fort Worth saw of Jim Courtright for a year.[24]

Jim McIntire, heavily ironed and guarded by four rangers and ten deputy sheriffs, arrived on the Fort Worth & Denver City train from Wichita Falls at seven o'clock. They found Fort Worth in a state of great commotion. The streets were again filled with people, all excitedly talking about Courtright's spectacular escape. McIntire described the scene, making himself, as usual, the center of the drama:

> The Rangers were all raving mad, and came to the depot to await the arrival of the train upon which I was coming. They swore by all that was good and holy that I wouldn't get away. When my train pulled in to the depot, there was the biggest crowd there to meet me that had ever filled that depot. Every hack was filled with officials, and I was lionized by everyone except the Rangers.... On the way from the depot to the jail, the Rangers covered me with drawn revolvers all the way. An immense crowd followed us, and in a few minutes the whole town had gathered at the jail.[25]

Courtright's legend-fostering biographer, Father Stanley Crocchiola, would have us believe that the man's immense popularity in Fort Worth was the reason for the extraordinary demonstrations to prevent his being returned to New Mexico. "What charm did Courtright possess to cause a whole city to place its very existence at his feet?" he asked.

> Why would over two thousand people give their blood for a man who would benefit them in no way? A detective at that. A man who made his living hunting down other

men. What answer can you give? A New Mexico paper called him a killer, responsible for the lives of fourteen men. He was wanted for murder. Some questions have no answers. They remain forever mysteries. Fort Worth never loved a man before or since as it loved Jim Courtright.... One man held the affection of the city in the palm of his hand.... Every man and lad able to pull a trigger was ready to die for him.[26]

But no mystery surrounds the outpouring of sympathy and support for Courtright, because it also extended to McIntire, who had never lived in Fort Worth and was unknown there. The fiction planted by Courtright that he and McIntire were wanted in New Mexico for the killing of Mexican thieves and, if returned, would most certainly be assassinated by Mexicans found fertile soil in the town. "Remember the Alamo!" "Remember Goliad!" the crowd had shouted. "The yells were terrible," reported a paper. "The governor has forgotten Travis and Crockett, but we have not," and "Courtright shall not be murdered by the greasers, By God!"[27] The two wanted men owed the remarkably wide outpouring of support they received in Fort Worth to deep-seated racial emotions in the citizenry and not to any particular affection felt for them personally.

On Monday, October 20, Captain Schmitt and Harry Richmond entrained for Austin to explain their actions in the affair to the governor. That afternoon a habeas corpus hearing into McIntire's arrest was held in district court. Since two important witnesses were not present, Doc Lewis and other lawyers representing McIntire requested and were granted a continuance. The threat of mob intercession in the legal process still remained and the prisoner was held in the Tarrant County jail under heavy guard by Texas rangers and deputy sheriffs.

In their journey south Schmitt and Richmond may well have passed a northbound train carrying Adjutant-General W. H. King. At the direction of Governor Ireland, King was on his way to Fort Worth to confer with the district judge, the county attorney, the sheriff and the mayor about the Courtright-McIntire affair. According to press reports, after this discussion he was "utterly disgusted" by Harry Richmond's actions and came to the conclusion that the New Mexico officer had been bribed by Courtright's friends.[28] In his report to the governor, however, King was much more circumspect. While attributing the escape to Richmond's poor judgment, he never alluded to a possible bribe. He exonerated his rangers, Grimes and Hayes, from any blame, saying they had turned the prisoner over to Richmond and were acting under his direction. As for the great uproar in Fort Worth precipitated by Courtright's arrest, he said:

> Courtright is reputed to be a man of fearless character, and of a friendly, free-and-easy style among his associates, and in his intercourse with quiet, orderly people, he was said to be unassuming and pleasant, and the union of these qualities gave him active friends among all classes, and strong sympathizers among some of the better. . . . The general belief about Fort Worth as to his offense, was, and is, that he had in a manly defense of valuable property committed to his care, been compelled to kill a Mexican greaser, or perhaps two, of the worst possible character. This impression. . . that his arrest was the result of an effort at kidnapping, and that his return to New Mexico would end in his death. Not by the law, but at the hands of a mob of Mexican greasers, was a prime factor in the attempt to rescue him and helped to imbue with lawless

zeal those of his friends who finally succeeded in procuring his escape.[29]

The extradition case and Courtright's sensational escape captured newspaper headlines around the state. Predictably, wild stories, feverish editorials and posturing by legal and political figures followed quickly.

McIntire's wife Kitty had come to Fort Worth from Wichita Falls and was staying in the Courtright home. She was quoted in one paper as saying that if her husband was returned to New Mexico she would accompany him, but would "kill him with her own hand" before "seeing him mobbed." The same paper reported that a "prominent Washington attorney" had offered to defend Courtright and McIntire without charge.[30]

Political opponents of Democratic Governor Ireland saw an opportunity to embarrass him. United States District Attorney J. C. Biggers, Republican candidate for Congress, announced that he would do all in his power to have the governor revoke the extradition requisition. "Hundreds of Democrats say they will vote for Republican or Independent candidates for governor," the *Dallas Weekly Herald* quoted him as saying. "A Texan who would deliberately surrender two Americans to be slaughtered by a mob is unworthy of their support."[31]

But the daily edition of the *Herald* took strong exception to this view. It deplored "the disgraceful demonstration by the citizens of [Fort Worth] in behalf of the notorious Courtright," and argued that the dignity of the law must be upheld.

It makes no difference whether this Courtright is innocent or guilty. If a proper demand is made for him by the governor of New Mexico, it is the duty of our governor to comply with it, or else New Mexico will become the asylum of all Texas offenders. Courtright is just as amenable to the law as anyone else, and should stand trial where he is said to have committed the bloody offenses charged against him. . . . He need not have one Mexican on the jury that tries him, and in all probability would not have one. Unless Governor Ireland has good and sufficient reason for knowing that Courtright would be mistreated, it is his duty to see him delivered to the New Mexican authorities.[32]

When McIntire's habeas corpus hearing was finally held on Friday, October 24, the courtroom was packed and looked, according to one dispatch, like "a military tribunal" with eight Texas rangers at stations around the room "with rifles in hand as if looking for a fight."[33] Judge Hood ruled against McIntire and his lawyers filed an appeal. One newspaper reported that Richmond offered a deal. In exchange for $1,000 in cash and a certified check for $10,000, he would not contest McIntire's immediate release.[34]

While the prisoner and his lawyers pondered this proposal, Captain Schmitt acted. On the night following the hearing he had McIntire quietly removed from the Tarrant County jail and taken under escort of a detachment of rangers to the lockup at Decatur, Wise County. If he thought that by getting his prisoner out of Fort Worth he had eliminated the possibility of his rescue attempt by supporters, he was mistaken. Within a week he received a communication from the jailer at Decatur that a mob was forming to make that attempt. The letter ended, "Send me assistance or come and get your man." Perhaps adhering to the legendary Texas Ranger tradition — one riot, one ranger — Captain Schmitt sent a single ranger private to help the jailer guard McIntire.[35]

In November Schmitt complained to Adjutant-General King about the calaboose at Decatur and the cost to him of maintaining a ranger there. "The jail," he said, "is now overcrowded and they came near breaking out the other day." He suggested moving McIntire to better facilities at Austin or San Antonio, but with a notation across the face of the letter King denied the request: "Gov. says let the prisoner remain at Decatur until further notice."[36]

Governor Ireland should have taken the advice of his ranger captain, for McIntire did not remain at Decatur long. On the night of December 11 he and five other prisoners escaped.[37] In his book McIntire described this breakout at length, adding his usual exaggerations and immodest accounts of his daring. There were, he said, thirteen other prisoners in the jail, guarded by five rangers, two deputies and the jailer. Through his cleverness he released every prisoner except one, a horse thief who had "peached" on him about an earlier escape attempt.[38]

Once again, all the gunmen who had participated in the callous American Valley murders were on the loose.

THE
FUGITIVE

*"Courtwright [sic] is recognized as being one of the most
desperate men in Texas, and is reverenced by certain people for
his daring deeds and quickness with the trigger."*

Silver City Enterprise,
October 24, 1884.

In November 1884 Tarrant County Attorney N. R. Bowlin called a special grand jury to consider bringing indictments against those who had
conspired in Jim Courtright's spectacular escape. Despite testimony by
Ranger Lieutenant Grimes and others, naming those who had held
guns on the officers as Courtright departed, the grand jury declined to
indict anyone. Many were suspected, including city and county law
officers in Fort Worth, and, of course, the detectives who worked for
Courtright. Harry Richmond was a prime suspect. After Adjutant
General King came to town to conduct his investigation in October he
was quoted as saying he was "utterly disgusted" with Richmond and
believed he had been bribed. "The charge is publicly made on the
streets that Richmond... sold out to Courtwright's [sic] friends, but the
rangers are thought honest," the *San Antonio Daily Express* reported.[1]

Captain Schmitt, however, was not so sure about one of the
rangers guarding Courtright at the time of the escape. In November
he fired Corporal Hayes, after learning that the ranger, for a $500 con-
sideration, had offered to allow another prisoner to escape. "I had also
suspicion on him that he was bribed in the escape of Courtright," he
wrote King.[2]

In the months following that escape rumors of Courtright's whereabouts abounded in Fort Worth. Ranger Captain Schmitt was certainly
confused by many of them. Ten days after the escape he received a tip
that Courtright had joined with fellow fugitive "Outlaw Bill" Moore in
Cooke County. He sent Lt. Grimes and another ranger to check out the
report, but it proved groundless.[3] A month later Schmitt reported to
King that Courtright was in Fort Worth and had "been seen at theatres
and other places a few days ago."[4]

Following McIntire's escape from the Decatur jail a newspaper
reported that the two fugitives from justice had hooked up again. On
the night of December 12, according to this account, they came into
Fort Worth, "took a drink at one of the principal saloons [and] each purchased a quart of whiskey." They were "armed to the teeth and riding
splendid animals. The supposition is that Courtright and McIntire have
a hiding place in Tarrant County."[5] On his return to Fort Worth more
than a year later, Courtright confirmed none of these stories.[6]

McIntire did claim that following his jail breakout he came back to
Fort Worth, not with Courtright, however, but with Henry Tickle, a
horse thief and fellow escapee from the Decatur jail. McIntire said
"one of the most popular and best lawyers" in Fort Worth helped him
hide out in the opera house. After ten days he grew bolder and ventured
out to visit friends in town.

> One night I slept in the next room to the captain of the
> Rangers. He was hunting me, and I overheard him talking
> to others about me in the next room. I only traveled at
> night, and was always disguised. One night, as I was step-
> ping off a streetcar, the Ranger captain and his lieutenant
> got on. They looked at me sharply, but did not penetrate my
> disguise, and I passed on. I stayed in Fort Worth about a

month longer, and saw and talked with the police every day
of that time, but, as I was only wanted in New Mexico, they
did not offer to arrest me."[7]

This whole story reeks of McIntire braggadocio. Fort Worth was the
most dangerous place Courtright and McIntire could be after their
escapes, and it is highly unlikely that either set foot in the town for
more than a year following their disappearance.

Rumors regarding Courtright's whereabouts, no matter how wild,
were eagerly picked up and repeated in the press. Shortly after his
escape a San Antonio paper said there was "reliable information" that
he was in Tucson, Arizona, and the very next day alleged that he was
concealed in the house of a friend in Waco. The city marshal of Waco
emphatically denied the latter report, saying the fugitive would find no
haven in his town.[8]

An old Fort Worth friend claimed to have seen him at the People's
Theater in St. Louis in June 1885. Courtright, he said, looked in good
health and "did not appear troubled about anything."[9]

He was said to have turned up in Caldwell, Kansas, where, under
an assumed name, he killed a man in a quarrel and was jailed but broke
out and fled to Arizona.[10]

He had gone to Dakota, where he "laid an officer low with a bullet
in his brain for suggesting Courtright give up his arms."[11] In another
version of this tale he merely shot the lawman in the leg. Arrested and
jailed, he stood trial but was acquitted.[12]

But the most persistent rumor was that he fled to Latin America.
Interviewed in Dallas in August 1885, Tom Wilson, an old New
Mexico friend of Courtright and McIntire, said that Courtright was
then in Chile, "perhaps in the Chilean army," he added rather vaguely.
"There are only three men who know of his whereabouts, but there

is not money enough in the country to induce them to give him away."[13]

Another detailed report published in a New Orleans newspaper had Courtright and McIntire together in Guatemala, where they joined the forces of President Justo Rufino Barrios, who was then leading a fight to unite all of Central America. There they organized "a large band of well known desperadoes from New Mexico and Texas" and planned to "either seize the country for themselves or to rob it extensively, divide the booty, return to the United States and scatter." Courtright was said to have passed through New Orleans in February 1885 "on his way to his old haunts to gather his men together and make arrangements for their departure to Guatemala, The war coming on, however, put the plans of the conspirators back, and Barrios' death compelled McIntyre [sic] to seek safety in flight to Hondorus [sic]."[14]

Another New Orleans paper ridiculed the account:

> There are a great many sensational stories afloat regarding the movements of McIntyre [sic] and Courtwright [sic] subsequent to their escape, but they are really nothing more than rumors. According to some of these yarns, Courtwright was at the same time breakfasting in New Orleans, playing billiards in Dallas, Tex., drinking in Montana and Nevada, organizing an army of 100 men in Mexico and fighting with Barrios in the Guatemalan army, and McIntyre was with him in all these places.[15]

Eugene Cunningham, in his initial fabrication of the Courtright legend, set it down as fact that Courtright and McIntire had indeed gone to Latin America, and most other writers have followed him uncritically ever since.[16] Interestingly, Father Stanley, after interviewing

Courtright's daughter and granddaughter, rejected these reports out of hand and probably correctly identified their source: "Courtright was never in South America any more than he was in Mexico, fighting the cause of some insurgents against the central government. True, word to that effect was spread around Fort Worth and Albuquerque [by his friends] to keep the authorities off the track as to the real whereabouts of Courtright."[17]

During the months of his expatriation from Fort Worth Courtright maintained contact with Abram Woody, the trusted friend and fellow officer who was a key figure in the escape. William A. Woody, Ab's son and later an eminent doctor in the city, has provided the best information on that escape and Courtright's subsequent movements.

Courtright had lived in the Woody home during one of his family's frequent visits to California, and teen-aged Will Woody came to know him well and idolized him. In interviews many years later he described how his father hid the pistols under the Merchant's Restaurant dining table and left the saddled horse in the alley for Courtright's escape.[18] Other officers no doubt had a hand in the plot. In his biography of noted lawman Henry A. "Heck" Thomas, who was on the Fort Worth police force at the time, western author Glenn Shirley hinted that Thomas was involved in the escape: "Nobody ever knew who fastened that six-shooter beneath the table, but Heck always smiled to himself when the affair came up for discussion in his presence."[19]

Abram Woody in 1884 was a man with many hats. In addition to carrying commissions as a Tarrant County deputy sheriff and a deputy United States marshal, he worked as a detective for Courtright and also served as a special agent for the Santa Fe Railroad Company. This last position gave him access to the rolling stock of the Santa Fe. On the evening of his escape, Courtright, after getting back in the saddle following his nearly disastrous tumble at the fire station, rode by prearrangement straight to the railroad yards. Even as Lt. Grimes was meeting the train from Wichita Falls carrying Jim McIntire and his ranger captors, Courtright was just down the tracks, being secreted by Woody in the baggage car of a train about to leave for Galveston.

Arriving at the port city the next morning, Courtright checked into the Washington Hotel under the alias "J. H. Armstrong." In disguise, he procured passage on the first departing steamship, the *Rio Grande*, bound for New York. He boarded the ship without incident but later told Woody that before the ship left port he had a few harrowing moments. Two law officers came aboard and began examining passengers. Hiding behind a bulkhead, Courtright eavesdropped on the lawmen's conversation and gathered they were not looking for him but for a black man. Just to be sure, he climbed into a bunk, covered his face with a blanket, and left his white hand sticking out. The officers walked right on by him.

The sailing was uneventful. On arriving in New York, he continued by train to Toronto, Canada. Later he re-entered the country and in a series of relocations, moved westward. He was in Chicago for a time and then Shell Rock, Iowa, where Betty, who was pregnant, and his two children joined him. He did not stay in one place very long but kept moving westward, supporting his family with whatever work he could pick up. He reportedly took a constable's job in Dakota Territory for a short period. Eventually he settled in Walla Walla, Washington, where he worked as a blacksmith.[20] There in May 1885 Betty presented him with another daughter. They called her Lulu May.[21]

Courtright might have remained in far-off Walla Walla indefinitely if Jim McIntire had not gotten himself arrested on April 20, 1885, in New Orleans.

By his own account, McIntire, after his escape from the Decatur jail and his brief sojourn back in Fort Worth, went to Denison, Texas, where he ran a gambling game in another saloon with the popular name, "White Elephant." By McIntire's lights, the officers at Denison were "all right," that is, not anxious to collect the reward outstanding for his capture. But soon "special officers, hungry for a piece of money," (i.e. bounty hunters), came sniffing around. Feeling the heat, McIntire hurriedly closed his game and caught a train for Shreveport, Louisiana, took a boat to Baton Rouge and another from there to New Orleans. There he bought passage on a ship bound for "the Honduras River."[22]

But before he sailed, the New Orleans police got a tip that a man registered at the City Hotel under the name C. T. Rogers was in fact Jim McIntire, the celebrated fugitive wanted on murder charges in

Lulu May Courtright Hart, one of Jim's daughters. *Author's personal collection.*

New Mexico. Captain Thomas Reynolds, assisted by Detectives T. J. Boasso, Tony Pecora and Dick Kerwin, cornered their man in the water closet of the hotel and took him into custody. With his usual hyperbole McIntire said it took five men to make the arrest, which, as he described it, must have been quite a scene:

> On finishing my dinner, I rose from the table and went to the toilet-rooms. While there, five big, stout men pounced on me unawares; they grabbed me in all sorts of positions and twisted my arms and neck around, until I thought they would break. When they were sure they had me, they picked me up bodily, and, without buttoning my clothes, carried me through the dining room out to the street, where a carriage was waiting. My appearance in the dining room with pants hanging down and person exposed created consternation among the lady guests at dinner, and they screamed and ran pell-mell for their rooms, knocking over tables and breaking dishes as they went.
>
> I never will forget the noise of the breaking dishes or the excitement which followed my forced trip through the dining room in my unpresentable condition. The officers who caught me didn't care for modesty or anything else, so long as they had captured Jim McIntire. They were a badly scared lot, and held on to me like grim death, even after we got into the hack. They didn't give me [a] chance to button up until I was safely locked up in the police station.[23]

A New Orleans newspaper described him as "tall, beardless, hair thrown back, [with a] clear piercing eye," wearing a wide-brimmed black slouch hat. He denied that he was Jim McIntire, the wanted fugitive.[24] But the arresting officers threw him in a cell and obtained a warrant to search his room. There they found "a handsome silver-mounted bone-handled six-shooter pistol"; twenty-five cartridges, three small fine-toothed saws "for cutting iron bars, with handles so made as to be taken apart and used as knives"; a bottle of chloroform; three packs of monte cards; "a gambler's device for marking cards on the back for swindling purposes"; and "a scrapbook containing memorandums of the money he had recently won in different parts of Kentucky, where it seems he has been lately."[25]

The arrest of the noted desperado triggered a new flood of press releases and many of the old stories and rumors about Courtright and McIntire were trotted out and reprinted. Out in New Mexico, Governor Sheldon fired off a telegram to New Orleans Chief of Police Zach Bachemin, asking him to hold the prisoner for receipt of a requisition that was on the way. The requisition did arrive as promised, but McIntire continued to cool his heels in the parish prison for more than a month while New Mexico and Louisiana officials haggled over the cost of returning him for trial.

Finally, on May 30 Chief Bachemin and Detectives Boasso and C. C. Cain started for New Mexico with the prisoner. The mob scenes in Fort Worth the previous October were still fresh in everyone's mind, and, to avoid a possible re-occurrence, they took McIntire to Albuquerque on a circuitous route by way of Memphis and Kansas City.[26]

Arriving back in New Mexico on June 3, 1885, McIntire was locked up in the Albuquerque jail. He could not raise bail, originally set at $10,000, but through the efforts of his lawyers, H. B. Ferguson and Thomas Phelan, the amount was reduced to $5,000.[27] Friends came up with the money, and he remained free on the streets awaiting trial.

Passions had cooled considerably in the more than two years that had passed since the infamous American Valley murders, and the trial

of Jim McIntire for complicity in those murders did not get the press
attention the trials of Casey and Scott had received in 1883. Witnesses
had scattered, and when the case came to trial on October 15 it
quickly became apparent the prosecution had no case and charges
against McIntire were dropped.[28]

Not everyone concerned in the case was pleased, least of all
Clotilde and Clemence Grossetete, but the editors of the *Albuquerque
Evening Journal* hailed what they called "McIntire's vindication":

> The whole history of this prosecution stamps it as mali-
> cious persecution. He was indicted on the evidence of a
> gang of scoundrels, all of whom are serving long terms in

Defendants in the
American Valley murder
trial were kept in the
Bernalillo County Jail at
Albuquerque, New
Mexico. *Courtesy
Albuquerque Museum
Photoarchives,
Albuquerque, New
Mexico.*

the penitentiary for various crimes or have died with their boots on. These men secured Mr. McIntyre's indictment, evidently to make him their victim, but his triumph over their machinations is now complete. He walks a free man, while his enemies are receiving their just rewards. Those who know McIntyre best, and have known him from boyhood, speak of him as a noble-hearted, brave, fearless man. . . . The Journal is glad to know that justice, tardy as it is, has been done at last.[29]

The paper was right in one respect: many of those who had testified against the accused defendants in the earlier trials had come to bad ends. Facing indictments on charges ranging from cattle and horse theft to embezzlement in Albuquerque, Dan McAllister fled to Utah. His beautiful blond wife Rhoda divorced him and ran off with Matthew Drya, another former American Valley ranch hand, who later dumped her in a Chicago brothel. Drya, also wanted on a number of charges, was captured in the Indian Territory and sent to prison. John W. Sullivan and Frank Hoagland, convicted of stealing stock, received five-year sentences in the territorial penitentiary at Santa Fe. D. L. Gilmore stole some horses in New Mexico and drove them to Colorado where he killed two men in a gunbattle and was summarily lynched. Hank Andrews, arrested in Socorro County for cattle and horse stealing, was taken from the arresting officers and hanged.[30]

Interviewed by a reporter for the *Albuquerque Evening Democrat* following his release, McIntire gave an amazing display of self-pity. "Thank God," he said,

I am once more Jim McIntyre [sic], and from this [time] on, the men who have insulted me and hurt my feelings,

because I was accused of crime, had better watch out. The
life I have had to endure in the past two years has almost
broken me down. I have tried to bear up and appear indif-
ferent, but when people pass you by continually, looking at
you as if you were a wild beast, and not a man of heart, and
soul, and feeling, it is enough to make you forget that you
possess such a thing as honor. The strain was terrible, and
no man can understand it unless he has been there. If I had
been guilty, it would have been different.[31]

The "man of heart, and soul, and feeling," whose sensitivities had
been so badly hurt, returned to Texas, resumed his gambling career, and
became a familiar figure in gambling resorts of the panhandle. In 1893
he joined the Cherokee Strip land run and opened a saloon in Woodward,
Oklahoma Territory. Selling out in 1898, he managed gambling operations in Guthrie and Mountain View. Struck down by smallpox in 1901,
he almost died. The near-death experience prompted him to publish his
autobiography, *Early Days in Texas: A Trip to Hell and Heaven*, the following year. He then dropped from sight, and the place and date of his death
are unknown.[32] Despite the false rumors that he and Courtright linked
up after their escapes, the two apparently never saw each other again
after splitting up on their return from New Mexico in 1883.

As soon as Ab Woody heard that the murder charge against
McIntire had been dropped, he wrote Jim Courtright, urging him to
return. If no case could be brought against McIntire, certainly the same
would apply to him and the cloud hanging over Courtright's head for a
year and a half could be lifted at last.[33]

The prospect of Courtright's return turned on the rumor mill again.
"Jim Courtright here," ran the headline on a story in the *San Antonio
Daily Express* of October 25, 1885:

Yesterday morning officers from Fort Worth in pursuit of the famous Jim Courtright, who made such a dashing and successful break for liberty, came to this city. Courtright was seen and recognized here by them, and they went to notify the officers here. When the deputy sheriffs arrived at the Volkfest grounds, where Courtright had boldly appeared, they were notified that he had taken a hack and driven to the international depot. When the officers had arrived there, the north-bound train had gone. The officers learned that Courtright had purchased a ticket for Waco and a description of him was telegraphed all along the line, and the fact of his going over the road announced. He made good his escape and is said to have been in the city several days and enjoyed the Volkfest until he learned that the officers were on the lookout for him. Wishing to save them the trouble of taking him, he gently sloped.[34]

Courtright, of course, was not in San Antonio, Waco, or anywhere else in Texas.He was still in Walla Walla and still wary. He waited three months before returning. Finally, after the receipt of $150 expense money advanced by Jake Johnson, an old Hell's Half Acre pal, he made the plunge, saying he "would rather be in a pine coffin in Fort Worth than be alive anywhere else in the world."[35] In January 1886, he went to Kansas City and telegraphed from there that he was ready to submit to arrest. By arrangement, he met two old friends, Deputy Sheriff Jim Thompson and theater man George B. Holland, at Colbert Station, Indian Territory.[36]

Holland later said that at the Colbert depot Courtright gave an exhibition of the strange sense of humor for which he was noted. He "nearly scared all the ladies in the car to death, because, as I was running up to meet the train, Jim jumped out on the platform, pulled down on me with both guns and shouted, 'throw up your hands!' The passengers thought there was going to be a fracas sure enough."[37]

The train to Fort Worth stopped in Denison, and news of the return of Panther City's most publicized resident was telegraphed ahead from that point. Word quickly spread throughout Fort Worth and "set all the city agog with excitement." An hour before the scheduled 8:10 P.M. arrival on January 20, "a stream of people began settling in toward the depot. The street cars running down Main and Calhoun Streets carried all they could hold, and a steady current of pedestrians lined the sidewalks and elbowed one another on the platform at the Union Depot. . . . As the tall form of Courtright emerged from the car there was a slight ripple of applause." The crowd followed as Courtright, Holland, and Thompson walked "through the slush and mud up Main Street to the variety show of George Holland, a short distance from the depot." There, upstairs in Holland's private office, "a levee was held" for Courtright "and his admirers talked with him and 'passed the bumper fair.'" Later Courtright went uptown and visited the White Elephant and Occidental saloons. "Everywhere he went a crowd gathered and listened with evident delight to the recital of his adventures since his memorable escape from the Rangers."[38]

New Mexico Governor Edmund G. Ross, who had replaced Sheldon, issued extradition papers for Courtright on January 25. Tarrant County Sheriff Walter Maddox was notified the same day that he would be receiving a warrant for the fugitive's arrest from Sheriff Charles T. Russell of Socorro County and that a deputy would be sent to return him. Interviewed again, Courtright said,

I am ready and willing to go back and stand my trial. But I want to go in custody of Sheriff Maddox or some

other friend of mine from Fort Worth, and I want to go
with my arms on like a free man. I don't want to go back
chained and hand-cuffed like the Rangers wanted to carry
me. I want to stand my trial and get this thing off my
mind.

I don't like the idea of their nolle prossin' [McIntire's]
case. It looks to me like they might re-indict him as soon as
they get me, so as to prevent his testimony from coming in
when I am tried. I want a square, fair trial, and if they give
me that and convict me, I'll walk on the scaffold and smoke
a cigarette as cool as a cucumber, while the sheriff is oiling
the trigger.[39]

(Although the last remark sounds more like guilty bravado than the
protestations of an innocent man, Father Stanley quoted it without
comment.)[40]

Maddox received the extradition papers on February 1, together
with a warrant for arrest and instructions from Sheriff Russell to hold
Courtright awaiting arrival of his deputy and further instructions.
Sheriff Maddox assigned his brother, Deputy Ed Maddox, to guard the
prisoner. Evidently surprised by the swiftness of action in New Mexico,
Courtright told a reporter:

I did not expect after I had come three thousand miles
to give myself up, that the New Mexican authorities would
put me to the trouble and expense of bringing me over
there to give bond, when my trial could not come up before
next May. I thought some arrangement would be made to
have the Sheriff look out for me here till the time the trial
would come off. I expect I can get a good bond made for

me when I get to Socorro. No, I don't think McIntyre [sic] wants to bring me back to Socorro. He was once Marshal there and always told me that the vigilantes often took men out of jail whom he had placed there for some slight offense and hanged them.

Within fifteen minutes of surrendering to arrest, Courtright said, he had received a telegram from his wife in Walla Walla, urging his immediate return, as their new baby was very ill.[41]

Courtright was not permitted to leave town, but when Under Sheriff C. A. Robinson of Socorro County arrived in Fort Worth on Wednesday, February 10, he agreed to delay his return with his prisoner, in order to give Courtright an opportunity to see his wife and baby Lulu May, who were on en route to meet him. Betty arrived in Fort Worth on Friday, but Robinson waited a full week before starting for Socorro.

Said the *Dallas Morning News*: "Neither the prisoner or his friends have the slightest apprehension of the final result of the trial. On this journey Courtright will be permitted the free use of his limbs, no hand-cuffs or shackles being used to prevent an attempt to escape."[42] Courtright had said that he wanted to return with his "arms on like a free man," but if Robinson allowed him to retain his weapons, no men-tion was made of it. Ab Woody, accompanied him on the trip.

According to press reports, on his arrival at Socorro Courtright received a reception more appropriate to a returning hero than a long-sought fugitive and suspect in a double murder case. The *Las Vegas Optic* said the *Socorro Chieftain* gave "Jim Courtright, the desperado… such a cordial welcome to that city that Jeems may take a notion to set-tle there after he has gone through with the formality of a trial."[43]

When he got back to Fort Worth, Ab Woody also commented on the surprisingly warm reception Courtright received at Socorro. The

passing of two-and-a-half years since the murders had somehow dissi-
pated the intense feeling against Courtright, he said, and those who
once would have helped lynch him now were "disposed to befriend
him. The prisoner is not subjected to close confinement, but is permitted to walk the streets in company with an officer, as he did after his
return to Fort Worth. . . . The trial, when it does come off, if ever, will
be a mere matter of form."[44]

On March 1, 1886, Courtright appeared before Judge William H.
Brinker of the Second Judicial District Court, charged with first degree
murder. As prosecutors had no better witnesses or evidence to present
than they had in the McIntire trial the previous October, they requested
that a nolle prosequi entry be made on the docket. Courtright objected
to this and demanded a trial. Judge Brinker ordered a continuance until
March 22 and release of the defendant under $5,000 bond.[45]

Courtright returned to Fort Worth but was back in Socorro three
weeks later for a second hearing. Again the prosecution, pleading the
absence of an important witness, requested and was granted a continuance until the next term of court.[46]

Eight months later Courtright made a third trip to Socorro and
finally got the result he sought—a complete dismissal of the charges.
Admitting they could never get together the necessary witnesses to
press the case, prosecutors threw in the sponge and asked that the
charges be dropped.

Thus the American Valley murder case ended, with none of the six
men who gunned down Alexis Grossetete and Robert Elsinger ever
being convicted. For his testimony against the others, Dan McAllister
escaped prosecution. After their two trials ended in hung juries, James
Casey and Mueller Scott were never retried. Despite the rewards
offered for him, W. C. Moore fled to Alaska and was never apprehended. By managing to evade the clutches of the law long enough

for witnesses to scatter and emotions cool, Jim McIntire and Jim Courtright avoided trial. Coincidentally, two of the central figures in the American Valley ranch sale, John A. Logan and Henry M. Atkinson, died in 1886, the year of Courtright's exoneration. James Casey died seven years later. John P. Casey, perhaps the man most responsible for the tragedy, outlived them all; he died in 1912.[47]

Following his release in New Mexico from all charges, Courtright returned home by way of El Paso, where he "demonstrated his prowess with the six-shooter in front of some properly awed citizens."[48] He showed them the quick draw with one gun or two. He demonstrated the "road-agent's spin," in which a pistol is offered, butt foremost, and then quickly reversed and cocked with one motion. The six-shooters danced in his hands in forward and backward spins and then flew in the air from one hand to the other in the "border shift." It was a display of pistol virtuosity that impressed all who saw it, including former City Marshal Jim Gillett, who shook his head in disbelief when, less than a year later, he heard what happened to this man "who handled his Colts as a sleight of hand performer juggled glass balls on the stage."[49]

Courtright had been dazzling observers with his handgun "wizardry" for years. "Jim was the fastest man I ever saw," one Fort Worth old-timer attested:

He could shoot as well with one hand as with the other and handled his guns in sort of slight-of-hand manner. He used to practice in the river bottoms just north of the present courthouse and I watched him lots of times. He would let any man face a tree while he would turn his back to it and bet any man $10 he could turn, draw and hit the tree before the man facing it could. And I never saw him lose a bet.[50]

Now, buoyed in spirits after his legal victory in Socorro and having properly astounded the citizenry of tough El Paso with his six-shooter artistry, Jim Courtright on November 29, 1886, arrived back in Fort Worth in triumph.[51] He had no way of knowing that in months all that six-shooter showmanship would avail him nothing and he would lie dead on a Fort Worth street, shot and killed by a gunfighter more deadly than he.

THE BATTLE
OF BUTTERMILK
SWITCH

*"Jim Courtright is largely responsible for the Fort Worth
massacre, but who is responsible for Jim Courtright?"*

San Antonio Light,
April 10, 1886

Conflict and controversy were always Jim Courtright's portion. Within
three months of his return to Fort Worth from his exile in Washington,
he was deeply involved in another violent episode.

Throughout 1885 and early 1886 trouble had been brewing
between the southwestern rail system controlled by railroad tycoon Jay
Gould and workers represented by the Noble Order of the Knights of
Labor. Things heated up considerably in March 1886 when the union
called a strike against Gould's Texas & Pacific Railway to protest the
firing of one of their members. There were incidents of violence, and
other lines were shut down as shopmen and crews walked out. Since
Fort Worth had become a major railroad terminus with the conver-
gence of three lines—the Missouri Pacific, the Fort Worth & New
Orleans, and the Texas & Pacific—the town became the focal point of
the bitter dispute. In an effort to disrupt all rail freight traffic through
Fort Worth, strikers damaged engines, pulled couplings from cars,
piled ties across tracks, and seized switch junctures. Wives of the striking men stood on the tracks in front of approaching locomotives and
defied the engineers to run over them. The tactics were successful.
Other than a single mail train a day permitted to pass through, freight
traffic in Fort Worth came to a halt.

March 1886 was the month Courtright made two train trips to Socorro for court appearances, and if the disruption of normal rail service at Fort Worth caused him any inconvenience, he was soon in a position to retaliate against those responsible.

Incredibly, after hiding from the law for more than a year with a price on his head and still facing unresolved double murder charges, Courtright on his return to Fort Worth was invested with police authority at federal, county, and municipal levels. U. S. Marshal William Lewis Cabell once again appointed him a deputy United States marshal. In anticipation of utilizing his services in the strike troubles, Sheriff John H. Boyd of Johnson County, lying just south of Tarrant, made him a deputy, and Mayor John Peter Smith of Fort Worth appointed him acting deputy city marshal.[1]

By the end of March railroad officials had enough of the traffic stoppage in Fort Worth and laid their plans to run a train through the blockade. To protect the train and crew from militant strikers they employed an armed guard headed by Courtright. Enlisted with him were a number of former or current city policemen and constables: John J. Fulford, Charles Sneed, James Thompson, W. B. "Bony" Tucker, Jr., R. W. "Dick" Townsend, R. Darby, J. C. Brannon, William Hale, Joseph Witcher, and Seth Maddox.

When the company issued injunctions enjoining the strikers from interference with the train's departure, word of the strikebreaking attempt spread throughout the city. On April 3, the day selected, a crowd estimated at about five hundred gathered at the yards. "The entire force of deputy sheriffs and nearly all the policemen of the city were stationed along the tracks, which was kept clear of the spectators and strikers, who presented an almost solid mass for several yards on either side."[2]

The railroad employees moved quickly about the tracks, making up the train, as the detail of officers stood calmly, the brown leather belts showing under their coats. Jim Courtwright [sic] was there, rather grave. He gave few directions, contenting himself with simply waving the pressing crowds farther back. At a word from him, the officers climbed on, some in the cab, some on the rear cars, Courtwright himself going in front. The few train hands looked beseechingly at the deputies, whom they expected to carry them through a very ticklish job. The whistle blew, and the heavy freight moved out.[3]

It had only moved about a hundred yards when "a wild-eyed woman, with disheveled hair and pale face" leaped between the rails directly in front of the locomotive and frantically waved a red flag. Standing her ground before the advancing engine, she was almost run over. At the last moment a man ran up and snatched her away. Whether the woman's action was intended as a show of revolutionary defiance or a warning to the crew was never determined.

As the train approached a place called Buttermilk Switch, the junction of the Fort Worth & New Orleans and Missouri & Pacific roads about two miles south of the depot, the engineer, Ed Smith, saw that the switch had been turned. Four men, apparently unarmed, were on the right of the tracks, walking away from the switch. Another group, five or more, was some distance off to the left, along a gully. They were armed with rifles.

Smith applied the brakes and stopped the train. Courtright leaped down and arrested the nearby four for throwing the switch. After searching them, he and Dick Townsend, a guard, walked around the front of the engine with their prisoners.

The men at the gully held weapons that Bill Hale, another guard, recognized, even at that distance, as "Winchester rifles, 45-60s, the best gun made."[4] Courtright called out: "Gentlemen, lay down those guns." Instead of complying, the riflemen knelt down and took deliberate aim. Again Courtright shouted: "For Christ's sake, don't shoot!"[5]

Unaccountably, Courtright and his guards were armed only with pistols. As Bill Hale later said ruefully, "We were at a big disadvantage as we had nothing but six-shooters. There wasn't a Winchester on the train." Perhaps railroad officials had thought it prudent not to incite the strikers and their sympathizers with a show of heavy armament at the station and had told Courtright to arm his men with handguns only, but that decision now put the guards in grave danger.

The riflemen opened fire. Dick Townsend went down with the first volley, struck with a bullet just above the heart. John Fulford, standing right beside Courtright, toppled over, hit in both legs. Charlie Sneed took a slug in the face. All the guards, including the wounded men, returned the fusillade as best they could with their revolvers. Even Townsend, mortally wounded, emptied his pistol at the riflemen before crawling into the cab and urging the fireman, C. E. Nicewarmer, to unbuckle his scabbard, reload his pistols, and use them.[6]

It seemed to Nicewarmer that the ambushing party was "particularly anxious to wing Courtright," who was firing from a position between the rails and behind the switch. Evidently they came very close, as two bullets reportedly passed through his hat.[7]

The gunbattle lasted twelve to fifteen minutes by most estimates. In all perhaps one hundred shots were fired before the riflemen withdrew. When the smoke cleared the four men who had been arrested had vanished. Courtright ordered Engineer Smith to back the train up to Fort Worth. There doctors ministered to the three wounded guards. Townsend's case was hopeless, and he died early the next morning. The other wounded guards survived, although Fulford was laid up for weeks and Sneed's face was "terribly disfigured."[8]

The ambushing party suffered two casualties, Tom Nance and Frank Pierce. Nance, formerly employed as a hostler at the Texas & Pacific roundhouse, received a bullet through the right thigh that shattered the bone. His friends took him by wagon to his home near the depot where a doctor dressed his wound. That afternoon officers took him in charge and lodged him in the county jail. Pierce, a well-known character about town, had only one arm, but before he was hit, loaded and fired his Winchester "with nonchalance and dispatch which invoked the admiration if not the approval of the officers." The day after the battle his dead body was found on the prairie where his confederates had left it.[9]

The only others the guards recognized were railroad employees J. T. Hardin, John May, and H. Henning. All seemed to have disappeared after the fight. Within a few days both the governor and the railroad company offered rewards for the apprehension of Hardin, who was believed to be the leader of the ambush party.

On April 3 Fort Worth was in its greatest state of excitement since the arrest and escape of Jim Courtright back in 1884. Fearing more violence, Mayor Smith sent an urgent wire to Governor Ireland: "We are threatened with serious trouble here. The presence of one or two companies of rangers or state militia would prevent a riot. Can you furnish the troops? Answer."[10] The governor responded that Adjutant-General King and companies of Texas Rangers were en route by special train. That night "squads of citizens, armed with repeating rifles and shotguns" stood guard at the Union Depot. "There is no loud talk or bluster," reported the *Gazette*, "No strikers are to be seen." In an editorial the paper added: "The issue is not now between the railroads and the strikers, but between law and anarchy."[11]

On orders from Governor Ireland, peacekeepers poured into Fort Worth the next day to present an overwhelming display of force. From

nearby Dallas came the Hibernian Rifles, Captain J. Mooney commanding, and the Dallas Light Guards, twenty-six strong, under the
command of Captain C. F. Cook. Shortly afterward the twenty-four-
man Grayson Rifles, commanded by Captain F. A. Ryan arrived from
Sherman. A special train from Harrold brought in Captain Samuel A.
McMurray and his company of ten Texas Rangers. Later in the day two
companies of infantry from Austin and a battery of artillery from Dallas
arrived on the scene, later to be augmented by another militia company
from Decatur. The state's highest legal dignitaries and military brass
were on hand, including Attorney General John D. Templeton,
Adjutant General Wilburn H. King, and Brigidier General A. S. Roberts
and Lieutenant Colonel J. C. Turner of the Texas National Guard. The
militia and rangers, together with a hundred armed citizens, patrolled
the streets of the city and there was no further violence. (Before the
excitement subsided, two more companies of Texas Rangers would be
ordered to Fort Worth, including the company of Captain George
Schmitt, whose rangers had been so embarrassed by Courtright's
escape two years earlier. Any pleasantries Captain Schmitt and
Courtright may have exchanged have gone unrecorded.)[12]

The story of the gunbattle put Courtright's name once again in
newspaper headlines across the state. "Deadly Work by the Strikers at
the Fort" ran the head in the *San Antonio Daily Express*, "Courtright's
Crew Ambushed and Outfought—A Wild Day with the Knights—
Rifles and Six-Shooters at One Hundred Yards—The Rangers Out—
Ireland and King En Route, Etc."[13]

On the day following the shootout, Courtright headed another
guard force on a train leaving Fort Worth. Unmolested, the freight
train ran south to Alvarado in Johnson County and was the first to
break the blockade.[14] He also led posses scouring the countryside for
the missing strikers without success.

Governor Ireland arrived in the city the next day and conferred with city officials and representatives of the railroads and the Knights of Labor. It was evident that the show of force by the governor had calmed the situation down considerably. By the seventh the Grayson Rifles and the Dallas Guards had departed and the rangers left soon afterward. A number of strikers were arrested and charged with rioting or the more serious offense of complicity in the murder of Townsend. Eventually indictments were brought against thirty-seven union members. Many were convicted on the riot charges and fined or jailed. "The juries have no trouble in reaching a verdict, agreeing in the last case in less than an hour," reported the *San Antonio Daily Express* in June.[15]

The paper noted that same month that the recovery of Tom Nance, the rifleman shot in the leg by Courtright's train guards, was not proceeding well and he was not expected to live. Nance had been indicted for the murder of Dick Townsend, but, due to his condition, lawyers succeeded in getting a series of case postponements and he apparently never came to trial.

Henning, one of the riflemen recognized by the guards, had fled but was later captured. On January 17, 1887, Courtright, Bony Tucker, John Fulford, and others testified at a district court hearing before Judge R. E. Beckham to determine the question of bail. After hearing the testimony, Judge Beckham "did not consume much time deliberating... but at once remanded the prisoner to the county jail to await his trial...."[16]

The following June a jury found Henning guilty of the murder of Dick Townsend and assessed his punishment at confinement in the state penitentiary for life.[17]

The labor unrest in the Southwest and particularly the Battle of Buttermilk Switch, as the fight involving Courtright came to be called, captured the interest of the nation and President Grover Cleveland requested that a congressional committee be formed to look into the matter. Accordingly, the House of Representatives on April 12, 1886 adopted a resolution to establish an investigative committee to look into the "cause and extent of the disturbed condition existing between the railroad corporations and their employees" in the states of Illinois, Missouri, Kansas and Texas. Congressman A. G. Curtin of Pennsylvania was the chairman. During hearings lasting from April 20 to May 14, the committee heard testimony from more than five hundred witnesses, including "strikers, strike sympathizers, railroad officials, loyal employees, strikebreakers, neutral observers, a Catholic priest, a reporter for the *Galveston* and *Dallas News*, business men, women boardinghouse keepers [and] Negro workers in the Marshall yards."[18] Jim Courtright was one of those called to testify. Some witnesses were grilled at length on their previous history, but Courtright "was asked no questions about himself although his answers would have made interesting reading."[19]

In the days following the labor explosion at Fort Worth, Courtright and the officials who had recently appointed him to law enforcement positions came under severe criticism in the press. The editor of the *San Antonio Light* was particularly outspoken in his editorial comment:

> **Jim Courtright is largely responsible for the Fort Worth massacre; but who is responsible for Jim Courtright? There seems to be a very grave doubt settled over the matter of his appointment as deputy marshal, but it is charged that he was acting without any legal warrant. It is a criminal act to place a man of his known antecedents in the lead, when the peace of society is threatened. The man who has been a terror of society, and who is gravely charged with the shooting of peaceable citizens heretofore, should not be entrusted**

with the delicate and very serious responsibility of keeping
the public peace when passion is at fever heat, as it was in
Fort Worth on that fatal day.... Those in a position to know,
affirm that the bullying threats by Courtright did more to
provoke that attack upon the trains than any other cause,
and that had he not been present, not one drop of blood
would have been shed.[20]

And in far-off Atlanta, Georgia, an editor penned a tongue-in-cheek
editorial headed "Texas Jim and Other Toughs." During the recent
turmoil at Fort Worth, Texas, he said,

> one of the most determined conservators of the peace
> was the notorious Jim Courtright. Everybody in this coun-
> try and Mexico, too, has heard of Texas Jim. The man is a
> typical border ruffian. He is a red-handed tough. In Texas,
> in the territories, and on the other side of the Rio Grande,
> he has killed a man whenever his pistol cracked, and it has
> cracked pretty often. He is wanted in New Mexico, for mur-
> der, as usual, and there is an urgent desire to have him
> stand and plead in several other places. Under the circum-
> stances the strikers were dumbfounded to see Jim at the
> head of a squad of citizens organized in the interests of law
> and order. . . . When Courtright, armed to the teeth, went
> to work running out the trains, the strikers weakened. Jim
> was for gore and plenty of it. When a regular desperado
> enrolls himself on the side of law there is trouble ahead if
> he is opposed.
>   Statesmen and other students of our social problems
> may learn something from this Courtright episode. Every

community has its toughs, hoodlums and plugs. If we cannot manage them, why not hire them to manage us? With sheriffs, deputies, metropolitan police, and with the army filled up with men of the Texas Jim stamp the country would be safe. In no other way can we utilize our dangerous classes to such advantage. It is to be hoped that the matter will receive due consideration.[21]

Shrugging off these imputations, Courtright turned to his detective business, a venture that had probably suffered by the extended absences of its chief. He now gave it his undivided attention.

ENTER
LUKE SHORT

---

*"Luke was a little fellow, so to speak, about five feet, six inches in
height, and weighing in the neighborhood of one hundred and forty
pounds. It was a small package, but one with great dynamic force."*

W. B. "Bat" Masterson, "Luke Short"

The Fort Worth City Directory for 1885-1886 contained a large ad for
the T.I.C. Detective Agency, headquartered at Houston and Second
streets. Officers were listed as T. I. Courtright, president and general
manager; A. N. Woody, general superintendent; James Maddox, assistant superintendent; and John Price, business manager. According to
the advertisement, this was a large organization, international in scope,
with branch offices headed by James B. Gillet [sic], captain in charge
of the El Paso district, and James T. Houston, captain in charge of the
Mexican division at Mexico City. A statement from the president and
general manager was included:

> The Undersigned have established a Detective Agency
> for the transaction of legitimate Detective business in all its
> branches, and respectfully tender their services in all cases
> requiring careful and skillful investigation.
>
> Evidence in criminal and civil actions obtained; missing
> persons found; absent witnesses located; collections made in
> all parts of the State, United States and Mexico; the mysteri-
> ous disappearance of goods inquired into; lost and stolen

property recovered; private watchmen furnished for stores, goods and dwellings when applied for through the office. All business strictly confidential. References furnished when required. Telephone in office.

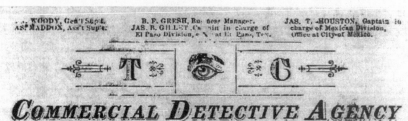

above: Advertisement for the T. I. C. Commercial Detective Agency. *Courtesy Craig Fouts Collection.*

right: Sign on building housing the T. I. C. commercial Detective Agency in Fort Worth. *Author's personal collection.*

Detective work by its very nature is secretive, and little is known of the activities of the T. I. C. Agency, but there were occasional mentions in the press when Courtright and his detectives assisted lawmen in making important arrests.

In January 1887 T. I. C. detectives nabbed C. L. Creek, a fugitive from Colorado, for whom a reward was offered. Creek had killed a Durango constable in a gunfight and jumped bail. His angry bondsmen offered a $600 reward for his capture, and the Courtright agency got on the case. Courtright, who still kept close tabs on Hell's Half Acre, and suspected that a gambler calling himself William Overton, who had worked the district and then suddenly disappeared, was in fact Creek, the wanted man. He traced him to Hot Springs, Arkansas, arrested him, brought him back to Fort Worth, and notified Sheriff J. C. Turner of La Plata County, Colorado. Turner came to Fort Worth, confirmed the identification, and took his prisoner back to Durango.[1]

Later that month Courtright was called on to assist in the capture of four men suspected of having robbed a Texas & Pacific train and almost got involved in another bloody shootout. Alerted by U. S. Marshal W. L. Cabell that the suspects were on a train approaching Fort Worth, Tarrant County Sheriff J. S. Richardson gathered Courtright and several officers, including City Marshal W. M. Rea, and policeman John Fulford, recently recovered from the leg wounds he suffered in the railroad gunbattle. The officers boarded the train and, with drawn guns, descended on the suspects as they lounged in the "reclining chair car." Mistaking the tough-looking intruders for train robbers and thinking *they* were being attacked, the four men resisted but were subdued before shots were fired. Further investigation disclosed their innocence.[2]

Jim Courtright may have been president and general manager of a viable company, but he was still only semi-literate, as is evident in an

undated letter he wrote tó Cyrus W. "Doc" Shores, sheriff of Gunnison
County, Colorado, about this time:

> Sir: I haf beean in formed that you want a man for mur-
> der committed in your county in 1882 that ansers to the
> following DisCription. . . . Should you want such a party &
> thair is Enuff in it to Justifie Ans. We can get him for you.
> Please favor Ous With and Eirly Reply & O Blige Yours
> Varie Respectfully T. I. Courtright. Commercial Detective
> Agency with offices Ft. Worth, El Paso, Mexico City.[3]

Courtright still frequented the dives of Hell's Half Acre where the
nightly bacchanal continued. An inveterate gambler, he probably
patronized the faro, monte, and keno tables. But he was never known
as a high roller in the class with the district's Nat Kramer, who ran
successful gambling operations there for four decades. In a professional gambling career lasting half a century Kramer was never known
to have taken a drink, engaged in a quarrel, or carried a weapon of any
kind. Luke Short, a gambler and gunman of note who was soon to
have his name forever linked with that of Courtright, said of Kramer:
"He is the most mysterious success I ever saw. How he does it I
would like to know, because I am tired of this business of packing
a gun."[4]

In an account of his life as a professional gambler, Charles "Rusty"
Coe, a veteran of the western gambling circuit, described a memorable
poker game held in the White Elephant Saloon in Fort Worth. Sitting
at the table with him, he said, were frontier luminaries Bat Masterson,
Wyatt Earp, Luke Short, and Jim Courtright. It was a high-stakes game;
Masterson alone had invested $9,000, money advanced him by wealthy
cattleman Jim Devine, and the exciting play drew a crowd of spectators.

In a final showdown Coe swept the table with four kings to beat Short's full house.[5]

Coe told a good story but one that lacks credibility. First of all, the game was said to have taken place in August 1885; Courtright was on the run at that time and far away from Fort Worth. Secondly, such a monumental clash of prominent western sporting men, witnessed by dozens, could not have escaped the notice of the city journalists, but no mention of the great game appeared in the papers. And lastly, Courtright was simply not in the same gambling league with the other players named.

Bat Masterson and Wyatt Earp were as widely known in the frontier West for their skills at the gambling tables as for their records as lawmen and gunfighters. They both were close friends and associates of Luke Short, who never wore a badge but who was famous throughout the West as a formidable gambler and gunman.

Luke Lamar Short was Texas-raised but Mississippi-born. One of ten children of Josiah Washington Short and Hettie Brumley, he was born February 19, 1854, near Laurel, Mississippi.[6] When he was two the family moved to Grayson County, Texas. According to family tradition, Luke was only thirteen years old when he stabbed a boy who had bullied him. Fearing punishment from both his stern father and the law, he joined a cattle drive to Kansas and did not see his family again for sixteen years.[7]

Short spent his teenage years in Kansas and Nebraska cowboying, buffalo hunting, and peddling whisky to hunters (legally) and Indians (illegally). For a period he took employment as a scout and dispatch rider for the U. S. Army.[8] But fascinated by the frontier gambling establishments and the well-dressed, distinguished-looking men presiding over the games, he resolved to follow the life of a sporting man. In the mid-1870s he spent several seasons in the tough cowtown of Ogallala and it was there he honed his skills as a gambler and gunman. One Nebraska pioneer, who watched Short practice the draw-and-shoot on the banks of the South Platte, a mile from Ogallala, said: "He could draw and fire a six-shooter more rapidly and accurately, at short range, than any other man I ever knew."[9]

Luke Short. *Author's personal collection.*

Short's name fit his physique, for he was indeed a little man. Bat Masterson described him as "about five feet, six inches in height, and weighing in the neighborhood of one hundred and forty pounds. It was a small package, but one with great dynamic force."[10]

With only rudimentary schooling, Short in his early years was what Bat Masterson called "a white Indian," a roughhewn border character who could barely write his name legibly. But, intelligent, ambitious, and an avid reader, Short transformed himself into a sporting dandy, well read and well spoken. Immaculately dressed, sporting a plug hat and often carrying a cane, he became a familiar figure in the gambling resorts of the Colorado, Wyoming, and Kansas boom towns. "He could," said Masterson, "write an excellent letter, always used good English when talking and could quote Shakespeare, Byron, Goldsmith and Longfellow better and more accurately than most scholars."[11]

Short quickly gained the respect of his gambling peers for his daring play and the alacrity with which he responded to personal attack. In Leadville a tough with a gunfighting reputation attempted to bully Short and reached for his gun, Masterson remembered, but "quicker than a flash," the little gambler outdrew the man, "jammed his own pistol into the bad man's face and pulled the trigger, and the bad man rolled over on the floor. The bullet passed through his cheek but, luckily, did not kill him."[12]

Short joined Masterson, Doc Holliday, Wyatt Earp and his brothers, and a horde of other fortune seekers in the rush to the new silver camp at Tombstone, Arizona. There his reputation as a deadly gunfighter was firmly established when on February 25, 1881, he shot and killed veteran gambler and gunman Charlie Storms. He was cleared on a plea of self-defense.[13]

Later that year Short took a lengthy trip to Chicago and points east. In New York City, according to some reports, he met and married "a

petite blond woman who had the same name as his mother, Hettie."[14]
Others believe his liaison with the "mysterious and alluring" beauty,
Marie Hettie Bimbo, began in Tombstone and the couple were never
legally married.[15] Common law marriage was prevalent among members of the sporting class; Short's close friends, Wyatt Earp and Bat
Masterson, both entered into lifelong arrangements of this type about
the same time.

On February 6, 1883, Luke Short, in partnership with William H.
Harris, purchased an interest in the Long Branch, the leading Dodge
City saloon. The transaction set off a chain of events that culminated
in the so-called "Dodge City War," one of the most publicized episodes
in the town's colorful history.

In April Harris, supported by "The Dodge City Gang," a coalition
of sporting men, merchants, and politicians favoring a wide-open town,
ran for mayor of Dodge. He was opposed by Larry Deger, a three-hun-
dred-pound former city marshal and bitter enemy of Bat Masterson
and Luke Short. Deger and a slate of city council candidates calling
themselves "moderates" were friendly to Alonzo B. Webster, the previous mayor and currently the proprietor of the Alamo Saloon, a Long
Branch competitor. Soon after the election, won handily by the "mod-
erate" candidates, the newly elected officials mounted a campaign to
drive Webster's major competitor out of business. They quickly passed
an ordinance suppressing prostitution. Two days later, on April 28,
Mayor Deger sent City Marshal Jack Bridges and City Clerk Louis C.
Hartman, the latter wearing the badge of a special policeman, to Harris
and Short's Long Branch, where they arrested three women and jailed
them on prostitution charges.

Furious when he learned that female habitues of other establishments, Ab Webster's Alamo saloon in particular, had not been bothered, Luke Short went on the prod. He and Lou Hartman exchanged

ineffectual shots in the street, but Hartman, in his haste to get away, tripped and fell headlong off the board sidewalk. Thinking he had killed the man, Short armed himself with a double-barreled shotgun, chased everyone out of the Long Branch, barricaded the door, and waited through the night, prepared to fight the entire Dodge City police department.

In the morning, after conferring with Marshal Bridges, who assured him he had not killed Hartman, Short agreed to surrender, plead guilty to a disturbance charge, and pay a small fine. But when he emerged from the Long Branch Bridges jailed him on a charge of criminal assault. Released on $2,000 bond, Short was promptly arrested again, together with several other gamblers, on charges of being "undesirables." On May 1 Mayor Deger and an armed posse escorted Short to the depot and gave him his choice of departing trains—east or west.

Short chose east. He went to Kansas City and telegraphed Bat Masterson in Denver that he had serious trouble in Dodge and required assistance. Bat himself was persona non grata in Dodge as a result of a little shooting affair back in 1881, but, always ready to drop everything to help a friend, he hurried east. He and Short called on Kansas Governor George W. Glick in Topeka and pled their case. Glick said the state would not interfere with their effort to "rehabilitate" Short in Dodge. Given the green light, the two gamblers separated to enlist the services of other gunmen of help achieve that end.

As the "Dodge City War" loomed, newspapers across the country picked up the story and Luke Short became something of a celebrity. On May 18, 1883, he was described by a writer for the *Topeka Daily Kansas State Journal* as presenting no appearance of the desperado. "In fact he is a regular dandy, quite handsome, and... a perfect ladies man. He dresses fashionably, is particular as to his appearance, and always takes pains to look as neat as possible. At Dodge City he associates with the very best element, and leads in almost every social event that is gotten up."

When Short, Masterson, Wyatt Earp, and a company of hard-eyed gunmen descended on Dodge City in the first week of June the Deger-Webster forces capitulated without a shot and the bloodless "Dodge City War" ended in complete victory for Short and his supporters. The well-publicized story, graphically illustrated by a photograph of Short, Masterson, Earp. and others sitting as a "Dodge City Peace Commission," that appeared in the *National Police Gazette* and other popular periodicals assured Luke Short's place in the hierarchy of western gun-packing sporting men.

W. B. "Bat" Masterson, a close friend of Luke Short, held Courtright in low regard. *Courtesy Kansas State Historical Society, Topeka, Kansas.*

The following November Short disposed of his interest in the Long Branch and by the summer of 1884 had settled in Fort Worth. He was a resident of the town at the time of Jim Courtright's spectacular escape from the rangers and yearlong exile. In October 1884 he contributed to a $500 purse raised to aid Betty Courtright in moving her family to her parents home in California, and following Courtright's return he helped finance his fight in the New Mexico courts.[16] During this period Short joined Nat Kramer and Jake Johnson in the top echelon of the town's professional gamblers. Newspapers soon came to refer to him as "the king gambler of Fort Worth."[17]

Arrested for conducting gambling games in Fort Worth, Short usually beat the charge, as in August 1884 when a paper reported: "The trial of gaming cases was continued to-day, William Atterbury and Luke Short being arraigned. The trial was by jury and six of our best citizens were in the box.... The evidence was exhaustive, but the jurors after being out a very few minutes acquitted. This makes seven different juries and not one guilty verdict. Public sentiment, so called, is not against gambling, or the law and the evidence fall far short of what they should be."[18]

In his memoirs veteran Texas cattleman John Loomis contributed a dubious addition to the Luke Short legend. At Fort Worth, he said, gambler Short also dabbled in cattle and land speculation. Even when working cattle, according to Loomis, Short wore a plug hat, a long tailed coat and a gun. "He had a ranch out from Fort Worth, and all his cattle were branded with a plug hat on the side of the jaw. It was said he only employed Negro cowboys, that they agreed in writing to call him Mr. Short and to work for a specified time. If they broke their contract Short reserved the right to shoot them. I did not know Luke Short, but I did know his brothers.... He was a gunman and a gambler, not a cattleman. He could not have handled white cowboys as he did his Negroes."[19]

Ad for the White
Elephant Saloon.
*Author's personal
collection.*

Luke Short's gambling peers in Fort Worth, Jake Johnson and Nat Kramer, had partnered for a time, but not long after Short's arrival in town Johnson teamed with him in the operation of the White Elephant Saloon, a large, two-story, drinking, eating, and gambling house at 308-310 Main Street.

Because of its location uptown, the White Elephant always attracted a better-class clientele and was considered several cuts above the dives of riotous Hell's Half Acre. By the mid-1880s the establishment, with its long, elaborate bar and fine dining room on the first floor and gambling rooms above, was already a Fort Worth landmark, famous throughout the West. Diners could choose from an extensive menu that included fresh fish, oysters, and wild game; bar patrons could indulge their tastes from a wide selection of choice wines, liquors, and cigars; and gamblers could try their luck at an assortment of games upstairs. It was, without a doubt, the finest establishment of its kind in the city. Many claimed it to be the best in Texas and some even said it could not be topped in the entire nation.[20]

Just before Short's involvement the White Elephant fell into some disrepute when it was closed by attachment and its proprietor charged with embezzlement, but after the place was reopened and Short set up a keno operation in the upstairs clubrooms business again picked up. In 1886 Short became a part owner, buying a share of the business with partners William and John Ward. William ran the saloon and restaurant downstairs while Luke handled the upstairs gambling. John was a silent partner. A little later Jake Johnson, who had previously operated the Cattle Exchange in partnership with Nat Kramer, also bought into the White Elephant.[21]

On February 7, 1887, Short sold his third interest in the establishment to Jake Johnson but continued to manage the upstairs gambling parlors. Whether this sale in any way contributed to the explosive events of the following day is not known, but within twenty-four hours Fort Worth was rocked by yet another episode of violence and at its center again was Timothy Isaiah "Jim" Courtright.

DEATH OF A GUNMAN – BIRTH OF A LEGEND

"The assassination of Jim Courtright in Fort Worth last night will cause regret. It is true Jim was not immaculate, but there were qualities about the man that atoned for his faults — one of which was his undaunted courage. He was such a character as strikes the popular eye. He was a representative of a class of men, now passing from Texas, who, whatever their faults, were types of brave and courageous manhood which always command respect and attract friends."

Austin Daily Statesman,
February 9, 1887

According to Courtright's original legend maker, Eugene Cunningham, his hero's fatal clash with Luke Short on the evening of February 8, 1887, came about because of a T. I. C. Detective Agency extortion racket. Courtright, he said, became "extremely unpopular with the gambling fraternity" when he began using his agency in a "shakedown" operation.

> For gambling was going on in Fort Worth, in violation of certain ordinances made, provided and comfortably ignored. To the gamblers came Courtright and his aides, "racketeering." The gambler paid certain amounts regularly, in return for shut mouths on the part of the T. I. C. A sorry business... certain to end in Colt Thunder.... Jim Courtright had slipped down a long, long way, from the place he had once occupied in men's esteem.[1]

The shakedown racket proved to be a lucrative business, it seems, and ran smoothly enough as long as the victims were the disreputable residents of the Bloody Third. But when Courtright tried to pull it on Luke Short of the White Elephant, said Cunningham, he "was invited to go jump in the Trinity River a few blocks north."[2]

This notion that Courtright's extortion racket was at the root of the trouble with Short originated in several newspaper reports. Courtright, said the *Dallas Morning News* of February 9, "exacted a certain sum each month as an inducement for him and his detective aide to keep their mouths shut. This was paid regularly to all accounts. Recently keno has been running, Short being the head of it, and Courtright wanted a certain sum from that game. Short refused to put up, and it is claimed that Courtright made threats to make Short bite the dust." The *St. Louis Globe-Democrat* of the same date expounded on the theme:

> Luke Short says that Courtright made a demand on all the gamblers that they pay him a salary, which he refused to do, remarking that he would not be blackmailed by any one. After this some one came to him and said:"Don't you think it better to pay Courtright and close his mouth?"He again replied that he would not submit to blackmail. These words were, it is said, aimed at Courtright, and word was brought back that Courtright had said he would "do up" Short....

The following day the *Brenham Daily Banner,* making use of an $18 word, repeated the allegation: "Since gambling was reopened in Fort Worth, it is stated that Courtright, who was in the detective business, had placed the gambling houses under monthly contributions. Short

LONG-HAIRED JIM COURTRIGHT
an Article by ᵕ Eugene Cunningham

Short-Courtright gunfight as depicted in Eugene Cunningham's 1929 article. *Author's personal collection.*

was running a keno bank and refused to be phlebotomized by Courtright, hence the tragedy."

The theory that Courtright used his detective agency to extort Fort Worth's gamblers and that the gunfight was precipitated by Short's refusal to pay up has been accepted by most writers and commentators on early Fort Worth history ever since.[3]

Alternate theories were put forward at the time, however. The *San Antonio Daily Express* quoted reports from Fort Worth that the keno craze "under the leadership of Short" had become of concern to "some leading citizens" and "prominent merchants" because young men of the city had been "fleeced" by the game. They had "employed Courtright to prosecute enough cases against the gamblers to put a stop to keno. That fact is what is supposed to have led to the shooting."[4] This explanation, less slanderous to Courtright's memory, was accepted by Fort Worth historian Oliver Knight.[5]

It was even suggested in print at the time that "certain parties" in Fort Worth had hired Courtright to dispose of Luke Short. Perhaps in an effort to leave no rumor unreported, the *Dallas Morning News,* one of the first papers to claim Courtright was running a shakedown operation, also made this allegation. It said that those mysterious "certain parties" had been instrumental in getting Courtright to return from exile "for the alleged purpose of putting Luke Short out of the way. Courtright came back, but the scheme miscarried, and was dropped, but Courtright still remembered what he was brought back for."[6]

In a statement to reporters after the shooting Short gave some credence to these rumors: "When Courtright came back here from New Mexico I was told he was brought back to kill me, but I could not say why, for I had never spoken a harsh word about him. On the contrary, when he went to Socorro to stand his trial, I gave him some money, being disposed to help him in his trouble. I thought after his return that the old trouble was all over, and paid no attention to the rumors I had heard."[7]

In his biography of Courtright, Father Stanley injected yet another motive for the fatal showdown, the always-dependable love triangle. Luke Short, he said, was smitten with Betty Courtright and intimated that he killed Courtright in order to marry the widow. When Short approached Betty with a marriage proposal shortly after the shooting, wrote Stanley, she "ran him off with a shotgun."[8] The good priest, who got this tale from Courtright's granddaughter in 1954, apparently never knew that Short was already married, albeit in a common law arrangement, when he lived in Fort Worth.

Other writers have scoffed at the suggestion of a Luke Short infatuation with Courtright's wife. "Hettie's head-turning beauty belies the rumor that Luke Short made a play for Betty Courtright," wrote Richard F. Selcer, historian of Hell's Half Acre.[9] Luke Short biographer William R. Cox called "the attempt to make capital of a conjectured romance with Mrs. Courtright...unfair both to the gambler and the lady."[10]

In the final analysis, most of the wild rumors and speculations about the cause of the celebrated Courtright-Short clash appear to be without basis.

Courtright, who in his entire life never had much money, in early 1887 had fallen on especially hard times. Despite contributions from friends, the expense of his fight to beat the New Mexico murder charges had drained what few funds he had. His detective agency was not prospering. He was dead broke and creditors were hounding him. Always a heavy drinker, he took more and more to the bottle. As he drank and cursed his ill fortune, he ruminated more and more on the dapper little gambler Luke Short and his prosperous gambling opera- tion at the White Elephant.[11] Short was cleaning up, especially with his popular keno games. Courtright had once operated keno games himself, but he no longer had the financial resources to get back in the business. Jealous of Short's success, he thought he saw a way to get in on the action, cut the little gambler down a notch, and improve his own fortunes. He approached Short and proposed that the gambler hire him as a security guard. Short's reaction infuriated him.

The story was told by Bat Masterson in his 1907 sketch of Luke Short's career. "In the spring of 1887," he wrote, "I visited Short in Fort Worth and learned soon after my arrival that he was having trouble which was likely to end seriously with a notorious local character by the name of Jim Courtright. It appears that this fellow Courtright... had asked Short to install him as a special officer in the White Elephant." Short not only rejected the offer, said Masterson, he told Courtright that rather than paying him to hang about the place, he would prefer to pay him to stay away. "You know," he said, "that the people about here are all afraid of you, and your presence in my house would ruin my business." Courtright took this as an insult, got "huffy at Luke and threatened to have him indicted and his place closed up."[12] This threat was probably the basis for the allegations of Courtright's extortion attempts.

Although one paper quoted Short as saying immediately after the shooting that there had been no previous disagreement or hard words between Courtright and himself and the deadly confrontation was "sudden, all unexpected" to him, there was the conflicting report that Courtright threatened to "do up" Short when the little gambler refused to give in to his extortion demands.[13]

If threats were made by the tall gunman with the awesome killer's reputation. Short would not have them taken lightly. Perhaps it was no coincidence that on Monday, February 7 Short sold out his interest in the White Elephant to Jake Johnson. In announcing the business trans-action, the *Gazette* noted that Short intended to remain in Fort Worth, presumably as manager of the gambling operation in the White Elephant,[14] but he may have had plans to move on after he got his affairs in order. Events of the next few days would drastically change those plans.

On the afternoon of February 8 Short approached Johnson and asked if he knew what Courtright had against him

"I don't know," Johnson answered. "I did not know that he had anything against you."

"He is doing a good deal of talking against me and the other gam-blers here, and threatens, unless money is given him, to break up every gambling game in the city."

"Now, I am a friend of Jim's," said Johnson, "and I don't under-stand what he means by that. I will see him and talk the matter over with him."[15]

Evidently it was common knowledge among the sporting gentry of Fort Worth that Courtright and the dapper gambler from the White Elephant were primed for a clash. On Monday, the very day that Short was selling out to his partner, Courtright was complaining loudly in John Stewart's saloon, a few doors down the street, that there was "a combination" against him at the White Elephant.

> He said God had made one man superior to another in muscular power, but when Colt made his pistol, that made all men equal. He called Short's name but said he didn't aim to do it and did not repeat it…. Courtright said he had lived over his time. No man on earth, he said, had any percentage over him. He said that this would be settled within a week, that he hadn't been treated with respect up stairs over the White Elephant.[16]

Sometime between seven and eight o'clock the next evening Officer Bony Tucker, his brother Rowan, and District Clerk L. R. Taylor were standing in front of the Cabinet Saloon at the corner of Main and Third, just down the street from the White Elephant. While they were trying to decide whether to go on downtown and attend a show, a man ran up, took Bony aside, and excitedly asked if the officer had two guns he would like to borrow one. He said that there was going to be trouble between Jim Courtright and Luke Short and, when the lid blew off he wanted to be armed. Tucker refused the request. Turning to his brother, he repeated the man's story and asked him to stay close. "If there was going to be trouble it must be stopped," he later said, "and I wanted somebody that I could rely on." A few minutes later he heard gunshots.[17]

As the Tucker brothers and Taylor stood on the corner discussing their plans for the evening, Bat Masterson and Luke Short were sitting in the billiard room of the White Elephant down the street. The subject of their discussion was Jim Courtright and what he might do to disrupt

Short's business. Jake Johnson came in the room and told Luke that at that moment Courtright, accompanied by Charlie Bull, one of his employees in the detective business, was in the outer lobby and wanted to talk to him

"Tell him to come in," said Short.

"I did invite him in," replied Johnson, "but he refused and said that I was to tell you to come out."

"Very well," said Luke, "I will see what he has to say."[18]

Short went to the entrance of the building with Johnson and met Courtright and Bull. The four men walked through the doorway and on the sidewalk separated, Courtright and Short continuing on, conversing quietly, as Johnson and Bull dropped behind.

Just north of the White Elephant was a shooting gallery run by a woman named Ella Blackwell. Courtright and Short stopped in front of this place and "had some quiet talk on private affairs," as Short put it. When the gambler reminded Courtright that he had contributed to a collection raised to help him in his defense at the time of the New Mexico troubles, "he assented, but not in a very cordial way."[19] Courtright grumbled that Short "had always been pleasant enough, but he had heard something lately he did not like." When asked what he had heard, he refused to answer. He "spoke very gruffly," Short thought.

> I had my thumbs in the arm-holes of my vest during the conversation, and casually dropped my hands and passed them over my vest front. As I did this Courtright said: "You needn't make any break for your pistol." I answered that I had no pistol there, and pulled up my vest front to show him. He stepped back, and threw his hand on his pistol. I drew my pistol from my pocket and fired five times.[20]

Hearing the shots only moments after being informed that Short and Courtright were about to tangle, Bony Tucker and his brother Rowan ran from the corner to the scene. It was dark and at first Bony could make out only Short, standing just north of the shooting gallery with a pistol in his hand. "Fearing that he might shoot me in the excitement of the moment," said the officer,

I dodged around him and grabbed his pistol. It was a Colt's 45-caliber. Rowan also grabbed him, and about that time Officer [J. W.] Pemberton came up. Then I saw Courtright. He had fallen just inside the shooting gallery, his feet extending out into the sidewalk. When I reached him he was dying, and though I bent over him, he never articulated a syllable. He grasped his gun in one hand, a "45" of the same make as the one that killed him. The chambers were full of cartridges, showing that he had failed to get in a shot. Three bullets had taken effect. One broke his right thumb, the second passed through his heart and the third struck him in the right shoulder. I believe it was the second shot fired that killed him. He was a dead man within five minutes after I reached him.[21]

Officer John J. Fulford, who, like Bony Tucker, had sided Courtright in the gunbattle during the railroad strike the year before, arrived on the scene of the shooting at almost the same moment. As the Tucker brothers disarmed Short, Fulford went directly to Courtright, who was on his lying back. "He had a pistol in his right hand, which I took, and another from the scabbard on his left side," the officer said. "The pistol held in his right hand was about half cocked and there was a cartridge in it which kept it from revolving smoothly." Courtright mumbled, "Ful, they've got me," just before he expired.[22]

Jake Johnson was only a few feet away and, other than Short, was the only witness to the actual shooting. Strangely, Charlie Bull somehow disappeared in the few minutes immediately before the action. A rumor spread that when the shooting started he had fired off one round at Short. Based on that report, Policeman Fulford later arrested him, and he spent the night in jail. It was soon determined that the story was untrue and Bull was released without even having to testify at the hearing the next day.[23] Jake Johnson's story followed that given by Short very closely:

> They were three or four feet apart while talking. Luke had his thumbs in the armholes of his vest, then he dropped them in front of him, when Courtright said, "You needn't be getting out your gun." Luke said, "I haven't got any gun here, Jim," and raised up his vest to show him. Courtright then drew his pistol. He drew it first and then Short drew his and commenced to fire.[24]

Within moments after the shooting a large crowd had gathered in the 300 block of Main Street. In his biography of "Longhair Jim," F. Stanley, following an account given him by Courtright family members, described the formation of a mob similar to the crowd that had protested Courtright's arrest by the rangers back in 1884. There was a Barnum show playing just a block away, they said, and a boy crawled under the tent and shouted: "Luke Short shot and killed Jim Courtright!"

> The entire audience was on its feet. Someone in the crowd yelled: "What are we waiting for [?] Let's go get Luke

Short." The cry was taken up all over the big top. The per-
formers played to an empty tent. The footsteps of the mob
was like the sound of flood waters. Now and then a man
shot his pistol into the air. There was a swiftness, a determination, a mob with a purpose. No place could hide Luke
Short. But the police were faster. They whisked Short to
jail. The mob followed. Guarding the entrance they called
for law and order. They would shoot the first man attempting to force his way in. The day of mob rule was over.
Courtright's death put an end to many things.[25]

Newspapers reported that Short was arrested and taken to the
county jail in the custody of Sheriff B. H. Shipp, City Marshal W. M.
Rea, and Bony and Rowan Tucker. Although "the affair created intense
excitement and in a few seconds after the shooting the street was
blocked with an excited throng of men eager to hear all the details of
the homicide,"[26] no threatening mob action was reported in the press.
Nor did Bat Masterson, in his account of the events of that night, mention a mob threat. Alfred Henry Lewis, Masterson's friend and legend
maker, however, wrote that "Mr. Masterson took his six-shooters and
begged the privilege of sitting in Mr. Short's cell all night, fearing mob
violence.... It turned out well, however, for the would be lynchers, told
by the Sheriff that Mr. Masterson and Mr. Short were together in the
jail, and each with a brace of guns, virtuously resolved that the law
should take its course, and went heedfully to bed."[27]

The body of the victim was removed to his home where "a wife and
three children, the eldest a girl of about fourteen years, were almost
distracted with grief. Their heart-rending sobs over the body of the lifeless husband and father were pitiable to hear."[28] Another paper
described "an effecting scene" when Courtright's eldest daughter,

Mary Ellen, was brought into the room where he lay. "She threw herself on the bloody corpse and kissed the hands and face of the dead man passionately, moaning, 'papa, papa.' Strong men, gambler, roughs, and officers wept like women at the sight."[29]

At an inquest held the next morning a coroner's jury found only that the deceased died of pistol shots fired by Luke Short. That afternoon witnesses were heard at an examining trial before Coroner and Justice of the Peace Smith. Ike Cantrell and W. A. James testified to having heard Courtright's earlier threats against the life of Short. Jake Johnson, the only admitted eyewitness to the shooting, told his story. Officers Bony Tucker, John Fulford, and J. W. Pemberton testified. Also examined were Ella Blackwell, proprietress of the shooting gallery, William Allison, her employee, and Frank Alstrop, a patron, none of whom admitted to having seen the actual shooting. Two of Short's attorneys, William Capps and Alexander Steadman, testified as to his character. At the conclusion of the hearing Justice Smith ordered Short bound over for the action of a grand jury. His attorneys immediately requested a bail bond be set and suggested $2,000 would be an appropriate amount. Justice Smith agreed, and, on a bond secured by Robert McCart, Walter T. Maddox, Alex Steadman, and Jake Johnson, Short was released from custody.[30]

Even while the examining trial was being held, the funeral of Timothy Isaiah Courtright, conducted by his brethren in the Odd Fellows lodge, was proceeding. At one o'clock the fire bells began ringing in honor of the former officer of the M. T. Johnson Hook and Ladder Company. At four a funeral procession began from the Courtright home and proceeded to Oakwood Cemetery, situated on the very land Courtright had briefly farmed when he first came to the area back in 1873. At its head was the Johnson Company fire wagon, "heavily draped in mourning and the splendid steeds that drew it themselves wearing the somber emblems of woe. One of these horses [was] called 'Jim' and was named for the dead man. Then came the other companies in line, and after them a long cortege that proceeded in solemn slowness to the place across the river where they were to part company with him forever." Courtright had always had many friends in Fort Worth and they all turned out to see him off. The string of carriages following the hearse was more than six blocks long.[31]

Contrary to the later stories that Courtright, through his detective agency, had been running a very lucrative shakedown operation, he left his family destitute. Only eighteen days after his death, Betty departed Fort Worth for her mother's home in California, never to return. Again a collection was taken up for the family, and again Luke Short was a generous contributor.[32]

Father Stanley, ever the apologist for his hero, accounts for Courtright's poverty by falsely claiming the man had "sunk every penny he had into the White Elephant."[33] Stanley was also in error when he said that Betty Courtright owned the shooting gallery next to the saloon and that Ella Blackwell leased the business from her.[34]

The Courtright-Short confrontation on Fort Worth's Main Street on February 8, 1887, has become one of the most celebrated man-to-man six-shooter conflicts in the history of the Wild West. It deserves recognition, for, despite a century of replays of similar scenes in countless western short stories, novels, motion picture and television plays, it was one of the very few actual face-to-face, quick-draw, gunfights ever recorded. All the elements of the classic duel are there: two determined fighting men, each with longstanding reputations for courage and fighting ability and each with killings to his credit, meet in a deadly showdown on the street of a tough western town; sharp words are exchanged, one reaches for a weapon, the other beats him to the draw, and shoots him dead.

Unfortunately for the Courtright legend makers, Cunningham and Stanley, their hero was the loser in this classic gun duel. So they ignored the facts and sworn eyewitness testimony in order to create a fictional scenario.

Cunningham began the fable with his original 1929 Courtright article and repeated it in most details in *Triggernometry*, in 1941. After following fairly closely the newspaper accounts of the events leading up to the climatic moment, including Courtright's warning, "Don't you pull a gun on me," and Short's denial, Cunningham said the little gambler

> lifted his hands and slapped those sections of his anatomy on which a gun would normally be found. Courtright stared narrowly. Suddenly Short's hand darted beneath his coat, to emerge with the gun from his shoulder-holster. Courtright was not to be taken nappin g. He drew like a rattler striking.
>
> But Short fired first, fired wild, too—or almost so. It was merest accident, it must have been, that shot of Luke Short's which tore from Courtright's hand the thumb which was pulling back the big hammer of his single-action Colt!
>
> From right hand to left. So Courtright threw the Colt, in that blurred twinkle of movement which the oldtimers called the "border shift." Luke Short had corrected his aim; had driven three bullets into Courtright's body. The long-haired man crumpled to his knees; to the floor; stone dead. Short gaped down, they say, seeming the most amazed of all in the place.
>
> So Jim Courtright died, the victim of perhaps the oddest bit of gun-play recorded in the annals of the Old West.[35]

In his later version of this tale, Cunningham said that Short "began pawing at his vest and all the time his hands got lower, closer to his belt, closer to the pistol *on his hip.* Too wise an old wolf to fall for this trick, Courtright drew first as he saw Short's hand "close to gun-butt." The result was as the writer had previously described it; Short's first shot blew away his opponent's hammer thumb, "as lucky a shot as the Old West ever heard of. It would be described for many a year around the cowboy's campfires, from the Rio Grande to Calgary." Instead of reaching for his left-hand gun, Courtright desperately tried the "border shift," but it was too late, Short finished him with three bullets in the body.[36]

Although Cunningham gave conflicting locations of Short's weapon—in a shoulder holster in the 1929 account, and on his hip in 1941—his account of the "lucky" thumb shot and the unsuccessful "border shift" has been followed and repeated by western writers ever since. But his story was based strictly on conjecture, for no one knew just which shot fired by Short hit Courtright's thumb. The attempt by Courtright to shift his pistol to the other hand, the "border shift," seems to have been an invention of the novelist's mind as well. No contemporary account mentions it, and officers Bony Tucker and John Fulford both testified that he still clutched his pistol in his right hand when he fell.

The "border shift" was one of the tricks Courtright performed for admirers, but there is absolutely no reason why he would employ it in this situation. He was wearing two six-shooters and, by all accounts, was equally adept at gun work with either hand. Two guns are normally carried for only one purpose: to provide a backup weapon if the first becomes ineffective for any reason. When a bullet struck his right hand and possibly the pistol it held, the experienced two-gun man would have immediately gone to his left-hand backup, not attempted the flashy but ineffective "border shift."

Father Stanley accepted and repeated the Courtright family's version of the shooting, a rendition completely at odds with all other accounts. According to this tale, the two men met in the upstairs rooms of the White Elephant, resolved their differences, and shook hands. "As Courtright turned to walk down the steps, Short shot him in the back, and then shot off Jim's thumb as Courtright turned to return the fire. Short fired four more bullets into his victim…. Mrs. Courtright examined her husband's body and found three bullet wounds in the back."[37]

Both legend makers distorted the facts in an effort to explain how their hero and his "uncanny speed and accuracy at weapon-play," who was "as fast as the twinkle of an eye when it came to drawing his six-shooters," could be beaten so badly in a stand-up sixgun encounter. To create the fable of the invincible gunfighter, "the fastest man with a six-gun in Texas," Cunningham had to characterize the outcome as the "merest accident, the oddest bit of gun-play recorded in the annals of the Old West." He also included the fiction of Courtright's employment of the "border shift" to show that even in his dying moments this marvelous gunfighter was still exhibiting his vaunted dexterity with pistols.

In his biography Stanley ignored the fanciful Cunningham details, but introduced the ancient "shot him in the back" excuse passed down in the Courtright family.

To any unbiased observer, however, it is clear from the available evidence that, despite having every advantage, when it came to the moment of truth, that instant when decisive action meant the difference between life and death, Jim Courtright, although enjoying every advantage, was beaten by a better gunfighter.

First of all, he was the aggressor in the confrontation, determined to have a showdown and settle his differences with Short. This gave him a certain edge: he knew what he was there for; Short could only guess.

Secondly, Courtright was much better outfitted for a gunfight. As Officer John Fulford's testimony clearly shows, he was wearing two pistols in scabbards hanging from a cartridge belt. Short, on the other hand, had one Colt's revolver with a cut-off barrel that he carried in a tailor-made leather-lined hip pocket.[38] When it came to a draw it is evident that Courtright had a distinct advantage.

Incidentally, it is plainly a canard that Courtright "wore two guns, butts forward, and drew the gun on the right side with his left hand," as reported by Stanley and repeated by later writers.[39] An early day resident of Fort Worth who claimed to know Courtright well, was quoted in 1929:

> He carried two guns at all times and I remember the holsters. They were made of patent leather and he wore them rather far back on each hip. The tops were cut away so that the whole hammer was free and his thumb could get a good grip on the gun while drawing. He used .45 caliber revolvers and they were real guns. Must have killed lots of men— those guns.[40]

A photograph reproduced in Father Stanley's book and purported to be an image of Jim Courtright shows a conventionally holstered pistol far back on the right hip as described. The left side is not visible in this photograph.

Note that Fulford said he took the pistol Courtright had drawn from his right hand and another from the scabbard on his left side. In their effort to identify their hero with the celebrated frontier scout and gunfighter, Wild Bill Hickok, who was known for his shoulder length hair and the butts forward style of gun wear, the Courtright legend makers have simply appropriated some of Hickok's known characteristics.

The *Gazette,* in the initial report of the shooting, suggested another explanation for Courtright's downfall other than the "lucky thumb shot":

> Courtright was a splendid shot. His dexterity with a six shooter was known far and wide. He could manipulate a weapon as well with one hand as another, and in a desperate situation his coolness and self-possession never left him. He was as quick, too, as lightning. It was singular, then, that he failed to fire his revolver at all, and owing beyond a doubt to the failure of his gun to operate smoothly that the tragedy was not a double one. Officers who examined it afterwards found that the cylinder failed to revolve and thus it was that it was useless when the crisis came.[41]

John Fulford, who took the pistol from Courtright's hand, testified at the examining trial the next day that it "was about half cocked and there was a cartridge in it which kept it from revolving smoothly."[42]

Based on these brief comments, some later writers have suggested that Short defeated Courtright because the latter's pistol was defective. It strains credulity that a man who had lived by the gun for so many years could have walked into what he knew was a dangerous situation with a defective six-shooter in his holster. It is much more likely that the same bullet that smashed his thumb also struck the weapon, disabling it, as others have postulated.[43] To accept this explanation, however, it is necessary to concede the obvious: that Short outdrew Courtright and fired before his adversary could cock his pistol and get off a shot. Unable to bow to the obvious, some have offered the feeble excuse that Courtright's pistol must have caught in his watch chain or in the sash around his waist.[44]

No one can know if it was Short's first shot that struck Courtright's thumb as Cunningham contended, or a later shot. In the end, it makes no difference, for with all his advantages and demonstrated dexterity with a six-shooter, Courtright should have gotten off the first shot. Short claimed, and sole eyewitness Jake Johnson confirmed, that Courtright made the first move for a weapon, an assertion to be expected, as it was vital to Short's claim of self-defense. But even if untrue, and Short reached for the pistol in his hip pocket first, Courtright, with his celebrated "lightning" draw and six-guns in scabbards, should have been able to get a weapon out and working before Short could pull a pistol from his hip pocket and fire a shot.

Bat Masterson, who had been involved in gunfights himself and had seen many of the noted practitioners of the art in action, claimed that three qualities were essential to the gunfighter's success: courage, skill with weapons, and deliberation at the critical moment. "I have known men in the West," he said, "whose courage could not be questioned and whose expertness with the pistol was simply marvelous, who fell easy victims before men who added deliberation to the other two qualities."[45] Deliberation in this sense he defined as coolness and nerve in a tense situation. He did not identify Jim Courtright as one of those who lacked that final vital quality, but he might well have, for there is no other plausible explanation for the outcome of the Courtright-Short fight.

From his confrontation with young Bingham Feild in 1875, in which he was almost killed without ever getting off a shot, to his final fatal showdown with Luke Short, Courtright never once demonstrated the ability to remain calm, cool, and deliberate when up against an armed opponent. And the lack of that essential quality cost him his life.

Afterword

"Jim Courtright is a brave man and proved an able and efficient officer in Fort Worth when he was City Marshal here."

Tarrant County Sheriff Walter Maddox,
January 1886.

"This is the West, sir. When the legend becomes fact, print the legend."

Editor Maxwell Scott
in *The Man Who Shot Liberty Valance.*

A gunfight remarkably similar to the Courtright-Short affair that took place on almost the exact spot a little more than a month later apparently escaped the attention of Cunningham, Stanley, and most other chroniclers of the Courtright story. In the early hours of March 16 gamblers Harry Williams and Robert Hayward met in front of the White Elephant and pulled pistols. Williams got off the first shot and put a bullet through his opponent's right eye. Hayward fell dead only twenty-five feet from the spot where Jim Courtright breathed his last.[1]

Today nobody in Fort Worth remembers Harry Williams or Robert Hayward, but, thanks to the legend makers, the names of Jim Courtright and Luke Short, the man who closed out his career, are recognized almost everywhere. The legend has been stretched even beyond that spun by Cunningham and Stanley. Today, as Fort Worth historian Richard Selcer has noted, "it is believed throughout the modern Fort Worth police department that Courtright was city marshal when he was killed and that he died heroically in the line of duty."[2] Of course, neither notion is correct.

The White Elephant Saloon, situated at 308-310 Main Street in Courtright's time, was relocated in the mid-1890s to the 600 block of the same street. Like all the buildings in the central downtown area, it became a casualty of Panther City's transition from a cow town to a great city. Today modern buildings stand where the White Elephant, Ella Blackwell's shooting gallery, John Stewart's Saloon, and other businesses flourished in an earlier time. There is a White Elephant Saloon in Fort Worth, however. A drinking establishment of that name is a popular tourist attraction on Exchange Avenue in the historic stockyards district of present-day Fort Worth.

After the death of Courtright, Luke Short stayed on in the town and enjoyed considerable success as "the king gambler of Fort Worth." When a crooked gambler named Charlie Wright, notorious from Omaha, Nebraska, to Las Vegas, New Mexico, began running brace games in rooms over the Bank Saloon at 1600 Main Street, Short exercised his authority as "king" to put a stop to it. One summer night in 1890 he walked into Wright's gambling den, chased out all the patrons, and tore the place up. Wright did not retaliate, probably in fear of the deadly gunman who had put out Jim Courtright's light. But when Short paid a second visit to Wright's bailiwick the following December, the proprietor, who had been tipped off, was waiting. He unloaded a charge of buckshot at Short, striking him in the back, side, and hand. Reeling from the blast, Short whipped out that short-barreled revolver from his leather-lined pocket and put a round through Wright's wrist. Both men survived, but from that time on Short's health deteriorated.[3]

As his small body wasted away from a combination of illnesses, the ever-faithful Hettie moved him to a health resort at Geuda Springs,

Kansas, and nursed him in his last days. When she knew the end was near she sent for two of Luke's brothers, Henry and Young. They arrived in Geuda Springs too late to say goodbye to their brother. Luke Short was only thirty-nine years old when he died, September 8, 1893. Hettie and the brothers took the body to Fort Worth by train, where for several hours on Sunday, September 10, crowds passed through the chapel of the Gause Funeral Home for one last view of the famed sporting man. A mile-long funeral cortege proceeded to Short's gravesite in Oakwood Cemetery. Hettie Short later married another of Luke's brothers, John, and moved to Arizona where she raised four children and died in 1940.[4]

In the spring of 1954 Jim Courtright's granddaughter, Mrs. Henry Meyerhoff, of Penticton, British Columbia, Canada, came to New Mexico and Texas to research the life of her famous forebear and, she said, "clear his name." Mrs. Meyerhoff was the daughter of Mary Ellen, eldest of the Courtright children. By 1954 Betty Courtright and two of her children, Mary Ellen and Jack, had died in California. The last surviving member of Jim Courtright's family, Mrs. Lulu May Hart, who had been born in Walla Walla, Washington, when Courtright was a fugitive, was now a resident of San Simon, California.[5]

In Albuquerque Howard Bryan, feature writer for the *Albuquerque Tribune,* interviewed Mrs. Meyerhoff, who told him a number of stories about her grandfather that she had heard from her mother. She also showed him several artifacts passed down in the family. There was a leather wallet containing a Christmas card that Jim was said to have been carrying when Luke Short killed him. Both wallet and card had been gifts from Betty Courtright to her husband only a few weeks before he died. There was a beaded tobacco pouch made, it was believed, by an Indian woman from the top of one of Wild Bill Hickok's boots and presented to Courtright as a gift by the great scout and gunfighter. There was a single pendant earring said to be the mate of the one Courtright playfully shot from Betty's ear.[6]

Mrs. Meyerhoff went on to Fort Worth where she had her grandfather's remains removed to a new location in Oakwood Cemetery. The site was only about two hundred feet from Luke Short's final place of rest. At the head of her grandfather's grave Mrs. Meyerhoff placed an impressive memorial stone. Its inscription memorialized the Courtright legend for all time:

Jim "Longhaired" Courtright

1845-1887

U. S. Army Scout, U. S. Marshal,

Frontiersman, Pioneer, Representative

Of a Class of Men Now Passing From

Texas, Who, Whatever Their Faults,

Were the Type of That Brave,

Courageous Manhood Which

Commands Respect and Admiration

It was at this time that Father Stanley met Mr. and Mrs. Henry Meyerhoff and began collecting the Courtright family tales that became the basis of his eulogistic biography of "Longhaired Jim" published three years later. Despite his many faults, Courtright was idolized by his children. They accepted all the favorable and rejected the unfavorable stories about him and passed on their heroic conception of the man to their children.

Mrs. Meyerhoff showed Father Stanley a fireman's shirt that had belonged to her grandfather. It had been made for a special celebration honoring the Fort Worth fire companies and bore Courtright's initials. Dark stains on the shirt, Mrs. Meyerhoff explained, told a story of Jim Courtright's gallantry, courage and fighting ability. The shirt had been

Mrs. Henry Meyerhoff stands beside her grandfather's new burial site in Fort Worth's Oakwood Cemetery. *Author's personal collection.*

stained, she said, by the blood of the great heavyweight-boxing champion, John L. Sullivan, who had twice been knocked down by City Marshal Courtright.

Sullivan was touring the saloons of Fort Worth, celebrating a ring victory in Waco the night before, according to this story, when he met a woman carrying a baby and forced her off the sidewalk. Observing this ungentlemanly behavior, Courtright stepped up to the prizefighter and demanded he apologize to the lady. Sullivan refused and Courtright, slipping on the "triple brace of brass knuckles" he always carried, punched the great prizefighter in the nose.

Blood spurted out and the champ went down. Courtright lifted Sullivan by the shoulder and told him to

Luke Short's gravestone, located only two hundred feet from Courtright's grave. *Author's personal collection.*

apologize. Again the fighter refused. Again he went down. Courtright left him lying in the gutter and himself escorted the woman and her baby across the street. When Sullivan slept it off he did nothing to 'get even' with the brass knuckle swinging marshal, saying he deserved what he got.[7]

Of course, had anything like this ever happened editor Buckley B. Paddock would have pounced on the story and emblazoned it across the pages of the *Democrat*. Fort Worth old timers would have been recounting it ever since. Like much of the Courtright myth, perpetuated in the family oral tradition, the John L. Sullivan yarn probably originated as one of Jim Courtright's "windies." He always liked to link his name with celebrities: he had saved the life of John A. Logan, he had scouted with Wild Bill Hickok, he had been a featured performer in Buffalo Bill's' Wild West Show, he had twice knocked down the great heavyweight boxing champion, John L. Sullivan. He spun the tales, his family believed every word, and the legend makers immortalized the yarns in print.

Timothy Isaiah "Jim" Courtright, a rough man in a rough time, was the right sort of individual to ride herd on turbulent Fort Worth as city marshal during its cow town period. A drinker, a gambler and a brawler himself, he understood the drinking, gambling, brawling types who caroused in Hell's Half Acre, and they related to and admired him. With very little scholastic education and no experience or training in law enforcement when he pinned on a badge, he nevertheless did a remarkable job as the chief police official of one of the toughest and most uproarious towns in the West.

Although he was involved in potentially fatal scraps with Bingham Feild, N. H. Wilson, O. C. Cheney, John C. Morris, Joe Young, Bud Davis, and probably others that went unrecorded, Courtright was never known to have killed a man during his years in Fort Worth. Had he not gone to New Mexico he might never have been branded a killer. But he did go to New Mexico, and he did participate in the brutal murders of the two inoffensive homesteaders in the American Valley. He seemed

The legend of "Longhaired Jim Courtright" is forever engraved on the stone placed at his new resting place by his granddaughter. *Author's personal collection.*

to exult in notoriety and played the role of the deadly, swift-handed gunfighting mankiller to the hilt. In so doing he sowed the seeds of his legend, seeds that were nurtured and brought to full bloom by Eugene Cunningham, Father Stanley Crocchiola, and their followers.

But Courtright's emerging legend also cost him his life, because a *real* gunfighter, a quiet, unassuming gambler named Luke Short, took no chances that his adversary's reputation was bogus. In the moment of truth Short acted with deadly skill and efficiency and shot Jim Courtright dead.

Once created, legends die hard. The legend of "Longhaired Jim" Courtright, "the fastest man with a sixgun in Texas," lives on, long after it should have been exploded along with the five cartridges in Luke Short's cut-down revolver.

INTRODUCTION

[1] Eugene Cunningham, "Long-Haired Jim Courtright," *Frontier Times*, (February 1929): 202.

[2] F. Stanley, *Longhair Jim Courtright, Two-Gun Marshal of Fort Worth* (Denver, Co.: World Press, 1957).

[3] Ramon Adams, *Six-Guns and Saddle Leather* (Norman: University of Oklahoma Press, 1969), 608-609.

[4] Thomas Penfield, *Western Sheriffs and Marshals* (New York: Grosset & Dunlap, Publishers, 1955), xii.

CHAPTER ONE.

[1] Joseph G. Rosa, *They Called Him Wild Bill: The Life and Adventures of James Butler Hickok* (Norman: University of Oklahoma Press, 1979), 8-9.

[2] Alfred Henry Lewis, *The Sunset Trail* (New York: A. S. Barnes & Co., 1905). Magazine articles include "Diplomacy in Dodge," (*Metropolitan Magazine*, April 1904); "An Invasion of Dodge," (*Colliers*, April 16, 1904); "The Fatal Gratitude of Mr. Kelly, (*Colliers*, September 17, 1904); "The Deep Strategy of Mr. Masterson," (*Saturday Evening Post*, December 17, 1904); "The King of the Gun-Players: William Barclay Masterson," (*Human Life*, November 1907).

[3] John Marvin Hunter and Noah H. Rose, *The Album of Gunfighters* (Bandera, Tex.: n. p.,1951), 159; Ed Bartholomew, *Biographical Album of Western Gunfighters* (Houston: Frontier Press of Texas, 1958); Denis McLoughlin, *Wild and Woolly: An Encyclopedia of the Old West* (Garden City, N.Y.: Doubleday & Company, Inc., 1975), 114-115; Bill O'Neal, *Encyclopedia of Western Gun-Fighters* (Norman: University of Oklahoma Press, 1979), 74-75; Carl Sifakis, *The Encyclopedia of American Crime* (New York: Smithmark Publishers, 1992), 180-181; Jay Robert Nash, *Encyclopedia of Western Lawmen and Outlaws* (New York: Paragon House, 1992), 87-88; Leon Claire Metz, *The Encyclopedia of Lawmen, Outlaws, and Gunfighters* (New York: Checkmark Press, 2003), 52-53

[4] Martin Donell Kohout, "Eugene Cunningham," in *The New Handbook of Texas*, Vol. 2 (Austin: State Historical Association, 1996), 448.

[5] Eugene Cunningham, "Long-Haired Jim Courtright," *Frontier Times* (February 1929): 202. The article originally appeared in a publication of the Hicks-Hayward Company of El Paso, manufacturers of "Rodeo Outdoors Clothes."

[6] W. B. "Bat" Masterson, "Luke Short," *Human Life* (April 1907). Despite Masterson's clearly expressed contempt for Courtright, a Fort Worth newspaperman as late as 1949 added a gratuitous and patently false element to the Courtright legend with an assertion that "Long-Haired Jim" came to Fort Worth from Colorado to take the city marshal's job at "the recommendation of his friend, the fabled Bat Masterson of Dodge City, Kan" (*Fort Worth Star Telegram*, October 30, 1949).

[7] Eugene Cunningham, *Triggernometry: A Gallery of Gunfighters* (Caldwell, Idaho: The Caxton Printers, Ltd., 1962), 205-206, 212.

8   Ramon Adams, premier collector and critic of gunfighter books, included
    Cunningham's work in his 1976 compilation, *The Adams One-Fifty: A Checklist of
    the 150 Most Important Books on Western Outlaws and Lawmen* (Austin, Tex.:
    Jenkins Publishing Company, 1976), 32, commenting: "This book has become a
    standard work and is reliable on most points" (32). The Western Writers of
    America in 1986 named *Triggernometry* one of the best non-fiction western books
    of all time.

9   Owen P. White, *My Texas 'Tis of Thee* (New York: G. P. Putnam's Sons), 78.

10 George D. Hendricks, *The Bad Man of the West* (San Antonio, Tex.: The Naylor
    Co., Publishers, 1941), 66.

11 Jack Martin, *Border Boss, Captain John R. Hughes, Texas Ranger*, (San Antonio,
    Tex.: The Naylor Co., Publishers, 1942): 27.

12 Carroll C. Holloway, *Texas Gun Lore* (San Antonio, Tex.: The Naylor Co.,
    Publishers, 1951), 192.

13 Stanley, *Longhair Jim Courtright*, ix, 68. The author contradicts himself a few
    pages later: "About his waist he wore two six-shooters, butts facing front, which
    normally meant cross-body draw, but Courtright trained himself to use the right
    hand for the gun on the right side and the left for the gun on the left side" (80).
    This depiction of Courtright's gun-carrying method seems to have originated with
    Dr. Will Woody, who claimed to have lived in the Courtright home at one time.
    Dr. Woody, the son of Courtright's close friend, Abram ("Ab" or "Abe") Woody,
    said that in the house Courtright carried his pistols in a sash. See Oliver Knight,
    Fort Worth: Outpost on the Trinity (Norman: University of Oklahoma Press, 1953),
    80, 266. In a photograph of Courtright reproduced in Father Stanley's book he is
    shown wearing a pistol in the conventional position on his right hip and not in the
    manner described.

14 Carl W. Breihan, "Luke Short's Mystery Gun Fight," *Real West* (March 1961): 32.

15 Cunningham, *Triggernometry*, 203-204. John Alexander Logan, born February 9,
    1826 in Jackson County, Illinois, served as a lieutenant in the U. S. Army 1846-
    48. He began law practice in 1851 and the following year was elected to the
    Illinois legislature. In 1855 he married a seventeen-year-old Missouri girl named,
    coincidentally, Mary Cunningham. Logan was elected to Congress from the
    eleventh Illinois district in 1858. With the outbreak of hostilities in 1861 he was
    made colonel of the Thirty-first Illinois Regiment and in 1862 promoted to gener-
    al. From 1866 to 1870 he served in the U. S. Congress as representative-at-large
    from Illinois. Elected to the U. S. Senate from Illinois in 1871 he served until his
    death at Washington, D. C. on December 26, 1886. In 1884 he was the vice pres-
    idential candidate on the Republican ticket with James G. Blaine.

16 Stanley, *Longhair Jim* Courtright, 2-7. Photographs of five women, all identified as
    Courtright's sisters, appear in Father Stanley's book, although he states clearly in
    the text that there were only four daughters. The brother, said to have been born
    four years after Timothy, is never named. The 1880 U. S. Census for Tarrant
    County, Texas, would seem to support the information provided by the family.
    Enumerated at Fort Worth was T. I. Courtright, born in Illinois, age thirty-five,
    which would indicate a birth in 1845. His father was said to have been born in
    Illinois and his mother in New York.

17 Ibid., 25.

18 Ibid., 39.

19 Ibid., 41-42.

20 Ibid., 55-56.

21 Ibid., 57-58.

22 Denis McLaughlin, *Wild and Woolly*, (New York: Doubleday, 1975), 114.

23 Harry Sinclair Drago, *The Legend Makers: Tales of the Old-Time Peace Officers and Desperadoes of the Frontier* (New York: Dodd, Mead & Company, 1975), 109-110.

24 Douglas Ellison to the author, November 6, 1998.

25 Shari Stelling, State Historical Society of Iowa, to the author, May 5, 2000.

26 John Daly, Director, Illinois State Archives, to the author, May 23, 2000.

27 Stanley, *Longhair Jim Courtright*, 47.

28 Joseph G. Rosa to the author, January 21, 1997.

29 Linda McDowell, The Butler Center for Arkansas Studies, to the author, April 26, May 9, 2002.

30 One oblique newspaper reference to the possible unusual length of Courtright's hair appeared in the *Dallas Morning News* of January 21, 1886. Reporting on Courtright's return to Fort Worth after more than a year's absence, the paper said one of the questions asked of him was, "When did you get your hair cut?"

31 *Fort Worth Daily Democrat*, March 30, 1879.

32 Arthur C. Wakely, *Omaha, the Gate City, and Douglas County, Nebraska* (Chicago: The S. J. Clarke Company, 1917), 118. Courtright is not listed in the Omaha city directories for the years 1866-73, nor was he enumerated in the 1870 Nebraska census (Cynthia E. Monroe, Nebraska State Historical Society to the author, January 9, 1997).

33 William R. Cox, *Luke Short and His Era* (Garden City, N. Y.: Doubleday and Co., 1961), 153.

CHAPTER TWO

1 *Fort Worth Weekly Democrat*, December 18, 1875.

2 *Galveston Daily News*, December 18, 1875.

3 *Fort Worth Weekly Democrat*, December 25, 1875.

4 B. B. Paddock, *Early Days in Fort Worth: Much of What I Saw and Part of Which I Was* (Fort Worth, Tex.: n.p., n.d.), 6.

5 Richard F. Selcer, *Hell's Half Acre: The Life and Legend of a Red Light District* (Fort Worth: Texas Christian University Press, 1991), 67.

6 Ibid., 68.

7 Ibid.

8 *Fort Worth Weekly Democrat*, April 8, 1876.

9 Ibid., April 22, 1876.

10 Ibid., May 20, 1876.

11 *Fort Worth Daily Democrat*, August 2, 1876.

12 Ibid., May 1, 1879.

13 *Fort Worth Weekly Democrat*, May 27, 1876.

[14] Charles Francis Colcord, *Autobiography of Charles Francis Colcord* (Tulsa, Okla.: Privately printed by C. C. Helmerich, 1970), 45-47. George and Mag Wood ran a succession of notorious dancehalls in the boomtowns of Kansas and Texas in the 1870s. George was shot to death in their "Red Light" establishment at Caldwell, Kansas, in August 1881.

[15] W. E. Oglesby in Jim Lanning and Judy Lanning, *Texas Cowboys: Memories of the Early Days,* (College Station: Texas A & M University Press, 1984), 8-9.

[16] *Fort Worth Daily Democrat,* July 20, 1876.

[17] Ibid., September 19, 1876

[18] Ibid., October 8, 1876.

[19] Ibid., December 8, 24, 1876

[20] Selcer, *Hell's Half Acre,* 93.

[21] *Fort Worth Daily Democrat,* July 15, 1876.

[22] Ibid., October 15, 1876.

[23] Ibid., October 20, 1876.

[24] Ibid., March 21, 1877.

[25] Ibid., March 23, 1877.

[26] Ibid., August 8, 1876.

[27] Joseph G. Rosa and Waldo E. Koop, *Rowdy Joe Lowe, Gambler With a Gun* (Norman and London, University of Oklahoma Press, 1989), 107. Joseph Rosa and the late Waldo Koop, both meticulous researchers, confessed to finding little information about Mollie Field. One wonders if the lady was related to the highly regarded Field family of Fort Worth or the equally respected Feild family of doctors.

[28] *Fort Worth Daily Democrat,* September 29, 1876; *Jacksboro Frontier Echo,* May 18, 1877.

[29] Selcer, *Hell's Half Acre,* 76-77.

[30] *Fort Worth Daily Democrat,* December 21, 1876.

[31] Ibid., December 22, 1876.

[32] Ibid., January 10, 1877.

[33] Cause No. 1476, State of Texas v. T. I. Courtright and W. A. Clower, assault with intent to murder, March 20, 1877.

[34] *Fort Worth Daily Democrat,* January 13, 1877.

[35] Ibid., January 16, 1877.

[36] Ibid., January 30, 1877. Later in the year "Marshal Courtright gave his special attention [to] a boisterous individual [with] the terrifying name 'Rocky Mountain Bill'" (Ibid., October 19, 1877).

[37] Ibid., March 17, 1877.

[38] *Fort Worth Standard,* March 27, 1877, quoted in Knight, *Fort Worth,* 80.

[39] *Fort Worth Daily Democrat,* March 7, 1877.

[40] Ibid.

[41] Ibid., July 29, 1880.

CHAPTER THREE:

[1] Also in the race were J. W. Williams, endorsed by the *Democrat*; O. F. Cheney, with whom Courtright would tangle later that year; George S. Andrews; J. H. Van Eaton; White Collins; W. L. Holt; and Lem Grisham.

[2] *Fort Worth Daily Democrat*, April 25, 1877.

[3] Ibid., June 5, 1877.

[4] Ibid., May 12, 1877.

[5] Ibid., January 10, 11, February 28, 1878.

[6] Ibid., September 25, 1877.

[7] Ibid., October 6, 1877.

[8] Ibid., February 13, 14, 16, 1878. It would seem that John Witt was not a very popular fellow in Fort Worth. Only a month before Rowdy Joe Lowe had been fined $1 in police court for assaulting the man (Ibid., January 13, 1878).

[9] Ibid., December 25, 1877.

[10] Ibid., January 5, 1878.

[11] Ibid., May 23, 27, 30, 1877. The latter issue reported that a campaign by the marshal to rid the city of stray dogs had resulted in sixty-four dead animals with "several precincts to hear from."

[12] Ibid., April 21, 1877.

[13] Ibid., June 17, 1877.

[14] Ibid., June 19, 1877.

[15] Ibid. Additional plaudits appeared in the same issue of the paper for the speedy apprehension by the police of two burglars who had broken into a wholesale liquor house on Houston Street: "Much credit is due the Marshal and his assistants in their promptness in capturing the burglars."

[16] Paddock, *Early Days in Fort Worth*, 31.

[17] *Fort Worth Daily Democrat*, October 20, 1877.

[18] Ibid., October 21, 1877.

[19] Ibid., September 25, 1877.

[20] Ibid., February 2, 8, March 3, 1878.

[21] W. B. "Bat" Masterson, "Ben Thompson," *Human Life* (January 1907).

[22] *Fort Worth Daily Democrat*, July 13, 1877; Karen Holliday Tanner, *Doc Holliday: A Family Portrait*, (Norman: University of Oklahoma Press, 1998), 106-108.

[23] *Fort Worth Daily Democrat*, January 26, 1878. By making bond, Wyatt Earp avoided the possible ignomy of an overnight stay in the noisome city hoosegow. On January 25, the day of Earp's arrest, the *Democrat* noted: "Marshal Courtright will be doing a commendable act by working the streets with the 'vag gang' who are now in the calaboose." Wyatt Earp was not a vagrant and, as a respected gambler and sometime police officer, it is highly unlikely Courtright would have further humiliated him by putting him to work on the streets.

[24] Ibid., January 22, 1878. Professional gambler Frank Loving and a man named Sam Banks were arrested and fined $3 each in February 1878 for assault and battery. The following year Loving would gain a kind of gunfighting celebrity by shooting

and killing Levi Richardson in the Long Branch Saloon in Dodge City, Kansas. In 1882 he was shot and killed in Trinidad, Colorado, by John Allen, another gambler.

25 Ibid., February 17, 1878. The paper would report a month later that Billy Simms, seeing "the error of his ways," had reformed a taken a job in a printing shop in Hot Springs, Arkansas.(March 5, 1878). But the desperate gambling life was in his blood and Simms returned to Texas and settled in San Antonio where he was associated with Jack Harris and Joe Foster, two other prominent gambling men, in the operation of the Vaudeville Theatre, the most notorious gambling, drinking and whoring establishment in the city. When his old mentor, Ben Thompson, shot and killed Harris in the place in July 1882, Simms swore revenge. It took him almost two years, but on March 11, 1884, Thompson and his companion, noted gunfighter King Fisher, were shotgunned to death by hidden gunmen in tbe Vaudeville. Simms and Foster were believed to have arranged the assassination but were never indicted, and the murders went unsolved.

26 Robert J. "Uncle Bob" Winders would later be in on the mining excitement at Tombstone, Arizona, where he had gambling and saloon interests as well as min- ing partnerships with Wyatt Earp and his brothers. See Allen Barra, *Inventing Wyatt Earp: His Life and Many Legends* (New York: Carroll & Graf Publishers, Inc., 1998), 71-72; Don Chaput, *Virgil Earp: Western Peace Officer* (Encampment, Wyo.: Affiliated Writers of America, Inc, 1994), 63. Also in Fort Worth at this time was a young lawyer named William R. McLaury, who would lose two brothers at the famous OK Corral fight in Tombstone and would go to the mining camp seeking revenge on their killers, the Earps and Doc Holliday.

27 *Fort Worth Daily Democrat,* June 12, 1877.

28 Ibid., July 10, 1877.

29 Ibid., July 10, 11, 12, 1877. Not everything went sour for Joe Lowe that summer. In August he won $340 and a gold watch and chain in a horse race bet and a few days later got another acquittal in county court of keeping a disorderly house (Ibid., August 7, 10, 1877). Perhaps not coincidentally, Lowe departed Fort Worth in April 1879 when Courtright lost his city marshal job. He went to Colorado and became a prominent vice figure in Canon City, Leadville, and finally Denver, where he was shot and killed by a former police officer in 1899.

30 Ibid., May 4, 1877.

31 Mrs. Henry Meyerhoff, Courtright's granddaughter, told this story in 1954 to both Father Stanley in Fort Worth (Stanley, *Longhair Jim Courtright,* 212) and newspa- perman Howard Bryan in Albuquerque. It was intended to impress the listener with Courtright's amazing skill with a handgun, but, as Howard Bryan notes, "she did not say what her grandmother's reaction was to this display of marksmanship." See Howard Bryan, *True Tales of the American Southwest: Pioneer Recollections of Frontier Adventures* (Santa Fe, N. Mex.: Clear Light Publishers, 1998), 48-50.

32 *Fort Worth Daily Democrat,* August 16, 1877. The Courtright residence was on Calhoun, between First and Weatherford. During the years they lived in Fort Worth the Courtrights also lived at 515 Belknap at the corner of Burnett and on Second Street, between Jones and Grove (Stanley, *Longhair Jim Courtright,* 88); Mack Williams, "In Old Fort Worth: A Series on the Life of Jim Courtright," *Fort Worth News-Tribune,* October 17, 1986).

33 *Fort Worth Daily Democrat,* March 3, 1878.

34 Ibid., August 12, 1877. The *Dallas Daily Herald* said that Courtright and Cheney were "full of tanglefoot" (August 15, 1877). According to the *Weatherford*

Exponent the crowd "became so turbulent that fears were entertained of a riot." This paper was still remarking on the affair two weeks later: "Fort Worth had a horse race a few weeks ago which ended in a big row, the most disgraceful ever witnessed in the city. The city marshal was pounded to a jelly, a deputy sheriff was knocked on the head and the sheriff was struck in the face with a revolver by a gang of roughs" (August 18, September 1, 1877).

35 *Fort Worth Daily Democrat,* August 12, 1877.

36 Evidently Courtright was held entirely responsible for the disturbance. Cheney was never charged.

37 Cause No. 15568, State of Texas v. T. I. Courtright, Malfeasance in Office, August 21, 1877.

38 *Fort Worth Daily Democrat,* October 14, 1877.

39 *Dallas Daily Herald,* February 11, 1880.

CHAPTER FOUR

1 Knight, *Fort Worth,* 102.

2 *Fort Worth Daily Democrat,* February 1, 1878.

3 Ibid., February 2, 1878.

4 Ibid., February 21, 1878.

5 Ibid., February 17, 1878.

6 *Dallas Daily Herald,* May 17, 18, 1878; Glenn Shirley, *Heck Thomas: Frontier Marshal* (Norman: University of Oklahoma Press, 1981), 30.

7 Letter from Thomas Martin, private secretary to Texas Governor R. B. Hubbard, to T. J. [sic] Courtright, Fort Worth City Marshal, September 24, 1877: "In reply to your letter…, His Excellency, the Governor, instructs me to inform you that there is no reward offered by the State for the arrest of George McCarty…." (Letter Press Book #320, Records of Governor R. B. Hubbard, Texas State Library).

8 *Fort Worth Daily Democrat,* December 11, 21, 1877

9 Letter Press Book #320, Records of Gov. R. B. Hubbard, Texas State Library. It is suspected that Courtright had someone else write his letter to the governor. Other Courtright correspondence reveals that his writing ability was considerably poorer than this example would indicate.

10 *Fort Worth Daily Democrat,* June 9, 11, 23, 1878; Charles L. Martin, *A Sketch of Sam Bass, the Bandit* (Norman: University of Oklahoma Press, 1968), 118-19; Wayne Gard, *Sam Bass* (New York: Houghton Mifflin Co., 1936), 165; Selcer, *Hell's Half Acre,* 105-106; Rick Miller, *Sam Bass & Gang* (Austin, Tex.: State House Press, 1999), 214, 218.

11 *Fort Worth Daily Democrat,* October 6, 1878; Richard F. Selcer, "Cowboy-Booted Gumshoes: The Private Detective in Texas," *True West,* (February 1992).

12 *Fort Worth Daily Democrat,* November 17, 1878.

13 *Fort Worth Daily Democrat,* November 9, 1878. An interesting but inexplicable addendum followed the account of this arrest. In October Texas Rangers had brought John Wesley Hardin, after his conviction for murder, to Fort Worth to catch the train to Huntsville penitentiary. The appearance of the notorious Texas outlaw and gunfighter created an uproar in town which was duly reported in the

Democrat, together with a reporter's interview with Hardin. Courtright was never mentioned. The story covering the arrest of Culbreth by Courtright a month later, however, added this: "During the trouble between Hardin and Marshall [sic] Courtright [Culbreth] espoused the cause of Hardin and it is said threatened to shoot Jim at the first opportunity."

14 Ibid., November 28, 1878.

15 Ibid., March 8, 1879.

16 Ibid., March 26, 1879.

17 Ibid., March 30, 1879. It was in this piece that the erroneous contention was made that Courtright "had many years experience as marshal of frontier towns, having filled the office in Omaha for a number of years to the perfect satisfaction of its citizens."

18 Ibid., March 26, 1879.

19 Ibid., March 20, 21, 1879; Selcer, *Hell's Half Acre,* 113

20 Fabric destroying "chintz bugs," like the boll weevil in the cotton belt, were thoroughly hated. Political foes and enemies were often branded with the derogatory terms.

21 *Fort Worth Daily Democrat*, March 25, 26, 27, 29, 1879.

22 Ibid., April 2, 1879.

CHAPTER FIVE

1 Cunningham, *Triggernometry*, 204-205.

2 Stanley, *Longhaired Jim Courtright*, 58, 91.

3 Cunningham, *Triggernometry,* 205.

4 Stanley, *Longhair Jim Courtright*, 58-59.

5 Selcer, *Hell's Half Acre*, 192-93; Nellie Snyder Yost, *Buffalo Bill: His Family, Friends, Fame, Failures, and Fortunes* (Chicago: The Swallow Press, Inc., 1979), 147; Don Russell, *The Wild West: A History of the Wild West Shows* (Fort Worth, Tex.: Amon Carter Museum of Western Art, 1978), 21.

6 *Fort Worth Daily Democrat*, February 8, July 20, 25, 1880. The "My" Theater was the former Centennial, kept by Joe Lowe. Animosity between Courtright and Morris dated all the way back to 1877 when Morris was the foreman of the grand jury that indicted Courtright for malfeasance in office.

7 Ibid., October 27, 1880. This was not the first reference by the paper to Courtright's "lead mine." An item in the issue of April 25, 1877 read: "Jim Courtright's lead mine was a little restless yesterday evening and he was a little roiled, which only makes him a better marshal."

8 Ibid., October 27, 1880. The story of the near duel was carried in papers across the state. The *Houston Daily Post* called Courtright and Morris "the two bullies of Fort Worth" (October 31, 1880).

9 Tarrant County Criminal Docket, "State of Texas vs. T. I. Courtright," Cause No. 1001C.

10 *Dallas Daily Herald*, December 2, 1880.

11 *Texas Penal Code*, February 21, 1879, p. 82, Chapter Sixteen (Dueling), 82; Cause No. 2230, State of Texas vs. T.I. Courtright, Unlawfully accepting a challenge to fight a duel with deadly weapons.

12 *Fort Worth Daily Democrat*, May 1, 1879.

13 Ibid, December 21, 22, 1881; January 21, 1882; *Houston Daily Post*, December 22, 1881. Rayner's bondsmen were local attorney Harry Furman, George Holland, who had succeeded Joe Lowe as manager of the "My" Theater, and Jake Johnson, cattleman and gambler, who would figure prominently in Courtright's final days in Fort Worth.

14 *Fort Worth Daily Democrat and Advance*, December 23, 1881.

15 Ibid., February 21, 23, 1882.

16 Ibid., March 3, April 6, 1882.

17 *Silver City Enterprise*, July 13, 1883.

18 Gary L. Roberts, "Gem Saloon Shootout," *Wild West*, June 1992. According to one report, Rayner was back in Fort Worth and present in the Merchant's Restaurant when Courtright made his dramatic escape from the rangers in 1884 (*Dallas Morning News*, June 9, 1929).

19 *Galveston Daily* News, November 12, 1875.

20 Ibid., January 31, 1880.

21 *Fort Worth Democrat and Advance*, February 2, 1882.

22 E. N. Herring, "Gunfight at Hunnewell," *Wild West*, August 2002. Prominent among the cowboy troublemakers at Hunnewell were the Halsell brothers, Oscar and Harry, who later became prosperous and highly respected cattlemen of Oklahoma and Texas. Another was "Little Dick" West, who turned outlaw, joined Bill Doolin's gang, and was shot and killed in 1898 by a posse led by famed Oklahoma lawmen Bill Tilghman and Heck Thomas.

23 *Dallas Daily Herald*, September 16, 1883.

24 In August 1884 Hamilton Rayner and his assistant, Ed Scotten, were shot in a fight with the cowboys. Scotten's wounds proved fatal and he died on September 2. Rayner survived. But, apparently having his fill of frontier violence, resigned in October and moved to New Orleans (Herring, "Gunfight at Hunnewell"). Will Rayner and Ed Scotten's brother Frank reportedly went from El Paso to Hunnewell seeking revenge, but nothing came of it (Roberts, "Gem Saloon Shootout").

25 *Dallas Daily Herald*, July 17, 23, 30, August 3, 1884.

26 Ibid., September 10, October 16, 17, 1884.

27 Ibid., October 24, 25, December 25, 1884; April 23, June 16, 17, July 22, August 18, September 11, 18, 1885.

28 *Fort Worth Daily Democrat*, December 11, 1877; January 11, 1878.

29 Ibid., November 21, 22, 1878. Almost a year later Hearn came to trial. For some reason Woody failed to appear to testify against him and was fined one hundred dollars (Ibid., October 29, 1879).

30 Ibid., May 14, 1879.

31 Ibid., February 25, March 1, 12, 20, 1879; *Galveston Daily News*, March 23, 29, 1879.

32 *Galveston Daily News*, April 12, 19, 25, 1879. Starrett was said to be the son of Robert Starrett of the Kentucky legislature (Ibid., May 2, 1879).

33 Ibid., May 24, 1879.

34 *Dallas Daily Herald*, February 11, 1880.

35 Ibid., May 8, 1880.

36 *Fort Worth Daily Democrat*, May 28, 1879.

37 Ibid., July 17, 1879.

38 Ibid., August 7, 8, 13, 1879. When Sheriff Edmondson found that a posseman named Jack Morris, left to guard the wounded John Jones, had allowed the prisoner to escape, he threw him in jail. That night twenty-five masked men overpowered the jail guards and shot Morris to death in his cell.

39 *Galveston Daily News*, December 4, 1879.

40 Jim McIntire, *Early Days in Texas: A Trip to Hell and Heaven* (Norman: University of Oklahoma Press, 1992), 69.

41 *Fort Worth Daily Democrat*, November 1, 1879.

42 McIntire, *Early Days in Texas*, 69-70.

43 *Galveston Daily News*, November 9, 1879; *Fort Worth Daily Democrat*, November 11, 1879.

44 *Galveston Daily News*, November 22, 23, 25, 30, December 1, 2, 4, 21, 28, 1879; *Fort Worth Daily Democrat*, November 26, 1879; James M. Oswald, "History of Fort Elliott," *Panhandle-Plains Historical Review* 32 (1959): 1-59; Jane Eppinga, *Henry Ossian Flipper, West Point's First Black Graduate* (Plano, Tex.: Republic of Texas Press, 1996), 63. Lieutenant Flipper was not court-martialed and thrown out of the Army over this affair as Jim McIntire asserted (*Early Days in Texas*, 70). While serving in a quartermaster capacity at Fort Davis, Texas, in 1882 Flipper received a dishonorable discharge when irregularities were found in his financial records. In 1976 the army rescinded this sentence and granted him a posthumous honorable discharge.

CHAPTER SIX.

1 *Galveston Daily News*, May 4, 1880; *Dallas Daily Herald*, May 4, 1880.

2 *Fort Worth Daily Democrat*, September 26, 1880.

3 Farmer was so well liked by Sheriff Pat Garrett of Lincoln County, New Mexico, that when that noted lawman shot and killed the notorious outlaw "Billy the Kid" Bonney, he made Farmer a present of Billy's hat and cartridge belt. "The hat is after the style of the Mexican sombrero, though it is evidently American made," said the *Fort Worth Democrat and Advance* of December 27, 1881. "It is almost white and has been a little worn. Around the band is written the words, 'Billy Bowny, alias Billy the Kid.' The cartridge belt is of red morocco, well quilted and lined. It is well filled with cartridges."

4 Ibid., April 6, 1881. The name of the paper changed that year.

5 Ibid., March 16, 21, 1881.

6 Ibid., March 26, 1881.

7 Ibid., April 15, 1881.

8 Ibid., August 11, 1881.

9 Ibid., April 11, 1882. Courtright's short sojourn in California apparently was the basis of the erroneous newspaper report a few years later that after losing his job

as Fort Worth city marshal he had "married a woman in Los Angeles [and] obtained work at the Calico mines in that vicinity" (*New Orleans Times-Democrat*, April 23, 1885.)

10 *Fort Worth Democrat and Advance*, May 22, 1882.

11 *Dallas Daily Herald*, May 24, 1882.

12 Ibid., May 27, 1882; *Fort Worth Democrat and* Advance, May 28, 1882.

13 *Sumner County Press*, June 29, 1882.

14 G. D. Freeman, *Midnight and Noonday* (Norman: University of Oklahoma Press, 1984), 207.

15 Cox, *Luke Short and his Era*, 154. This story was drawn from the *Dallas Morning News*, June 9, 1929.

16 A November edition of the *Las Vegas Optic*, quoted in F. Stanley, *The Lake Valley (New Mexico) Story* (Pep, Tex.: n. p., 1964), 6.

17 Ibid.

18 McIntire, *Early Days in Texas*, 11-17.

19 Ibid., 16-19.

20 *Albuquerque Journal*, June 8, 1885.

21 T. C. Richardson, "A Quart of Bullets," *Frontier Times* (August 1937): 494.

22 *Las Vegas Optic*, November 3, 1882.

23 Lou Blachly interview with Ellen Lucy Capp, May 1952.

24 Cunningham, *Triggernometry*, 206.

25 Stanley, *Longhair Jim Courtright,* 91.

26 In his little monograph, *The Lake Valley Story,* Father Stanley corrected his mistake and told of McIntire's role.

27 *Fort Worth Democrat and Advance*, August 18, 19, 1882; *El Paso Lone Star,* December 20, 1882.

28 Ibid., December 30, 1882.

29 McIntire, *Early Days in Texas,* 76.

30 Cunningham, *Triggernometry,* 206; Stanley, *Longhair Jim Courtright*, 91-92; Stanley, *The Lake Valley Story,* 10. These unverified claims have been repeated almost verbatim by later writers, i.e.Ralph Looney, *Haunted Highways: The Ghost Towns of New Mexico* (New York; Hastings House, 1968), 173. Other contributors to the Courtright legend have expanded on the undocumented claims. In his 1986 series of articles on Courtright in the *Fort Worth News-Tribune* Mack Williams wrote that "in the newly-discovered gold [sic] fields and ranches around Lake Valley and American Valley, Courtright killed 14 men" (October 14, 1886).

31 Cunningham, *Triggernometry*, 207.

32 Frederick Nolan, "'Boss Rustler,' The Life and Crimes of John Kinney," *True West* (September 1996), 14; (October 1996), 13.

33 *Dallas Daily Herald,* April 3, 1883. Fountain's report is quoted in Stanley, *Longhair Jim Courtright,* 93-98; Stanley, *The Lake Valley Story,* 10; Larry D. Ball, *The United States Marshals of New Mexico and Arizona Territories, 1846-1912* (Albuquerque: University of New Mexico Press, 1978), 148-149. An enigmatic item appeared in the January 27, 1883 issue of the *El Paso Lone Star:* "Governor

Sheldon refused to accept the resignation of the Lake Valley guards, but he summarily dismissed them." The identity of the "guards" was never made clear.

[34]   Fountain report, quoted in Stanley, *Longhair Jim Courtright*, 93.

[35]   The name is given variously in Fountain's reports and newspaper stories as "Leland," "Zillard," "Dillard," and "Gillliard." McIntire called him "Butch Hill" (McIntire, *Early Days in Texas*, 77).

[36]   According to the *El Paso Lone Star* of March 28, 1883, John Watts "was a rustler from pure love of the business, and not from want or necessity. He recently sold a mine from which he realized something like $20,000 and yet, with the money in his pocket, he deliberately 'jined the gang' and chose the life of a thief and outlaw, rather than that of an honest man."

[37]   *Dallas Daily Herald*, April 1, 1883, reprinting a story in the *Lake Valley Herald*.

[38]   Ibid.

[39]   McIntire, *Early Days in Texas*, 77.

[40]   *Lake Valley Herald* story in the *Dallas Daily Herald*, April 1, 1883.

[41]   Fountain report quoted in Stanley, *Longhair Jim Courtright*, 96.

[42]   *Lake Valley Herald* story in the *Dallas Daily Herald*, April 1, 1883.

[43]   A. M. Gibson, *The Life and Death of Colonel Albert Jennings Fountain* (Norman: University of Oklahoma Press, 1965), 125; Philip J. Rasch, "The Rustler War," *English Westerners Brand Book* (April 1965), 2-7.

CHAPTER SEVEN.

[1]   Cunningham, *Triggernometry*, 207; Stanley, *Longhair Jim Courtright*, 39.

[2]   B. B. Paddock's *Democrat* in Fort Worth took a dim view of this possibility, of course, commenting in its May 2, 1883 issue: "It is said that John A. Logan really expects to be nominated for the presidency. That he should even want the nomination is evidence of softening of the brain and national degeneracy."

[3]   Victor Westphall, "The American Valley Murders" (unpublished manuscript), 11, 34-35. Information in this manuscript was drawn primarily from contemporary newspapers, transcripts of the American Valley murder trials, and interviews with descendents of the principals involved in the case.

[4]   R. K. DeArment, "The Mystery of Outlaw Bill," *True West* (January 1992).

[5]   "Muster Roll of Company C, First Regiment of New Mexico Volunteer Militia," New Mexico State Records Center, Santa Fe. The company consisted of three officers, five sergeants, four corporals, and thirty-eight privates.

[6]   McIntire, *Early Days in Texas*, 78.

[7]   Westphall, "The American Valley Murders," 11, 29-30; Bryan, *True Tales*, 135.

[8]   Westphall, "The American Valley Murders," 45-46, 52. The name was sometimes reported in the press as "Montinay" or "Montanay." It is not known if, like Courtright and McIntire, he was also a deputy U. S. marshal.

[9]   Ibid., 33-34.

[10]   Ibid., 26, 36.

[11]   Ibid., 45.

[12]   Ibid., 52.

[13] Ibid., 54. The account of the murders is drawn from trial testimony, particularly that of McAllister, who turned state's evidence, and accounts of those who discovered the bodies

[14] Ibid., 65.

[15] Ibid., 79-80; *Albuquerque Morning Journal*, May 11, 18, October 10, 18, 1883; *Albuquerque Daily Democrat*, May 17, 1883.

[16] Westphall, "The American Valley Murders," 81-82; *Albuquerque Morning Journal*, May 18, October 19, 1883.

[17] *Albuquerque Daily Democrat*, May 17, 1883.

[18] The following year the Republican Party nominated Logan as its vice presidential candidate to run with James G. Blaine. The ticket was defeated and Logan died two years later in Washington.

[19] Philip J.Rasch, "Murder in American Valley," *English Westerners' Brand Book* 6 (April 1965): 2-7;

[20] *Albuquerque Morning Journal*, May 17, 18, 1883. Among those released was Christopher "Kit" Joy, a desperado Morrison had brought from Fort Wingate. Later that year Joy led an outlaw gang in the robbery of a Southern Pacific train near Deming, New Mexico. In a spectacular escape from the Silver City jail all three of his cohorts were killed or lynched. Joy got away, only to be recaptured in 1884. He lost his leg resisting arrest and his freedom when he was sent to the territorial prison for life (Dan L. Thrapp, *Encyclopedia of Frontier Biography, In Three Volumes,*(Glendale, Calif.: Arthur H. Clark Co., 1988): Vol. II, 747-48.

[21] Westphall, "The American Valley Murders," 91-92; *Albuquerque Morning Journal,*May 26, 1883; *Albuquerque Daily Democrat*, May 26, 29, 1883; DeArment, "The Mystery of Outlaw Bill," 20.

[22] Westphall, "The American Valley Murders," 92-93; *Albuquerque Morning Journal*, May 31, 1883; *Albuquerque Daily Democrat*, May 29, 1883. The latter paper, in its issue of May 30th said that Sheriff Simpson called at the office of the *Democrat* and gave his account of what happened. He believed that Courtright, after reading in the paper of the indictments, slipped away from his guard and "immediately started away to Kingston, by the trail, which is miles shorter than the stage road, [and] warned McIntyre [sic] and they both escaped before the stage, with the officers, got there." In his memoirs Jim McIntire gave a greatly distorted account of this escape with Courtright, making no mention of the murder indictments, but saying they were being hunted by the hated "Greaser Militia" of Major Fountain (McIntire, *Early Days in Texas*, 79-80).

[23] McIntire, *Early Days in Texas*, 80-83.

[24] *El Paso Lone Star*, June 2, 16, 1883.

[25] McIntire, *Early Days in Texas*. 84.

[26] *El Paso Lone Star*, June 9, 1883, "Hotel Arrivals."

[27] McIntire, *Early Days in Texas*, 84.

[28] *Dallas Daily Herald*, June 21, 1883.

[29] Ibid., June 26, 1883.

[30] *El Paso Lone Star*, June 30, 1883.

[31] *Dallas Daily Herald*, June 29, 1883.

[32] Ibid.

33 Ibid., June 30, 1883.

34 *San Antonio Daily Express,* July 14, 1883.

35 Ibid., July 8, 1883.

36 *Dallas Daily Herald,* July 22, 1883.

37 Ibid., October 21, 1883.

38 Ibid., November 25, 1883.

39 Ibid.

40 Rick Miller, *Bounty Hunter,* (College Station, Tex.: Creative Publishing Company, 1988), 143-145.

41 *Dallas Daily Herald,* July 23, 24, 1884; *San Antonio Daily Express,* July 23, 1884.

CHAPTER EIGHT

1 During the trials, Clotilde, the mother of the murdered Alexis, was said to have carried into court a hidden knife with which she intended to exact her own revenge on one of the Casey brothers if the opportunity presented itself (Westphall, "The American Valley Murders," 131-32).

2 Ibid., 128; Rasch, "Murder in American Valley," 4-5.

3 Newspapers reported that the jury in the second trial "had undoubtedly stood 11 to 1 in favor of acquittal," (Westphall, "The American Valley Murders," 156).

4 *Albuquerque Morning Journal,* October 28, 1883.

5 DeArment, "The Mystery of Outlaw Bill." In a recent book, *William C. Moore, Good Guy or Outlaw Bill?* (Salt Lake City, Utah: Jaffa Printing Company, 1998), Frank H. Slaven, Jr., a grandson of Moore's wife, attempts to vindicate Bill Moore. He postulates a theory that Moore was murdered in the American Valley on the order of John P. Casey at the same time that Grossetete and Elsinger were killed and his body secretly hidden there. All of the elements of Moore's reported escape from Albuquerque, his interview in a Las Vegas paper, his alleged bogus check paper trail, his pursuit by Detective Tony Neis, were part of an elaborate scheme concocted by Casey and his cronies to rid themselves of ranch partner Moore and at the same time leave him with the blame for the murder of the young partners. This hypothesis is ridiculous, of course, as Moore was seen by dozens of people at the ranch, on the trip back, and at Albuquerque, between May 6, the day of the murders, and May 23, when the grand jury handed down murder indictments and Moore disappeared from Albuquerque.

6 *San Antonio Daily Express,* December 23, 1883; *Dallas Daily Herald,* December 23, 1883.

7 *Las Vegas Optic,* January 30, 1884, quoting the *Fort Worth Daily Democrat.*

8 *San Antonio Daily Express,* February 19, 1884.

9 *Dallas Weekly* Herald, April 24, 1884, quoted in Stanley, *Longhair Jim Courtright,* 145-46.

10 *Dallas Daily Herald,* September 11, 1884.

11 *San Antonio Daily Express,* September 11, 12, 1884. Sheriff Thomas R. Allen of Wise County, Texas, told Captain George Schmitt of the Texas Rangers that he went to Fort Worth to arrest Courtright and was refused assistance by Sheriff Walter Maddox and City Marshal W. M. Rea. Both told him that Courtright could

not be taken back to New Mexico alive (Report of Captain Schmitt to Adjutant-General King, October 30, 1884).

12 Territory of New Mexico, Governor's Records, 1881-1885.

13 The details of Courtright's arrest are drawn from the *Fort Worth Daily Gazette*, October 19, 1884; *Dallas Daily Herald*, October 18, 1884; *San Antonio Daily Express*, October 19, 1884; Report of Captain Schmitt to Adjutant-General King, October 30, 1884. Some newspaper accounts included a Texas Ranger named Beard in the arrest, but Schmitt's report mentions only Grimes and Hayes. Coincidentally, on October 18, the day of Courtright's capture, the *Las Vegas Optic* announced that John P. Casey (of all people!) had offered a $10,000 reward for Courtright's arrest (Rasch, "Murder in American Valley," 6-7).

14 McIntire, *Early Days in Texas*, 86.

15 Schmitt to King, October 30, 1884.

16 Amos Melton in the *Dallas Morning News*, June 9, 1929.

17 *San Antonio Daily Express*, October 19, 1884. Dispatches from Fort Worth printed in the eastern press estimated the crowd at 1,500 persons. The arrest was made, according to these erroneous reports, by "New Mexico rangers" (*New York Times*, October 20, 21, 1884).

18 *Fort Worth Daily Gazette*, October 19, 1884; Schmitt to King, October 30, 1884. The *San Francisco Chronicle*, one of the many papers around the country carrying the story of the events in Fort Worth, reprinted a dispatch from Galveston that gave the crowd figure as fifteen hundred. The fiction that Courtright had spread was reflected in the headline: "Arrest of Two Men Accused of killing Mexicans" (October 19, 1884).

19 Wilbur Hill King, *Report of the Adjutant-General of the State of Texas* (Austin, Tex.: State Printing Office, D&D Asylum, December 1884), 23.

20 Schmitt to King, October 30, 1884. Affixed to Schmitt's letter in the Texas Archives is an undated and unidentified newspaper clipping with a statement attributed to Courtright exonerating both Jim Maddox and his brother, Sheriff W. T. Maddox, from having had any part in the arrest. "I know neither of them had anything whatever to do with helping to capture me," he is quoted. "They are both now, and always have been, my warm personal friends and such a statement being circulated on them mortifies me almost as much as my arrest."

21 *San Antonio Daily Express*, October 19, 1884.

22 *Dallas Morning News*, January 22, 1886.

23 *Fort Worth Daily Gazette*, October 20, 1884.

24 Accounts of Courtright's escape, one of the most dramatic events in western outlaw history, have appeared in every publication dealing with Fort Worth's early years. The version given here is drawn primarily from contemporary news stories: *Fort Worth Daily Gazette*, October 20, 1884; *Dallas Daily Herald*, October 20, 1884; *San Francisco Chronicle*, October 20, 1884; *San Antonio Daily Express*, October 21, 1884.

25 McIntire, *Early Days in Texas*, 87.

26 Stanley, *Longhair Jim Courtright*, 150-51.

27 *Dallas Daily Herald*, October 20, 1884.

28 *San Antonio Daily Express*, October 22, 1884.

[29] King, *Report of the Adjutant-General of the State of Texas*, December 1884, 23-24.

[30] *San Antonio Daily Express*, October 24, 1884.

[31] *Dallas Weekly Herald*, October 23, 1884.

[32] *Dallas Daily Herald*, October 21, 1884.

[33] *San Antonio Daily Express*, October 25, 1884.

[34] *Dallas Daily Herald*, October 24, 1884.

[35] Monthly Return, October 31, 1884, Company C, Frontier Battalion, Texas Rangers, Adjutant General's Files, (A.G.F.) Archives Division, Texas State Library, Austin.

[36] Letter, Schmitt to King, November 22, 1884 (A. G. F).

[37] *Dallas Weekly Herald*, December 13, 1884.

[38] McIntire, *Early Days in Texas*, 87-89.

CHAPTER NINE

[1] *San Antonio Daily Express*, November 22, 23, 1884.

[2] Letter, Schmitt to King, November 22, 1884 (A.G.F.).

[3] Letter, Schmitt to King, October 31, 1884 (A.G.F.).

[4] Letter, Schmitt to King, November 30, 1884 (A.G.F.).

[5] *Dallas Daily Herald*, December 14, 1884. The story was picked up and repeated in newspapers around the country, including the *San Antonio Daily Express* of December 14, 1884 and the *Las Vegas Optic*, of December 16, 1884.

[6] *Dallas Morning News*, January 21, 1886; *San Antonio Daily Express*, Jan. 21, 1886.

[7] McIntire, *Early Days in Texas*, 90.

[8] *San Antonio Daily Express*, October 23, 24, 1884.

[9] *Dallas Daily Herald*, June 7, 1885.

[10] Ibid., August 22, 1885.

[11] *San Antonio Daily Express*, April 17, 1885.

[12] *New Orleans Times-Democrat*, October 21, 1885.

[13] *Dallas Daily Herald*, August 22, 1885. Wilson was also the source for the unsubstantiated Caldwell shooting story.

[14] *New Orleans Times-Democrat*, April 22, 1885.

[15] *New Orleans Daily Picayune*, April 23, 1885.

[16] Cunningham, "Long-Haired Jim Courtright," *Frontier Times*, (February 1929), 204; Cunningham, *Triggernometry*, 212. Among many later writers who accepted and repeated the fable of Courtright's South American sojourn were Hunter and Rose in *The Album of Gunfighters*, 158, Cox, *Luke Short and his Era*, 155, and Leon Metz, *The Shooters*, (El Paso, Tex.: Mangan Books, 1976), 170.

[17] Stanley, *Longhaired Jim Courtright*, 162-163.

[18] *Fort Worth Star-Telegram*, October 30, 1949; Williams, "In Old Fort Worth," October 24, 1986. According to Father Stanley (Ibid., 152), Woody was aided in planting the pistols by Caroline Brown, a waitress in the restaurant, who "was

particularly grateful to Courtright who had helped her on occasion when over amorous gentlemen gave her a rough time." To Stanley, Courtright was always chivalrous.

[19] Glenn Shirley, *Heck Thomas: Frontier Marshal* (Norman: University of Oklahoma Press, 1981), 38.

[20] Ab Woody's son, Dr. W. A. Woody, recounted the story of Courtright's escape and fugitive experience in an interview in the *Fort Worth Star Telegram*, October 30, 1949. Courtright himself told much the same story to a reporter for the *Dallas Morning News* of January 21, 1886, quoted in Stanley, *Longhair Jim Courtright*, 163-169. Part of this interview was reported under the headline, "Arrival of the Panther City's Pet" in the *San Antonio Daily Express*, of January 21, 1886. Perhaps to protect Ab Woody, Courtright said that he remained in Fort Worth a week before catching the train to Galveston.

[21] U. S. Census, Shasta County, Washington, 1900. According to the Daggett Papers of Fort Worth, Lulu was born in 1886, but the location of the birth is also given as Walla Walla.

[22] McIntire, *Early Days in* Texas, 90-92.

[23] Ibid., 92-93.

[24] *New Orleans Times-Democrat*, April 21, 1885; *Denver Tribune-Republican*, April 27, 1885.

[25] *New Orleans Times-Democrat*, April 23, 1885; *New Orleans Daily Picayune*, April 23, 1885.

[26] *New Orleans Times-Democrat*, June 4, 1885; *Albuquerque Evening Journal*, June 8, 1885.

[27] Rasch, "Murder in American Valley," 6.

[28] *Albuquerque Evening Democrat*, October 15, 1885.

[29] *Albuquerque Evening Journal*, October 19, 1885.

[30] Ibid., October 15, 1885; *New York Times*, October 22, 1884; *Silver City Enterprise*, October 31, 1885; Rasch, "Murder in American Valley," 5; Westphall, "The American Valley Murders," 160-61.

[31] *Albuquerque Evening* Democrat, October 15, 1885.

[32] DeArment, "The Frontier Adventures of Jim McIntire," (*True West*, February 1999).

[33] *San Antonio Daily Express*, October 25, 1885.

[34] Ibid.

[35] *Dallas Morning News*, January 21, 1886.

[36] Ibid., *San Antonio Daily Express*, January 21, 1886. Jim Thompson was reportedly one of Courtright's friends who helped him escape from the Rangers (*Dallas Morning News*, June 9, 1929). Holland ran a succession of disreputable variety theaters in Fort Worth and in the eighties was said to be the richest man in the county "as far as ready money was concerned" (Selcer, *Hell's Half Acre*, 298).

[37] *Dallas Morning News*, January 21, 1886.

[38] Ibid.

[39] Ibid., January 25, 1886.

[40] Stanley, *Longhair Jim Courtright*, 170.

41 *Dallas Morning News*, February 2, 1886.

42 Ibid., February 16, 1886.

43 *Las Vegas* Optic, February 23, 1886. The least Courtright could do to show his gratitude, suggested the *Optic* editor, was to take out a subscription to the *Chieftain*.

44 *Dallas Morning News*, February 25, 1886.

45 Ibid., March 3,1886; Stanley, *Longhair Jim Courtright*, 172-73.

46 *Las Vegas Optic*, March 26, 1886.

47 Westphall, "The American Valley Murders," 159-60.

48 Metz, *The Shooters*, 170.

49 Cunningham, *Triggernometry*, 206. Courtright was said to have had a "slightly crippled right hand" (Knight, *Fort Worth*, 80), but this didn't seem to hamper him with his six-shooter tricks. The damage to his hand may have resulted from a severe bite he received from one of a pair of bear cubs on display in the Pacific Saloon in Fort Worth on June 30, 1877 (*Fort Worth Daily Democrat*, July 1, 1877).

50 *Dallas Morning News*, June 9, 1929.

51 *San Antonio Daily Express*, November 30, 1886; *Las Vegas Optic*, December 2, 1886.

CHAPTER TEN

1 *Fort Worth Daily Gazette*, April 6, 1886; Stanley, *Longhair Jim Courtright*, 200-201, quoting Courtright's testimony at later hearings into the April 3 shootings.

2 *Fort Worth Daily Gazette*, April 4, 1886. The crowd was estimated as high as 1,000 in telegraphic dispatches from Fort Worth (*New York Times*, April 4, 1886).

3 *San Antonio Daily Express*, April 4, 1886.

4 Ibid.

5 *Fort Worth Daily Gazette*, April 4, 1886; Courtright's testimony, Stanley, op. cit.

6 *San Antonio Daily Express*, April 4, 1886; *Fort Worth Daily Gazette*, April 4, 1886. Erroneous dispatches to newspapers around the country said that Charles Sneed, shot through the jaw, also received a bullet in the heart (*New York Times*, April 4, 1886) and in the head (*Coshocton Semi-Weekly Age*, April 6, 1886).

7 *Coshocton Semi Weekly Age*, April 6, 1886; Stanley, *Longhair Jim Courtright*, 186.

8 *San Antonio Daily Express*, April 6, 1886. Dick Townsend was another old Courtright friend and supporter who reportedly assisted him in his escape from the Texas Rangers in 1884 (*Dallas Morning News*, June 9, 1929).

9 Stanley, *Longhair Jim Courtright*, 186, 192. Exaggerated newspaper reports across the nation reported that "seven men are now dead and a number are wounded" (*New York Times*, April 4, 1886).

10 *Fort Worth Daily Gazette*, April 4, 1886.

11 Ibid.

12 Ibid., April 5, 6, 1886; *Coshocton Semi Weekly Age,* April 6, 1886; Robert M. Utley, *Lone Star Justice: The First Century of the Texas Rangers* (Oxford, N.Y.: Oxford University Press, 2002), 231.

13 *San Antonio Daily* Express, April 4, 1886.

14 *Fort Worth Daily Gazette,* April 5, 1886.

15 *San Antonio Daily Express,* June 26, 1886

16 Ibid., January 18, 1887; *St. Louis Globe-Democrat,* January 18, 1887.

17 *Austin Daily Statesman,* June 19, 1887.

18 Ruth A. Allen, *The Great Southwest Strike* (Austin: The University of Texas Press, 1942), 92.

19 Ibid., 106.

20 *San Antonio Light,* April 10, 1886.

21 *Atlanta Constitution,* April 9, 1886.

CHAPTER ELEVEN

1 *St. Louis Globe-Democrat,* January 4, 10, 1887.

2 Ibid., January 27, 1887.

3 Al Look, *Unforgettable Characters of Western Colorado* (Boulder, Colo.: Pruett Press, Inc., 1966),103.

4 Herbert Asbury, *Sucker's Progress: An Informal History of Gambling in America From the Colonies to Canfield* (New York: Dodd, Mead & Company, 1938), 338.

5 The story appeared in *My Life as a Card Shark*, ghost-written for Coe by Hugh Walters and published as a paperback in 1903. No copy seems to have survived, but writer Tom Bailey, who once owned a copy, drew on it for his article, "King of Cards," published in *See: New Magazine for Men* Vol. 17, No. 3 (May 1958): 13-15, 72-74.

6 There is some confusion regarding the location of Short's birth. His first biographer, William R. Cox, said he was born in Mississippi in the year 1854 (*Luke Short and His Era*, 9). His source was the great grandson of Henry Short, Luke's younger brother, and the Short family Bible (Ibid., 193). In a later biography, Wayne Short, a great-nephew of Luke, wrote that his great-uncle was born in Arkansas in 1854 (*Luke Short: A Biography of One of the Old West's Most Colorful Gamblers and Gunfighters,* Tombstone, Ariz.:Devil's Thumb Press, 1996), but seems to have relied only on Texas census data (2, 241). The *San Antonio Daily Express* of September 28, 1895 gave January 22, 1854 as the date of Short's birth, but no location. Here I have used the date and place provided by Jack DeMattos, a careful researcher (W. B. [Bat] Masterson and Jack DeMattos, *Famous Gun Fighters of the Western Frontier*, Monroe, Wash.: Weatherford Press, 1982) 65.

7 Short, *Luke Short*, 20-23.

8 Ibid., 64-71, 108-110; Cox, *Luke Short and His Era,* 18, 194; Masterson and DeMattos, *Famous Gun Fighters,* 65.

9 Cox, *Luke Short and His Era,* quoting J. H. Cooks, "Early Days in Ogallala," *Nebraska History Magazine,* (April-June 1933).

10 Masterson, "Luke Short," *Human Life,* (April 1907).

11 Ibid.

12 Ibid.

[13] Ibid. Defended by W. J. Hunsacker, Short appeared before a justice of the peace on May 2, 1881, and was released on bail. His case was called on July 7 in the Tucson district court and "ignored by the grand jury" (Masterson and DeMattos, *Famous Gun Fighters,* 65; Short, *Luke Short,* 155, 159). According to Wayne Short, Luke and Storms had run-ins prior to Tombstone. They clashed over a card game in Cheyenne and in Leadville over "a handsome widow" (Short, *Luke Short,* 151).

[14] Short, *Luke Short,* 171.

[15] Selcer, *Hell's Half Acre,* 178, 197-98. Short biographer William Cox doubted that there was ever a formal marriage between Luke and the woman known by some family members as "Cousin Brumley Anderson" and "Aunt Hettie" (*Luke Short and His Era,* 185).

[16] *San Antonio Daily Express,* October 25, 1884; *St. Louis Globe-Democrat,* February 9, 1887.

[17] *San Antonio Daily Express,* February 9, 1887.

[18] Dispatch from Fort Worth printed in the *Dallas Daily Herald,* August 27, 1884.

[19] John A. Loomis, *Texas Ranchman: The Memoirs of John A. Loomis* (Chadron, Nebr.: The Fur Press, 1982), 28. Loomis casts further doubt on his credibility when he adds gratuitously and erroneously that Short was killed in a gunfight.

[20] Selcer, *Hell's Half Acre,* 172, 306.

[21] Ibid., 172. Father Stanley falsely asserts in *Longhair Jim Courtright* (210-11) that "Luke Short owned no part of the White Elephant," and that "Jim, Jack and Mary Courtright were the joint owners."

CHAPTER TWELVE

[1] Cunningham, *Triggernometry,* 213.

[2] Cunningham, "Long-Haired Jim Courtright," *Frontier Times,* (February 1929): 205.

[3] Selcer, *Hell's Half Acre,* 182; O'Neal, *Encyclopedia of Western Gunfighters,* 74; Cox, *Luke Short and His Era,* 162-63.

[4] *San Antonio Daily* Express, February 9, 1887.

[5] Knight, *Fort Worth,* 120. F. Stanley, who made the unfounded assertion that Courtright owned the White Elephant, wrote that the "city fathers" came to him with "the admonition that he close Luke Short's gaming room" and this led to the gunfight (*Longhair Jim Courtright,* 211).

[6] *Dallas Morning* News, February 9, 1887.

[7] *St. Louis Daily Globe-Democrat,* February 9, 1887.

[8] Stanley, *Longhair Jim Courtright,* 212-13. This story was repeated in an article on Courtright in the *Fort Worth News-Tribune* of November 7, 1986. The author, Mack Williams, followed the Stanley biography uncritically.

[9] Selcer, *Hell's Half Acre,* 178.

[10] Cox, *Luke Short and His Era,* 203. Cox was in error in describing Betty Courtright as "a matronly woman, a couple of years older than Luke" (Ibid). Betty was thirty years old in 1887, three years younger.

[11] Selcer, *Hell's Half Acre,* 179-80.

[12] Masterson, "Luke Short," *Human Life* (April 1907).

13 *Fort Worth Daily Gazette*, February 9, 1887; *St Louis Daily Globe-Democrat*, February 9, 1887.

14 *Fort Worth Daily Gazette*, February 8, 1887.

15 Testimony of Jake Johnson reported in the *Dallas Morning News*, February 10, 1887.

16 Testimony of Ike Cantrell and W. A. James at the inquest into Courtright's death, quoted in the *Fort Worth Daily Gazette*, February 10, 1887.

17 Ibid., February 9, 1887.

18 Masterson, "Luke Short."

19 *Fort Worth Daily Gazette*, February 9, 1887.

20 *St. Louis Daily Globe-Democrat*, February 9, 1887.

21 *Fort Worth Daily Gazette*, February 9, 1887. The post-mortem report basically confirmed Tucker's original findings. Courtright had been struck by three bullets. His right thumb was broken and "he was shot in the region of the heart, through the left shoulder and the right lung" (*St. Louis Daily Globe-Democrat*, February 9, 1887).

22 *St. Louis Daily Globe-Democrat*, February 9, 1887.

23 Ibid., *Fort Worth Daily Gazette*, February 9, 1887.

24 *Fort Worth Daily Gazette*, February 10, 1887.

25 Stanley, *Longhair Jim Courtright*, 212-13.

26 *Fort Worth Daily Gazette*, February 9, 1887.

27 Lewis, "The King of the Gun-Players: William Barclay Masterson."*Human Life* (November 1907). Masterson's presence in Fort Worth at the time was never mentioned in the press, causing some historians (i.e. Jack DeMattos in *Famous Gun Fighters of the Western Frontier*, 69) to question whether he was even there. But unlike many frontier veterans, Masterson in his published recollections did not falsely place himself at the scene of dramatic events and his account was probably accurate. Another gunfighter historian has suggested rather ludicrously that Masterson not only was there, but that it was he who killed Courtright and not Short (Bartholomew, *The Biographical Album of Western Gunfighters*).

28 *Fort Worth Daily Gazette*, February 9, 1887.

29 *St. Louis Daily Globe-Democrat*, February 9, 1887.

30 *Fort Worth Daily Gazette*, February 10, 1887; *Dallas Morning News*, February 10, 1887.

31 Ibid.

32 *Dallas Morning News*, February 10, 1887; *Brenham Daily Banner*, February 10, 1887; *Fort Worth Daily Gazette*, February 25, 1887.

33 Stanley, *Longhair Jim Courtright*, 224.

34 Ibid., 211.

35 Cunningham, "Long-Haired Jim Courtright," 205. The first mention of this theory was in a special dispatch from Fort Worth describing the shooting that appeared in the February 9, 1887 issue of the *St. Louis Daily Globe-Democrat*: "[Courtright's] right thumb was broken and this accounts for his not using his pistol." A later dispatch said: "It seems almost certain that had Courtright's thumb not been broken at the first fire he would have killed Short" (Ibid., February 10, 1887).

36 Cunningham, *Triggernometry*, 216.

37 Stanley, *Longhair Jim Courtright*, 212-13.

38 Cox, *Luke Short and His Era*, 35.

39 Stanley, *Longhair Jim Courtright*, 68; Knight, *Fort Worth*, 80.

40 *Dallas Morning News*, June 9, 1929.

41 *Fort Worth Daily Gazette*, February 9, 1887.

42 Ibid., February 10, 1887.

43 Cox, *Luke Short and His Era*, 173; Metz, *The Shooters*, 171.

44 *Fort Worth Press*, November 21, 1927.

45 Masterson, "Ben Thompson."

ENDNOTES: AFTERWORD

1   *Fort Worth Daily Gazette*, March 17, 1887; *St. Louis Globe-Democrat*, March 18, 1887; Selcer, *Hell's Half Acre*, 210.

2   Richard Selcer to the author, October 12, 1998.

3   Cox, *Luke Short and His Era*, 180-82, 186; Robert K. DeArment, *Knights of the Green Cloth: The Saga of the Frontier Gamblers* (Norman: University of Oklahoma Press, 1982), 112-13; Selcer, *Hell's Half Acre*, 195-97.

4   Selcer, *Hell's Half Acre*, 198-98; Short, *Luke Short*, 240. According to Selcer, the children were fathered by Luke Short (*Hell's Half Acre*, 175). A man named Charles William Borger, who claimed to be a grandson of Luke's, became so identified with the famous gambler and gunman that he changed his name to Luke Short III (Ibid., 309). However, Wayne Short, a great-nephew of Luke Short, wrote that Luke had no children (*Luke Short*, 239).

5   Stanley, *Longhaired Jim Courtright*, 223-26. Lulu May was apparently married more than once. The Mary Daggett Lake Papers in the Genealogical and Local History Department of the Fort Worth Public Library has a copy of the marriage license of Wesley W. Shilling, 22, and Lulu M. Courtright, 18, made out at San Luis Obispo, California on September 2, 1904.

6   Bryan, *True Tales of the American Southwest*, 148-49; Stanley, *Longhair Jim Courtright*, 225-26. Bryan introduced Mrs. Meyerhoff to Fred Landon, nephew of Alexis Grossetete, one of the men Courtright had been accused of murdering seventy-one years before.

7   Stanley, *Longhair Jim Courtright*, 226.

Books:

Adams, Ramon F. *The Adams One-Fifty: A Checklist of the 150 Most Important Books on Western Outlaws and Lawmen.* Austin, Tex.: Jenkins Publishing Company, 1976.

——. *Burs Under the Saddle: A Second Look at Books and Histories of the West.* Norman: University of Oklahoma Press, 1964.

——. *More Burs Under the Saddle: Books and Histories of the West.* Norman: University of Oklahoma Press, 1979.

——. *Six-Guns and Saddle Leather: A Bibliography of Books and Pamphlets on Western Outlaws and Gunmen.* Norman: University of Oklahoma Press, 1969.

Allen, Ruth A. *The Great Southwest Strike.* Austin: The University of Texas Press, 1942.

Asbury, Herbert. *Sucker's Progress: An Informal History of Gambling in America From the Colonies to Canfield.* New York: Dodd, Mead & Company, 1938.

Ball, Larry D. *The United States Marshals of New Mexico and Arizona Territories, 1846-1912.* Albuquerque: University of New Mexico Press, 1978.

Barra, Allen. *Inventing Wyatt Earp: His Life and Many Legends.* New York: Carroll & Graf Publishers, Inc., 1998.

Bartholomew, Ed. *The Biographical Album of Western Gunfighters.* Houston: Frontier Press of Texas, 1958.

Browning, James A. *The Western Reader's Guide.* Stillwater, Okla.: Barbed Wire Press, 1992.

Bryan, Howard. *True Tales of the American Southwest: Pioneer Recollections of Frontier Adventures.* Santa Fe, N. Mex.: Clear Light Publishers, 1998.

Chaput, Don. *Virgil Earp: Western Peace Officer.* Encampment, Wyo.: Affiliated Writers of America, Inc., 1994.

Colcord, Charles Francis. *Autobiography of Charles Francis Colcord.* Tulsa, Okla.: Privately printed by C. C. Helmerich, 1970.

Cox, William R. *Luke Short and His Era.* Garden City, N. Y.: Doubleday and Co., 1961.

Cunningham, Eugene. *Triggernometry: A Gallery of Gunfighters.* Caldwell, Idaho: The Caxton Printers, Ltd., 1962

DeArment, Robert K. *Bat Masterson: The Man and the Legend.* Norman: University of Oklahoma Press, 1979.

——. *Knights of the Green Cloth: The Saga of the Frontier Gamblers.* Norman: University of Oklahoma Press, 1982.

Drago, Harry Sinclair. *The Legend Makers: Tales of the Old-Time Peace Officers and Desperadoes of the Frontier.* New York: Dodd, Mead & Company, 1975

Eppinga, Jane. *Henry Ossian Flipper, West Point's First Black Graduate.* Plano, Tex.: Republic of Texas Press, 1996.

Gaddy, Jerry J. *Dust to Dust: Obituaries of the Gunfighters.* Fort Collins, Colo.: The Old Army Press, 1977.

Gard, Wayne. *Sam Bass*. New York: Houghton Mifflin Co., 1936.

Gibson, A. M. *The Life and Death of Colonel Albert Jennings Fountain*. Norman: University of Oklahoma Press, 1965.

Goodnight, Charles, Emanuel Dubbs, John A. Hart, and others. *Pioneer Days in the Southwest from 1850 to 1879*. Guthrie, Okla.: The State Capital Company, 1909.

Grove, Pearce S., Becky J. Barnett, and Sandra J. Hansen, ed. *New Mexico Newspapers: A Comprehensive Guide to Bibliographical Entries and Locations*. Albuquerque: University of New Mexico Press, 1975.

Hendricks, George D. *The Bad Man of the West*. San Antonio, Tex.: The Naylor Co., Publishers, 1941.

Holbrook, Stewart H. *Little Annie Oakley & Other Rugged People*. New York: The Macmillan Company, 1948.

Holloway, Carroll C. *Texas Gun Lore*. San Antonio, Tex.: The Naylor Co., Publishers, 1951.

Hunter, John Marvin, and Noah H. Rose. *The Album of Gunfighters*. Bandera, Tex.:1951.

King, Wilbur Hill. *Report of the Adjutant-General of the State of Texas*, Austin, Tex.: State Printing Office, D & D Asylum, 1884.

Knight, Oliver. *Fort Worth: Outpost on the Trinity*. Norman: University of Oklahoma Press, 1953.

Lanning, Jim and Judy Lanning, ed. *Texas Cowboys: Memories of the Early Days*. College Station: Texas A & M University Press, 1984.

Lewis, Alfred Henry. *The Sunset Trail*. New York: A. S. Barnes & Co., 1905.

Look, Al. *Unforgettable Characters of Western Colorado*. Boulder, Colo.: Pruett Press, Inc., 1966.

Loomis, John A. *Texas Ranchman*. Chadron, Neb.: The Fur Press, 1982.

Looney, Ralph. *Haunted Highways: The Ghost Towns of New Mexico*. New York: Hastings House, Publishers, 1968.

McIntire, Jim. *Early Days in Texas: A Trip to Hell and Heaven*, 1902. Edited by Robert K. DeArment. Norman: University of Oklahoma Press, 1992.

McLoughlin, Denis. *Wild and Woolly: An Encyclopedia of the Old West*. Garden City, N.Y.: Doubleday and Co., 1975.

Martin, Charles L. *A Sketch of Sam Bass, the Bandit*. Norman: University of Oklahoma Press, 1968 reprint of 1880 edition.

Martin, Jack. *Border Boss: Captain John R. Hughes, Texas Ranger*. San Antonio, Tex.: The Naylor Co., Publishers, 1942.

Masterson, W. B. (Bat). *Famous Gun Fighters of the Western Frontier*. (Annotated and Illustrated by Jack DeMattos). Monroe, Wash.: Weatherford Press, 1982.

Miller, Rick. *Bounty Hunter*. College Station, Tex.: Creative Publishing Company, 1988.

——. *Sam Bass & Gang*. Austin, Tex.: State House Press, 1999.

Nash, Jay Robert. *Encyclopedia of Western Lawmen and Outlaws*. New York: Paragon House, 1992.

O'Neal, Bill. *Encyclopedia of Western Gun-Fighters*, Norman: University of Oklahoma Press, 1979.

Paddock, B. B. *Early Days in Fort Worth, Much of What I Saw and Part of Which I Was*. Fort Worth: n.p., n.d.

Rosa, Joseph G. *They Called Him Wild Bill: The Life and Adventures of James Butler Hickok*. Norman: University of Oklahoma Press, 1964.

———. and Waldo E. Koop. *Rowdy Joe Lowe: Gambler With a Gun*. Norman and London: University of Oklahoma Press, 1989.

Russell, Don. *The Wild West: A History of the Wild West Shows*. Fort Worth, Tex.: Amon Carter Museum of Western Art, 1978.

Schoenberger, Dale T. *The Gunfighters*. Caldwell, Idaho: The Caxton Printers, Ltd., 1971.

Selcer, Richard F. *Hell's Half Acre: The Life and Legend of a Red Light District*. Fort Worth: Texas Christian University Press, 1991.

Short, Wayne. *Luke Short: A Biography of One of the Old West's Most Colorful Gamblers and Gunfighters*. Tombstone, Ariz.: Devils' Thumb Press, 1996.

Sifakis, Carl. *The Encyclopedia of American Crime*. New York: Smithmark Publishers, 1992.

Slaven, Frank H., Jr. *The Wright Brothers Were There Too!* Salt Lake City, Utah: Jaffa Printing Company, 1998.

———. *William C. Moore: Good Guy or Outlaw Bill?* Salt Lake City, Utah: Jaffa Printing Company, 1998.

Stanley, F. *Longhair Jim Courtright: Two Gun Marshal of Fort Worth*. Denver, Colo.: World Press, 1957.

———. *The Lake Valley (New Mexico) Story*. Pep, Tex.: F. Stanley, 1964.

———. *The Las Vegas (New Mexico) Story*. Denver, Colo.: World Press, Inc., 1951.

Streeter, Floyd Benjamin. *The Complete and Authentic Life of Ben Thompson, Man With a Gun*. New York: Frederick Fall, Inc., Publishers, 1957.

Tanner, Karen Holliday. *Doc Holliday: A Family Portrait*. Norman: University of Oklahoma Press, 1998.

Thrapp, Dan L. *Encyclopedia of Frontier Biography, In Three Volumes*. Glendale, Calif.: Arthur H. Clark Co., 1988.

Tise, Sammy. *Texas County Sheriffs*. Albuquerque, N. Mex.: Oakwood Printing, 1989.

Tyler, Ron, Editor in Chief. *The New Handbook of Texas*. Six Volumes. Austin: The State Historical Association, 1996.

Utley, Robert M. *Lone Star Justice: The First Century of the Texas Rangers*. Oxford, N.Y.: Oxford University Press, 2002.

Wakely, Arthur C. *Omaha: The Gate City and Douglas County, Nebraska*. Chicago: The S. J. Clarke Publishing Company, 1917.

White, Owen P. *My Texas 'Tis of Thee*. New York: G. P. Putnam's Sons, 1936.

Yost, Nellie Snyder. *Buffalo Bill: His Family, Friends, Fame, Failures, and Fortunes*. Chicago: The Swallow Press, Inc., 1979.

ARTICLES:

Bailey, Tom. "King of Cards." *See: New Magazine for Men*, Vol. 17, No. 3 (May 1958) pp. 12-15, 74-84.

Breihan, Carl W. "Courtright's Last Gunfight." *Westerner*, (March 1971) pp. 10-13, 54-56.

——. "Luke Short's Mystery Gun Fight." *Real West*, (March 1961).

Bryan, Howard, "Off the Beaten Path." *Albuquerque Tribune*, (February 16, 1959).

Campo, Matt. "Longhair Jim Courtright Quiets Lake Valley – Then Ends Up Hiding in Mexico From Fountain." *The Southwesterner*, (March-April, 1965).

Cheney, Louise. "Longhair Jim Courtright: Fast Gun of Fort Worth." *Real West*, (November 1970), pp. 26-28, 77.

Cook, J. H. "Early Days in Ogallalah." *Nebraska History Magazine,* (April-June, 1933).

Cunningham, Eugene. "Courtright the Longhaired." *True West*. Vol. 4, No. 5, (May-June 1957) pp. 12-13, 35-37.

——. "Long-Haired Jim Courtright." *Frontier Times*, Vol. 6, No. 5, (February 1929), 202-205.

DeArment, R. K. "The Frontier Adventures of Jim McIntire." *True West*, Vol. 46, No. 2 (February 1999) pp. 10-17.

——. "Gunfighters and Lawmen: Jim Courtright." *Wild West,* (October 2003) pp. 16, 60-61.

——. "The Mystery of Outlaw Bill." *True West*, Vol. 39, No. 1 (January 1992) pp. 14-21..

Herring, E. N. "Gunfight at Hunnewell." *Wild West*, August 2002.

Kildare, Maurice. "American Valley Went Up in Smoke." *Frontier Times*, New Series, No. 98, October-November, 1975, pp. 8-11 ff.

——. "Gunman Courtright in New Mexico." *New Mexico Lawman*, Vol. 35, No. 11 (November 1969) pp. 3-11.

Lewis, Alfred Henry. "An Invasion of Dodge." *Colliers*, April 16, 1904.

——. "The Deep Strategy of Mr. Masterson." *Saturday Evening Post*, December 17, 1904.

——. "Diplomacy in Dodge." *Metropolitan Magazine*, April 1904.

——. "The Fatal Gratitude of Mr. Kelly." *Colliers*, September 17, 1904.

——. "The King of the Gun-Players: William Barclay Masterson." *Human Life,* November 1907.

Masterson, W. B. "Bat." "Ben Thompson." *Human Life*, January 1907.

——. "Luke Short." *Human Life*, April 1907.

Nolan, Frederick. "Boss Rustler": The Life and Crimes of John Kinney." *True West*, (September 1996):14-21; (October 1996): 12-19.

Oswald, James M. "History of Fort Elliott." *Panhandle-Plains Historical Review* 32, (1959): 1-59.

Rasch, Philip J. "Murder in American Valley." *English Westerners' Brand Book* Vol. 7, No. 3 (April 1965) pp. 2-7.

——. "The Rustler War." *New Mexico Historical Review,* Vol. XXXIX No. 4. (October 1964) pp. 257-73.

Richardson, T. C. "A Quart of Bullets." *Frontier Times* Vol.14, No. 11 (August 1937) pp. 490-94.

Roberts, Gary L. "Gem Saloon Shootout." *Wild West*, Vol. 5, No. 1 (June 1992) pp.22-28.

Scott. Jay. "Marshal of Fort Worth," *True Western Adventures,* (December 1959) pp. 23-24, 67-69.

Selcer, Richard F. "Cowboy-Booted Gumshoes: The Private Detective in Texas." *True West*, Vol. 39, No. 2 (February 1992) pp.14-20.

——. "Fort Worth's Wild White Elephant Saloon." *Wild West* (October 2003) pp. 23-28, 70.

Stanley, Samuel. "Jim Courtright, Gunfighter." *Real West,* Vol. 28, No. 208 (June 1986) pp. 14-16.

Walker, Wayne T. "Jim Courtright, Gunfighter." *Great West*, (June 1970) pp. 10-13, 39- 40.

——. "Jim Courtright, Professional Gunfighter." *Pioneer West,* (November 1977) pp. 8-10, 38-44.

——. "Killer in Fancy Pants." *True West,* Vol. 4, No. 1 (September-October 1956) pp. 14-15, 35-36.

Westphall, Victor. "The American Valley Murders," *Ayer y Hoy en Taos* No. 9 (Fall 1989): 3-8.

Williams, Mack "In Old Fort Worth: A Series on the Life of Jim Courtright." *Fort Worth News-Tribune*. Six-part Series, October 3 through November 7, 1986.

NEWSPAPERS:

Albuquerque Daily Democrat, May-June, 1883; October 15, 1885

Albuquerque Evening Democrat, October 15, 1885.

Albuquerque Evening Journal, June 8, October 15, 19, 1885.

Albuquerque Morning Journal, May-June; October 10, 18, 19, 28, 1883; June 8, 1885

Atlanta Constitution, October 21, 1884; April 9, 1886

Austin Daily Statesman, June 19, 1887.

Brenham Daily Banner, February 10, 11, 1887.

Coshocton (Ohio) *Semi-Weekly Age,* April 6, 1886.

Dallas Daily Herald, August 15, 1877; May 17, 18, 1878; February 10, 11, May 4, 8, October 27, December 2, 3, 1880; February 25, 1881; May 24, 27, 1882; June 21, 26, 29, 30, July 8, 22, August 19, September 16, October 21, 25, November 25, December 23, 1883; July 17, 23, 24, 30, August 3, 27, September 10, 11, October 16, 17, 18, 20, 21, 23, 24, 25, December 14, 25, 1884; April 23, June 7, 16, 17, July 22, August 18, 22, September 11, 18, 1885.

Dallas Morning News, January 21, 22, 25, February 2, 16, 25, March 3, 1886; February 10, 1887; June 9, 1929

Dallas Weekly Herald, October 23, December 13, 1884

Denver Tribune-Republican, April 27, 1885.

Dodge City Times, November 8, December 20, 17, 1879.

El Paso Lone Star, August 5, December 20, 30, 1882; January 27, March 28, June 2, 9, 16, 30, 1883

El Paso Thirty-Four, August 19, 1882

Fort Worth Daily Democrat, July 1876-December 12, 1881

Fort Worth Daily Gazette, October 19, 20, 1884; April 2, 4, 5, 6, 7, 1886; February 8, 9, 10, 25, March 17, 1887

Fort Worth Democrat and Advance, December 13, 1881-May 1883

Fort Worth News-Tribune, October 24, November 9, 1986.

Fort Worth Press, November 21, 1927.

Fort Worth Star Telegram, October 30, 1949; November 7, 1986.

Fort Worth Weekly Democrat, 1873-June 1876

Galveston Daily News, November 12, December 18, 1875; March 23, 29, April 12, 19, 25, May 2, 24, November-December 1879; January 31, May 4, 1880.

Houston Daily Post, October 31, 1880; December 22, 1881.

Jacksboro Frontier Echo, May 18, 1877

Las Vegas Daily Optic, November 3, 1882; January 30, October 18, December 16, 1884; February 23, March 26, December 2, 1886.

New Orleans Daily Picayune, April 21, 22, 23, 1885

New Orleans Times-Democrat, April 21, 22, 23, May 19, 22, June 4, October 21, 1885

New York Times. October 20, 22, 1884; April 4, 1886

St. Louis Daily Globe-Democrat, January 14, 10, 18, 27, February 9, 10, 14, March 18, 1887.

San Antonio Daily Express, July 8, 14, December 23, 1883; February 19, July 10, 23, September 11, 12, October 19, 21, 22, 23, 24, 25, November 22, 23, December 13, 14, 1884; April 17, October 25, 1885; January 21, April 4, 6, June 26, November 14, 30, 1886; January 4, 18, February 9, 10, 1887; September 28, 1895.

San Antonio Light, April 10, 1886.

Santa Fe New Mexican, May 1883

San Francisco Chronicle, October 19, 20, 1884.

Silver City Enterprise, April 6, May 25, July 13, 1883; October 31, 1885.

Sumner County (Wellington, Kansas) *Weekly Press,* June 29,1882..

Topeka Daily Kansas State Journal, May 18, 1883.

Weatherford Exponent, April 21, August 18, September 1, 1877.

GOVERNMENT DOCUMENTS:

Adjutant-General's Files [A. G. F.] (Archives Division, Texas State Library, Austin, Texas).

Cause No. 200, District Court, Second Judicial District, May Term 1883: Territory of New Mexico vs. John P. Casey, Larceny (New Mexico State Records and Archives, Santa Fe, New Mexico).

Cause No. 204, District Court, Second Judicial District, May Term 1883: Territory of New Mexico vs. John P. Casey, Assault with intent to murder (New Mexico State Records and Archives, Santa Fe, New Mexico).

Cause No. 205, District Court, Second Judicial District, May Term 1883: Territory of New Mexico vs. John P. Casey, Larceny (New Mexico State Records and Archives, Santa Fe, New Mexico).

Cause No. 210, District Court, Second Judicial District, May Term 1883: Territory of New Mexico vs. William C. Moore, James Casey, James McIntyre, James Courtright and Moeller W. Scott, Murder (New Mexico State Records and Archives, Santa Fe, New Mexico).

Cause No. 212, District Court, Second Judicial District, May Term 1883: Territory of New Mexico vs. James Casey and Moeller W. Scott, Murder (New Mexico State Records and Archives, Santa Fe, New Mexico).

Cause No. 1001C, State of Texas v. T. I. Courtright (Tarrant County Criminal Dockets, Special Collections, University of Texas at Arlington).

Cause No. 1476, State of Texas v, T. I. Courtright and W. A. Clower, Assault with Intent to Murder, March 20, 1877 (Tarrant County Criminal Dockets, Special Collections, University of Texas at Arlington).

Cause No. 1568, State of Texas v. T. I. Courtright, Malfeasance in Office, August 21, 1877 (Tarrant County Criminal Dockets, Special Collections, University of Texas at Arlington).

Cause No. 2230, State of Texas v. T. I. Courtright, Unlawfully Accepting a Challenge to Fight a Duel with Deadly Weapons, February 14, 1881 (Tarrant County Criminal Dockets, Special Collections, University of Texas at Arlington).

Extradition papers for James Courtright issued by Edmund G. Ross, Governor of New Mexico, dated January 25, 1886 (Texas State Archives, Austin, Texas).

Muster Roll of Company C, First Regiment of New Mexico Militia (New Mexico State Records and Archives, Santa Fe, New Mexico)..

Requisition for W. C. Moore, James McIntire and James Courtright issued by Lionel A. Sheldon, Governor of New Mexico, September 29, 1884 (New Mexico State Records and Archives, Santa Fe, New Mexico).

Reward notice for William C. Moore, James McIntyre and James Courtright issued by Lionel A. Sheldon, Governor of New Mexico, October 29, 1883 (New Mexico State Records and Archives, Santa Fe, New Mexico).

Territory of New Mexico, Governor's Records, 1881-1885, New Mexico State Records Center and Archives, Santa Fe.

Texas Penal Code, February 21, 1879, p. 82, Chapter Sixteen (Dueling).

U. S. Census Reports, Tarrant County, Texas, 1880; Shasta County, California, 1900.

UNPUBLISHED MATERIALS:

"Dreesen Files" (Albuquerque Public Library, Albuquerque, New Mexico).

"Mary Daggett Lake Papers" (Fort Worth Public Library, Fort Worth, Texas).

Westphall, Victor, "The American Valley Murders," (unpublished manuscript).

LETTERS AND INTERVIEWS:

Lou Blachly interview with Mrs. Ellen Lucy Capp, May 1952 (Southwest Oral Histories, Southwest Archives, Western New Mexico University Museum, Silver City, New Mexico.

T. I. Courtright, Fort Worth City Marshal, to R. B. Hubbard, Governor of Texas, March 12, 1878 (File No. 301-103, Letter Press Book #320, Records of Governor R. B. Hubbard, Texas State Library).

John Daly, Director, Illinois State Archives, to the author, May 23, 2000.

Douglas Ellison to the author, November 6, 1998.

Linda McDowell, The Butler Center for Arkansas Studies, Little Rock, Arkansas, to the author, April 26, May 9, 2002.

Thomas Martin, private secretary to Texas Governor R. B. Hubbard, to T. J. [sic] Courtright, Fort Worth City Marshal, September 24, 1877 (File No. 301-102, Letter Press Book #320, Records of Governor R. B. Hubbard, Texas State Library, Austin, Texas).

Cynthia E. Monroe, Nebraska State Historical Society, Lincoln, Nebraska, to the author, January 9, 1997.

Joseph G. Rosa to the author, January 21, 1997.

Shari Stelling, State Historical Society of Iowa, Iowa City, Iowa, to the author, May 5, 2000.

John Swindells, acting private secretary to Texas Governor R. B. Hubbard, to T. I. Courtright, Fort Worth City Marshal, March 13, 1878 (File No. 301-103, Letter Press Book #320, Records of Governor R. B. Hubbard, Texas State Library, Austin, Texas.).

M. S. Winon, jailer, Wise County, Texas, to Texas Ranger Captain George Schmitt, October 29, 1884 (Texas State Archives, Austin, Texas).

Index